Who Judges?

Designing Jury Systems in Japan, East Asia, and Europe

RIEKO KAGE
University of Tokyo

CAMBRIDGE
UNIVERSITY PRESS

CAMBRIDGE
UNIVERSITY PRESS

University Printing House, Cambridge CB2 8BS, United Kingdom

One Liberty Plaza, 20th Floor, New York, NY 10006, USA

477 Williamstown Road, Port Melbourne, VIC 3207, Australia

4843/24, 2nd Floor, Ansari Road, Daryaganj, Delhi – 110002, India

79 Anson Road, #06-04/06, Singapore 079906

Cambridge University Press is part of the University of Cambridge.

It furthers the University's mission by disseminating knowledge in the pursuit of education, learning, and research at the highest international levels of excellence.

www.cambridge.org
Information on this title: www.cambridge.org/9781107194694
DOI: 10.1017/9781108163606

First published 2017

Printed in the United Kingdom by Clays, St Ives plc

A catalogue record for this publication is available from the British Library.

Library of Congress Cataloging-in-Publication Data

Names: Kage, Rieko, 1973– author.
Title: Who judges? : designing jury systems in Japan, East Asia, and Europe / Rieko Kage.
Description: Cambridge [UK] ; New York : Cambridge University Press, 2017. I Includes bibliographical references and index.
Identifiers: LCCN 2017035936 I ISBN 9781107194694 (hardback)
Subjects: LCSH: Jury—Japan I Jury selection—Japan. I Justice, Administration of—Japan. I Jury. I Justice, Administration of.
Classification: LCC KNX1585 .K34 2017 I DDC 347/.0752—dc23 LC record available at https://lccn.loc.gov/2017035936

ISBN 978-1-107-19469-4 Hardback

Contents

Figures

Tables

Acknowledgments

This book has truly been a collective endeavor. Numerous scholars and friends helped me improve and refine its message every step of the way. In the early stages of this project, Yuriko Takahashi organized the edited volume project that first sparked my interest in the lay judge system. Yutaka Shinada generously offered the dataset that provided the initial inspiration for this project. Takeshi Ito, Hiroshi Okayama, Masako Suginohara, Naoki Takahashi, and in particular Yu Uchiyama offered insightful comments that helped to orient this work in the right direction. Yoshiko Herrera, Airo Hino, and Kenneth McElwain read through the entire manuscript and generously offered their time and insights at an author's conference at the University of Tokyo on a sizzling August day in 2015. The Kansai Group for Public Administration is among the best fora in Japan for presenting works-in-progress, and I thank Wataru Kitamura, Haruka Kubo, Shunsuke Kyo, Kengo Soga, and other participants of this group who selflessly devoted their time to giving me feedback on a cold, rainy day in Kobe in February 2016. Celeste Arrington and Jiyeoun Song carefully read draft chapters and offered their expertise on Korean politics. As I am a newcomer to the field of criminal law/criminal procedures, this book would not have been possible without the legal expertise and extensive feedback of Takayuki Shimaya. David Welch kindly arranged talks for me at highly productive seminars at the Japan Foundation in Toronto and the University of Waterloo. At the final stages of this book project, I benefited tremendously from participating at a seminar at the Graduate School of Law, Kobe University. I thank Professors Atsumi Kubota and Shimaya for organizing the event, as well as Takuya Hatta, Tamotsu Isomura, Shintaro Koike, Yukio Okitsu, Hiroshi Takahashi, Kazutaka Ueshima, Takashi Uto, and other participants at the event. The book has also benefited greatly from insightful comments, suggestions, and support from Eric Feldman, Darryl Flaherty, Carlo Guarnieri,

Takuya Iwata, Reid Krell, Michio Muramatsu, Shozo Ota, Jeffrey Sachs, and Chin-shou Wang. Kazuhiko Nishihara and Ryoko Yabuki at the Honmachi International Law Office kindly offered highly professional legal support. I also thank the three anonymous reviewers for this book for their careful reading of the manuscript and extremely helpful comments.

The Taiwan portion of the book would not have been possible without the incredible warmth with which many individuals there opened their doors and minds to me. In particular, I thank the Judicial Reform Foundation, which kindly facilitated numerous interviews that I had not dreamt would be possible. Jerry Cheng, Chuang Chiao-ju, and Kao Jung-chi helped me become oriented with the Taiwanese debates over introducing the jury/lay judge system. Senior officials at the Judicial Yuan kindly offered their candid views on the debate, and Professor Yu-shun Lin generously shared his insightful expertise based on his knowledge of both Taiwanese and Japanese legal systems, while Professor Wang Yeh-lih filled me in on the nuances of Taiwanese politics. Ker Chien-ming, Yu Mei-nu, Tien Chiu-chin, and Wan-Ling Chu kindly offered their insightful views on both the legislative and the NGO worlds in Taipei. I also thank Professor Wang and the Taiwanese Political Science Association for generously hosting my stay in Taipei to present an early version of this work at their annual meeting in December 2014.

The book has benefited from the work of three superb research assistants. Ronan Tse-min Fu provided research assistance for the Taiwanese case study and also served as an excellent interpreter in my interviews in Taipei. Nick Horton also conducted crucial background research for the Taiwanese case. So-hyung Lee cheerfully undertook the painstaking task of preparing the index, as well as assisting in research on the Korean case. I wish these young scholars all the best in their future endeavors.

I am fortunate to have an incredibly smart and generous group of colleagues at the Department of Advanced Social and International Studies at the University of Tokyo. I am deeply grateful for their unwavering commitment to research, which has made this book possible.

It has been a great pleasure to have the opportunity to work with the superbly efficient and dedicated Joe Ng and the whole team at Cambridge University Press. Thanks to Joe, the path to publication has moved forward much more quickly and smoothly than I had thought possible. I am also grateful to Karen Oakes and Grace Morris at the Press.

Two individuals in particular have helped me enormously on this project and also serve as tremendous role models for my career overall. I have been very fortunate to have the opportunity to work with Frances Rosenbluth, who kindly invited me to speak about this project at Yale University in September 2015. We also spent a fun day together shopping in New Haven, picking up Frances' boys, and exchanging ideas over bottles of kombu-cha. Frances has an incredible ability to balance family and cutting-edge research and I continue to learn much from her through our collaborative projects.

The book has also benefited greatly from the sharp insights of Susan Pharr. Ever since I embarked on my Ph.D. dissertation project at Harvard fifteen years ago, Susan has continued to offer incisive yet kind suggestions, consistently encouraging me to "think big." During the final stages of writing this book manuscript, Susan once again helped me to sharpen and broaden the scope of my argument.

I also thank a third (but really first) mentor, Hideo Otake. When I embarked on this project, little did I know that this would become a book on the new left. In true new left fashion, I will not dedicate this book to him, but I hope that he is well.

Finally, I thank my teammate-in-life and co-owner of our "struggling small business," Jacques Hymans, for his unfailingly loyal support. This book would not have been possible without him.

This project was generously supported by JSPS KAKENHI Grant Number 15K03267.

1 | *Introduction*

Overview

Jury/lay judge systems are a distinctive institution in developed democracies. Unlike in ancient Athens, most avenues for political participation in contemporary democracies only offer citizens the opportunity to participate *indirectly* in state decision-making. Elections, for instance, allow citizens to elect public officials who, in turn, make policy, but they do not allow citizens to engage in policymaking themselves. Similarly, petitions and protests enable citizens to exert pressure on elected officials, but the elected officials are the ones who ultimately make policy decisions. In contrast, serving as a juror or a lay judge presents a rare opportunity for the average citizen to take part directly in the making of consequential state decisions (Gastil et al. 2010: 19).[1]

Aristotle argued that in a democracy, "judges selected out of all should judge, in all matters, or in most and in the greatest and most important."[2] Indeed, the practice of lay participation in trials can be traced back to ancient Greece, where citizens directly engaged not only in legislating and administrating but also judging (Jackson and Kovalev 2006/7). Historians have located the origins of the English jury in the Norman era (Lloyd-Bostock and Thomas 1999). Trial by jury is deeply embedded in the histories of other countries in the English "common law" tradition, such as Australia, Canada, and New Zealand. The American colonies inherited this legacy, and the right to criminal trial by jury is stipulated in the 1787 US Constitution (Article 3). Many continental or "civil law" systems also have long histories of lay judge participation. In Germany and France, historians have found precedents going

---

[1] The referendum offers another example. For the growth in the use of the referendum, see Scarrow (2003).

[2] Aristotle, *The Politics*, Book VI, in Stephen Everson, ed., *Aristotle: The Politics and The Constitution of Athens* (Cambridge: Cambridge University Press, 1996), p. 155.

back to the seventh century (Dawson 1960). Other civil law countries with longstanding traditions of lay participation in court trials include Austria, Italy, Portugal, Sweden, and Switzerland (Malsch 2009).

Not all countries have such long traditions of lay participation in their criminal trials, however. Another option is the bench trial, in which the task of verdict and sentencing is left entirely in the hands of professional judges. Yet the period since the 1990s has seen a wave of countries around the world introducing new lay judge or jury systems in place of professional judge-dominated criminal trial proceedings. Among developed democracies, Spain, Japan, and South Korea legislated new jury or lay judge systems in 1995, 2004, and 2007, respectively. In the Republic of China (Taiwan), both major political parties have introduced competing legislative proposals to achieve this reform, although as of writing none has yet been formally adopted. The wave has also swept over countries outside the developed world. Russia, Ukraine, Georgia, Azerbaijan, Kazakhstan, Uzbekistan, Thailand, the People's Republic of China, Bolivia, and parts of Argentina have established systems of lay participation since the 1990s (Fukurai et al. 2010: iii–vi).

The recent adoption of jury/lay judge systems for criminal proceedings in these countries represents a potentially major shift in the delivery of justice, one of the core functions of the modern state. Citizens in many countries are sitting in judgment of their peers for the first time; others are doing so after many decades of hiatus. In Japan, for instance, from the introduction of the Japanese "*saiban-in*" (lay judge) system in April 2009 up to October 2016, 53,828 randomly selected citizens served as lay judges on trials involving 9,350 accused individuals (Saiko Saibansho n.d.[1]).

From the perspective of state elites, allowing this many members of the public to take part in criminal proceedings clearly entails both opportunities and risks. First and foremost, juries/lay judges are likely to use different bases than professional judges for deciding whether the accused is guilty or not guilty or what sentence might be appropriate. Precisely for this reason, some elites may view the introduction of jurors/lay judges as a means of making trial outcomes more reflective of common sense. But juries/lay judges may also undermine the practices and norms that professional judges have created and adhered to for decades, and that citizens have come to expect. This uncertainty could erode public trust in the justice system, despite the fact that the new systems are often introduced to promote it.

Second, another potentially double-edged sword from the perspective of state elites is the civic education function of participation as a juror/lay judge. Numerous studies of the American jury have found that the experience of serving as a juror often enhances the civic-mindedness of citizens and makes them more aware of various social and political issues (e.g. Diamond 1993; Gastil et al. 2002). Surveys conducted by the Secretariat of the Supreme Court of Japan also confirm that many citizens found that serving as lay judges opened their eyes to new issues and made them more aware of the world around them (see Chapter 9). While some policymakers may welcome a more empowered and civic-minded citizenry, it may cause worries for others. For instance, since the introduction of the *saiban-in* system in Japan, some of the ex-lay judges have formed a movement to oppose the death penalty.[3]

Political scientists have often noted the expansion of judicial independence across the globe in recent decades, in form if not in substance (e.g. Hirschl 2002; Linzer and Staton 2015). Judicial independence gives courts greater space to rule according to judges' professional beliefs without political interference (Helmke and Rosenbluth 2009). But the political science literature has almost entirely overlooked the contemporaneous spread of jury/lay judge systems, which have made the courts *less* independent vis-à-vis citizens in many countries, both in the developed and the developing world. In short, just as a growing number of countries have given courts greater space vis-à-vis the political sphere, they have also increasingly constrained the courts vis-à-vis the public, albeit to varying degrees in different countries. To what extent they have done so, and why, requires systematic investigation.

Part of the explanation for the introduction of new jury/lay judge systems since the 1990s is international diffusion, or "legal transplantation" as it is known in the comparative law literature. The mere fact of diffusion, however, fails to explain why different countries have adopted jury/lay judge systems that delegate quite varying degrees of power from professional judges to jurors/lay judges. For instance, the rulings of jurors/lay judges are binding on professional judges in Japan and Spain, but they are not binding in South Korea or the proposed

---

[3] "Shikei Shikko Teishi Hoshorahe Youseie Moto Saiban-in 'Kokumintekina Gironwo' [Ex-Lay Judges to Call on Justice Minister to Suspend the Death Penalty, Urging a 'National Discussion,'" *Nikkei Shimbun*, February 1, 2014.

system in Taiwan. What factors account for the differences in the extent to which the four countries have empowered juries/lay judges? Why have different states chosen to undermine their own powers to different degrees?

This book advances a new, two-step framework to account for this variation. First, the more that parties embrace new left causes, the more they may be expected to favor jury/lay judge systems that considerably undermine the powers of professional judges. Leftist parties in many developed democracies in recent decades have become champions not only of greater government intervention in the economy and income redistribution, but also so-called "new left" or "postmaterialist" causes such as environmental protection, decentralization, and participation. As Herbert Kitschelt (1994) has noted, these new left-oriented parties express concern not only over the achievement of substantive policy outcomes, but also the "quality of the process" through which those outcomes come about. Enthusiasm for strong new jury/lay judge systems epitomizes their postmaterialist preferences. But the extent to which leftist parties have taken up new left concerns varies considerably, both across different parties within the same country and across different countries.

Second, the book hypothesizes that the extent to which the preferences of new left-oriented parties actually translate into a major transfer of powers from professional judges to juries/lay judge depends on the relative power of those parties vis-à-vis other parties within the political system at the time that the issue of jury/lay judge participation emerges onto the policy agenda. *Ceteris paribus*, the stronger the new left-oriented parties vis-à-vis conservative parties and "old left" parties, the more the new jury/lay judge systems may be expected to delegate powers to juries/lay judges.

The book draws on both mixed-method analysis of the Japanese case and comparative case studies of Taiwan, South Korea, and Spain to support the hypotheses offered above. Japan presents a particularly crucial case for this study because it has the oldest democratic regime among the four countries and thus also the most entrenched professional judicial bureaucracy, yet it introduced a lay judge system in the 2000s that imposed relatively strong constraints upon the power of professional judges. The study presents quantitative content analyses of over fifty years of postwar parliamentary discussions over the possibility of reviving a jury/lay judge system, as well as qualitative process-tracing of the precise mechanisms through which partisan dynamics shaped the design of the new Japanese system in the late 1990s and early 2000s. The book also reports the results of in-depth original field research on the case of Taiwan. As Taiwan has not yet introduced a new jury/lay judge system, it offers an especially useful case for this book. Not only do the reform proposals advanced by different Taiwanese parties provide additional opportunities to test the validity of the hypotheses presented in this study, but the case also illuminates the conditions under which no transfer of power from professional judges to ordinary citizens may occur. The book also features shadow case studies of Spain and South Korea, which offer important variation in jury/lay judge system design.

The case studies demonstrate that judicial reform granted more power to juries or lay judges in countries where leftist parties had adopted new left issues to a greater extent and were stronger vis-à-vis other parties in the system. Spain presents a prototypical case of this constellation of factors, whereby a new left-oriented governing party legislated an extensive transfer of powers to the jury. In Japan, new left-oriented parties had enough power at key junctures to achieve a substantial transfer of power from the professional judges, despite the reluctance of the conservative ruling party. In South Korea, the new left orientation even of the leftist parties was weak, and the leftist president faced a conservative legislature, so the resulting jury system was weak. In Taiwan, new left-oriented parties controlled neither the legislature nor the executive branch during the period under study, and this situation severely hampered their efforts to introduce a system that transferred extensive powers from professional judges to lay judges.

It should be noted at the outset that the term "jury" is typically reserved for the Anglo-American lay judge system. "Lay judge" is a generic term for the institution in both common law and civil law systems. Thus, in the remainder of the book, the term "jury" or "pure" jury will refer to lay judge systems of the Anglo-American tradition, while the term "lay judge system" will refer more generally to systems of public participation in criminal trials.

Transfer of Powers: Substantive Impact

Jury and lay judge systems are only one component in the complex of institutional arrangements that support the criminal justice system in a country. Nevertheless, the introduction of a jury or lay judge system can have important impacts on the delivery of justice, in terms of verdicts and sentencing as well as criminal procedures. Chapter 9 of this book will detail some of those impacts in the case of Japan, with briefer remarks on the cases of South Korea and Spain. These impacts include a rise in the percentage of acquittals of defendants who had been charged with committing the most serious crimes. The launch of the system was also followed by a decline in the percentage of the heaviest sentences, such as death sentences and life sentences, and a rise in the percentage of suspended sentences with probation. Moreover, the introduction of the system was followed by a large drop in the percentage of cases booked by police that ended up being charged by prosecutors, a rise in the percentage of denied prosecutorial requests for detentions, and a rise in the percentage of detainees released before final ruling. Many of these trends were already underway before the system came into effect in 2009, so the new lay judge system may not have been the only cause of these trends, but it can at least be said that it reinforced and often accelerated them. Overall, the changes that have occurred since the introduction of the lay judge system thus far seem to have been in a pro-defendant direction.

In addition to their impacts on verdicts, sentencing, and criminal procedure, lay judge systems also have important impacts on the lay judges themselves. In Japan, South Korea, and Spain, thousands of citizens have participated in trials as jurors or lay judges since the new systems were created. For many of these people, it was the first significant interaction they had ever had with the criminal justice system. Survey data collected from Japanese people who served as lay judges overwhelmingly indicate that they found the experience rewarding, empowering, and educational. These findings lend support to Tocqueville's view that the jury may serve as a "school for democracy."

A Brief History of Lay Judge Systems

In an influential article, the economists Glaeser and Schleifer (2002) claim that countries with common law systems, such as the United Kingdom, are characterized by jury systems, while those with civil law systems, such as France, typically lack juries. This institutional difference, they argue, accounts for the higher economic growth rates in common law countries than in civil law countries today. But historians and comparative legal scholars have long known that many civil law countries actually do incorporate lay participation in trials. Indeed, these lay judge systems often have at least as long a history as the English jury (Dawson 1960; Malsch 2009; Donovan 2010).

As noted earlier, evidence of lay judge systems in Germany and France can be found as early as the seventh century (Dawson 1960: Chapter 2). According to Dawson (1960), early forms of lay judge systems used local notables as a way to address the shortage of professional judges during Merovingian rule. Continental states' reliance on local notables to dispense justice generally declined over subsequent centuries, but the situation changed dramatically as a result of the French Revolution and the Napoleonic empire, which played a key role in instituting the modern jury, not only in France but elsewhere in continental Europe as well (Hans and Germain 2011). In 1791, during the French Revolution, France adopted a new penal code that provided for jury trials. The system that France adopted was similar to the English jury, with professional and lay judges performing separate functions (ibid). As Napoleon expanded his empire across Europe, he transplanted the institution of the jury to the occupied areas (Langbein 1981). In many countries, this institutional innovation remained popular even after Napoleon's defeat, and thus the nineteenth century saw a wave of now-independent European countries formally adopting lay judge systems. For instance, Belgium, which had seen the brief introduction of a jury system while it was under French rule, reintroduced the system after gaining independence in 1831 (Traest 2001). Portugal introduced the jury in 1830. Greece began to experiment with a jury in 1834, and its 1844 constitution guaranteed trial by jury (Vidmar 2000). The German Reich constitution of 1849 stipulated for jury trials for more serious offenses (Casper and Ziesel 1972).

In 1850, the Kingdom of Hanover innovated the modern German lay judge system as we know it today, with lay judges sitting alongside professional judges. This "mixed jury" system quickly spread to other parts of Germany and Europe. Austria informally adopted a German-style lay judge system in 1850, then formally in 1869. Most Eastern European states retained the system after the fall of the Austro-Hungarian empire and even after World War II (Vidmar 2000; Bobeck 2015). The current lay judge systems in many Eastern European countries thus typically predate, and continued during, communist rule

(Leib 2007). Scandinavian countries formally introduced lay judge systems during the late nineteenth century as well, although the forerunners of Scandinavian lay judge systems go back much further into the past; in fact, some scholars have argued that early forms of the Scandinavian lay judge system served as the model for the medieval English jury (Turner 1968). Even France was not immune to the appeal of the German-style lay judge system. Despite the English-influenced jury system established by the Napoleonic Criminal Code, over time the French lay judge system underwent a number of reforms that strengthened the power of professional judges, and Vichy France in 1942 saw the introduction of a German-style system that was retained after the war (Vidmar 2000; Hans and Germain 2011).[4]

Despite the widespread use of this institution, however, a handful of developed countries still lacked any system of public participation in criminal trials as of 1990. Among the OECD countries, these included Japan, Luxembourg, the Netherlands, South Korea, and Spain. The Netherlands had briefly had a jury system during the French occupation (1811–13), but it was cancelled shortly after the end of occupied rule and was never restored (Malsch 2009). Luxembourg had long had a lay judge system for its criminal trials but abolished it in 1987 (ibid). The reason given for the cancellation of Luxembourg's lay judge system was that its verdicts could not be appealed, and this potentially violated the European Convention of Human Rights (ibid: 57). Nor did Estonia, Mexico, and Turkey (which were not yet OECD members in 1990) have any system of public participation at the time (Jackson and Kovalev 2006/7). Finally, Taiwan, which has levels of income commensurate with other OECD countries, although not a member of the OECD, also lacked such a system.

But several of these countries introduced some form of lay participation in subsequent years, as part of the "global proliferation" of jury/lay judge systems in the post-Cold War era (Wilson et al. 2015).

The overall distribution of OECD member countries and Taiwan as of 2015 in terms of whether they had "pure" jury systems, "mixed" jury systems, both, or neither is shown in Table 1.1. Underlined countries/regions are recent adopters, since 1990.

---

[4] Of course, the French and German systems are not the same. For instance, one major difference is that lay judges in Germany serve a fixed term (typically five years), while French lay jurors only sit on one case. See Jackson and Kovalev (2006/7).

Table 1.1 *Distribution of jury/lay judge systems among OECD countries (as of 2015) and Taiwan*

"Pure" juries	"Mixed" juries	Both "pure" and "mixed" juries	No jury/lay judge system
Australia, Belgium, Canada, England and Wales, Ireland, New Zealand, Northern Ireland, Scotland, South Korea, Spain, the United States (11 countries and regions)	Austria, Croatia, Czech Republic, Estonia, Finland, France, Germany, Greece, Hungary, Iceland, Italy, Japan, Norway, Poland, Portugal, Slovakia, Slovenia, Sweden, Switzerland (19 countries)	Denmark (1 country)	Chile, Israel, Luxembourg, Mexico, Netherlands, Republic of China (Taiwan), Turkey (7 countries and regions)

Underlined countries/regions are recent adopters since 1990. Scotland and Northern Ireland adopt different systems than England and Wales and are thus listed separately.
Sources: Jackson and Kovalev (2006/7), Leib (2007), and Malsch (2009).

Table 1.1 shows that the overwhelming majority, or thirty-one of thirty-eight OECD countries and regions, now have some form of public participation in criminal trials. Of these thirty-one countries and regions, nineteen rely on the "mixed" jury system in which lay and professional judges deliberate together to reach sentence and verdict. As noted earlier, the civil law countries of continental Europe typically opt for this system, as did Japan more recently. Meanwhile, eleven countries and regions rely on the "pure" jury system, in which the jury deliberates and votes separately from professional judges. Most of these are Anglo-American common law countries, but "pure" jury systems can also be found in civil law Belgium,[5] Spain, and, somewhat less clearly, in South Korea as well. Denmark uses *both* "pure" and

[5] In early 2016, Belgium adopted a reform that moves its system closer to a "mixed" jury system. Professional judges will now be present during jury deliberations, although they will not have a vote.

"mixed" juries.[6] Finally, seven countries/regions do not have any systems of jury/lay participation, including Taiwan, although in Taiwan a pilot "lay observer" system was launched in 2012.

OECD countries that newly introduced or re-introduced jury or lay judge systems from the 1990s are shown underlined in Table 1.1. This group of countries includes Estonia, Japan, South Korea, and Spain. This group of countries forms the focus of the present book. The case of Estonia will not be discussed in this book as it was not a member of the OECD at the time that it adopted its lay judge system in the early 1990s (Wilson et al. 2015).

The Configuration of Different Lay Judge Systems

Table 1.1 conceals a much more complicated institutional reality. It is important to recognize that lay judge systems are designed very differently in different countries. Simply noting that states have decided to adopt a lay judge system, or even making the distinction between "pure" and "mixed" juries, obscures rich variation among those systems. Indeed, the question that lies at the heart of this book is that of explaining the *variations* in the design of new jury/lay judge systems. In particular, this book seeks to explain the different extents to which the new lay judge systems in Japan, South Korea, Spain, and the proposed systems in Taiwan *transfer powers* from professional judges to juries/ lay judges. The extent to which countries empower juries/lay judges and undermine the powers of professional judges may be viewed as the single most significant measure of the extent to which countries have broken from their preexisting bench trial systems, in which professional judges held monopoly power over verdicts and sentencing. In short, this book asks: how much genuine change is represented by the reforms in different countries, and why might some countries have chosen to make a more dramatic break from the past than others?

The extent to which different states transfer powers from professional judges to juries/lay judges may be conceptualized along seven

---

[6] In Denmark, "pure" jury trials are held for cases in which the prosecution asks for imprisonment of four or more years or those in which the defendant may be placed in custody or other forms of detention (Courts of Denmark n.d.). "Mixed" jury trials are held for cases in which the defendant pleads not guilty but the prosecution asks for imprisonment (ibid). According to the Courts of Denmark, the number of "pure" jury trials is very small (ibid).

dimensions: (1) the scope of crimes that are subject to jury/lay judge trial; (2) whether or not professional judges have the authority to decide which cases should be ruled by jurors/lay judges; (3) whether or not the lay judges deliberate separately from professional judges; (4) whether or not the professional judges can overrule the decisions of jurors/lay judges; (5) in "mixed jury" systems, the relative number of lay and professional judges; (6) the degree of consensus required between lay and professional judges to reach a decision; and (7) whether lay judges take part in determining the verdict only or both the verdict and sentence.[7]

Jury/lay judge systems are "stronger," i.e. impose greater constraints over professional judges, if (1) the scope of cases on which jurors/lay judges may serve is broader; (2) professional judges have limited discretion over which cases should be ruled by jury/lay judge trial; (3) the jurors/lay judges deliberate in isolation from professional judges; (4) the decisions of jurors/lay judges are binding; (5) in "mixed jury" systems, the number of jurors/lay judges vis-à-vis professional judges is smaller; (6) the votes of professional judges are not required to reach a decision; and (7) jurors/lay judges take part in determining both verdict and sentence.

Let us consider these seven criteria in greater detail. First, there is the matter of scope. Virtually no country stipulates that jurors/lay judges must serve on *all* criminal trials; the scope of crimes subject to jury/lay judge trials may be broader or narrower. Spain, for instance, provides for jury trials not only for violent crimes but also some categories of white-collar crime. In contrast, lay judges in Japan do not serve on

---

[7] In addition to the seven criteria outlined above, it could also be of interest to examine the system of appeals. First, juries/lay judges may serve solely in courts of original jurisdiction, or they may also serve at the appellate level. For instance, in France and Italy, citizens serve both at the original and appeals courts (Kaplan et al. 2006: 112). *Ceteris paribus*, the relative power of citizens should be greater in systems where they serve at multiple levels of the court. Second, jury/lay judge systems may vary in the extent to which they allow for appeals. For instance, the French mixed jury system traditionally had limited grounds for appealing jury verdicts in the *Cours d'assises*, but France has significantly expanded the opportunities for appeal in recent decades (Hans and Germain 2011). *Ceteris paribus*, the power of the citizens vis-à-vis professional judges should be greater if jury/lay judge verdicts cannot be appealed, and especially if jury/lay judges do not serve on appellate courts. I thank Professor Atsumi Kubota for these points. This book, however, focuses on the power of jurors/lay judges in the context of courts of original jurisdiction.

cases of white-collar crime. *Ceteris paribus*, the broader the scope of cases on which jurors/lay judges may serve, the greater the constraints on the power of professional judges.

Second, professional judges retain more of their powers if they have broader discretion to determine which cases should be decided by lay judges and which by professional judges. Given a choice, professional judges may choose to hand only the more ordinary or most trivial cases to lay judges, while jealously guarding the professionals' jurisdiction over the more "important" cases.

Third, *ceteris paribus*, professional judges will be able to retain greater influence over rulings if they deliberate and rule together with lay judges, whereas jurors should enjoy greater autonomy from the views of professional judges if they deliberate and rule in isolation from professional judges. Social-psychological studies of juries and of small group deliberation typically find that when lower status individuals are placed in the same group with higher-status individuals, the former tend to participate less actively than the latter (e.g. Kaplan and Martin 1999; Bliesener 2006). Moreover, these studies also find that less trained individuals tend to participate less than those with greater expertise (ibid). Thus professional judges, who are typically of higher status and better trained in law than jurors/lay judges, should generally dominate discussions if both sides are to deliberate together. Jurors in the Anglo-American tradition typically deliberate and make rulings separately from professional judges, whereas in "mixed" jury systems of the civil law tradition, the lay judges typically deliberate and rule *with* professional judges. There are ways to limit the influence of professional judges over lay judges when they deliberate together. For instance, in Taiwan's proposed "lay observer" system, professional judges do not speak until lay jurors have voiced their opinions. Nevertheless, *ceteris paribus*, systems in which jurors/lay judges deliberate separately should constrain the power of professional judges to a greater extent than those in which they deliberate together.

Fourth, very importantly, the decisions of jurors/lay judges may or may not be binding on professional judges. The influence of jurors/lay judges will obviously be greater in systems where their decisions are binding on professional judges. In countries such as the United States, juries' rulings are binding on professional judges, but in others, such as South Korea or prewar Japan, the decisions of jurors can be overruled and do not constrain the professional judges in any formal way.

Of course, the fact that decisions are non-binding does not mean that jurors/lay judges will have no influence over professional judges. Since the jurors/lay judges represent the broader public, professional judges may feel at least some normative pressure to respect jurors'/lay judges' rulings. Nevertheless, there is a qualitative difference in the power of juries/lay judges between systems in which their rulings are legally binding on professional judges and those in which they are not.

A fifth dimension that shapes the balance of power between professional judges and juries/lay judges in "mixed" jury systems has to do with the number of lay judges vis-à-vis professional judges that are empaneled for a trial. There is great cross-national variation in the number of jurors/lay judges. In some countries, such as Austria or Germany, only two or three lay judges sit on a trial, while in others, such as Japan, there are six and in the United States there are twelve (Leib 2007). There is an intriguing disconnect between academic theory and political actors' conventional wisdom on this point. Political actors often believe that *ceteris paribus*, the larger the number of lay judges that serve on a trial, the more influence they should wield over professional judges. Indeed, as will be shown in Chapter 5, the LDP in Japan sought to limit the number of lay judges because it wanted to preserve the power of professional judges. By contrast, the Komeito, the LDP's coalition partner, pushed for a larger number of lay judges, believing that greater numbers would give citizens more power. However, the social-psychological research on juries, and on small-group deliberation more generally, actually suggests that the social influence of higher-status individuals (such as professional judges) is more limited in smaller groups than in larger ones (e.g. Moscovici 1985; Chud and Berman 2000; Devine et al. 2001).

Sixth, voting rules also shape the balance of power between jurors/lay judges and professional judges. This issue also applies only to "mixed" jury systems in which jurors/lay judges deliberate and rule together, in the continental European tradition. Voting rules may take different forms in different countries, and the Anglo-American tradition of requiring a consensus is not common among civil law "mixed" jury systems. At one end of the spectrum, one can conceive of a system in which lay and professional judges rule by majority, but which requires all presiding professional judges to be part of the majority. Such a system would keep most of the power in the hands of the professional judges. At the other end, the lay judges may also rule by majority without any professional judge concurring. Such a system would transfer considerable powers from professional judges to jurors/lay judges.

Seventh, lay judge systems also vary in the decisions that they ask jurors/lay judges to make. In some countries, jurors/lay judges only rule on the basic verdict of guilt or innocence, while in others, they also make decisions on sentencing. Typically, in Anglo-American jury systems, jurors rule solely on verdict and not on sentence, while by contrast, in civil law "mixed" jury systems, lay judges typically take part in deciding both verdict and sentence.[8] *Ceteris paribus*, the powers of jurors/lay judges will be greater if they take part in determining both verdict and sentence, and more limited if they rule only on verdict.

Jury/lay judge systems also vary along other dimensions that are important, but less relevant to the question of the relative power of jury/lay judges versus professional judges. For instance, some systems may leave the decision of whether to have a jury/lay judge trial entirely up to the defendant. Such was the case in prewar Japan (Tokyo Bar Association 1992). These are important institutional issues, but since the relative power of professional and jury/lay judges is not clearly affected by them, this study devotes less attention to explaining why they were chosen. Different countries also adopt different selection rules for jurors/lay judges. For instance, in Japan, both the prosecution and the defense may each exclude three individuals from the lay judge pool without providing a reason, but judges' discretion in dismissing a candidate for lay judge service is very limited. Since jury selection typically affects the relative chances of the prosecution and defense more than the balance of power between professional judges and juries/lay judges, the issue of jury selection will not be discussed further in this book.

Among the seven criteria for differentiating jury/lay judge systems that have been highlighted here, two are particularly important in

---

[8] In the Belgian "pure jury" system, however, jurors ruled on both sentence and verdict (Jackson and Kovalev 2006/7). Belgian jurors determined their verdict in isolation from professional judges, but once they found a defendant guilty, they collaborated with professional judges to determine sentence. This system was reformed in early 2016 and now the jury determines verdict in the presence of professional judges (see Footnote 5).

shaping the power of juries/lay judges vis-à-vis professional judges: whether the professional judges have broad discretion to determine if a case should be ruled by juries/lay judges, and whether decisions of the juries/lay judges are binding on professional judges. Even if the jury/ lay judge system appears robust in other respects, it is fundamentally weak if the professional judges have the power to relegate juries/lay judges only to the "less important" cases, or if they can simply ignore jury/lay judge rulings.

It should also be stressed that the distinction between systems that transfer greater powers to juries/lay judges and those that transfer less does not necessarily correspond to the distinction between "pure" and "mixed" juries. Since, as noted earlier, lay judges are often found to participate less actively in the deliberation process in "mixed" juries than "pure" juries (Kaplan and Martin 2006), they are sometimes seen as cosmetic institutions. This bias against "mixed" jury systems is especially pronounced in the Anglo-American world. However, as the preceding discussion shows, "mixed" juries often enjoy greater powers than "pure" juries in important respects. For instance, mixed juries typically rule on both verdict and sentence, while "pure" juries typically only decide on verdict. The scope of crimes for which jury/lay judge trials are used may also be broader or narrower, regardless of whether the country adopts a "pure" or "mixed" jury system. Thus, the extent to which different jury/lay judge systems empower citizens and undermine the power of professional judges depends on the precise configuration of each system, rather than simply on whether they belong to the family of "pure" or "mixed" jury systems.

Four Countries in Comparative Perspective

As noted above, during the 1990s and 2000s, a number of developed democracies that had conspicuously lacked systems of lay participation for many decades introduced such systems: Spain, Japan, and South Korea. In addition, Taiwan moved gradually toward the adoption of such a system and launched a pilot system in 2012, although its legislature still had not passed the full-scale reform as of late 2016. This book focuses on the four cases of Spain, Japan, South Korea, and Taiwan.

A key advantage of comparing these four countries is that they present considerable variation in the extent to which their lay judge systems constrain the power of professional judges. The systems are summarized in Table 1.2.

Of the four countries' systems, the Spanish, introduced in 1995, represents the most extensive transfer of power from professional to lay judges. In the Spanish system, professional judges have no authority to rule on which cases should be decided solely by professional judges and which by a jury. The empaneling of a jury is required for a relatively broad range of crimes, including not only those that carry heavier sentences, such as murder and homicide, but also robbery and trespassing of dwelling (Thaman 1997). Some categories of white-collar crime, such as "crimes against honor" (mainly libel cases), are also subject to a jury trial (ibid). Following the French model, nine jurors sit on a trial versus only one professional judge (Thaman 1997: 263; Jimeno-Bulnes 2004).[9] The Spanish jury deliberates and rules separately from professional judges (Thaman 1999; Jimeno-Bulnes 2004). The rules require five votes to acquit and seven to convict, and the jury's decisions are binding on the professional judges. The jurors rule on verdict but not sentence, although they may recommend a suspended sentence (Thaman 1997). Unlike in most jury systems, the Spanish jury is required to present a reason for their verdict (Leib 2007), and as part of this process, the jury also votes on questions regarding facts that are posed by the professional judge (Martín and Kaplan 2006).

Japan's system was passed in 2004 and launched in 2009. Japan's reform represented a significant transfer of power out of the hands of professional judges, but not to the same extent that Spain's did. Like Spain, the Japanese system has a list of crimes for which lay judges must be empaneled. But the list of such crimes is more limited in Japan than in Spain and covers only the more serious criminal offenses, such as murder, burglary leading to injury or death, and injury leading to death. "Lesser" offenses such as robbery, which are subject to jury trial in Spain, are not covered in Japan. Also in contrast to Spain, white-collar crimes such as bribery are not subject to a lay judge trial. Judges in Japan only have the legal authority to exclude cases from

---

[9] The French lay judge system has since moved from a nine-juror system to a six-juror system (Gadbin-George 2012).

Table 1.2 *Configuration of lay judge systems in Spain, Japan, South Korea, and Taiwan*

	Spain	Japan	South Korea	Taiwan (proposed "lay observer" system)
Formal introduction of lay judge system?	Yes (1995)	Yes (2004)	Yes (2007)	No, but bill submitted to legislature (2012)
Scope of cases to be judged by lay judges?	Broader	Narrower	Broader (requires defendant request)	Narrower
Professional judges determine which cases to be tried by lay judges?	No	Very limited	Yes	Yes
Number of lay/professional judges	9 lay, 1 professional	6 lay, 3 professional	5, 7, or 9 lay, 3 professional	5 lay, 3 professional
Lay judges deliberate separately from professional judges?	Yes	No	Yes on verdict; No on sentence	No
Lay judge decisions binding?	Yes	Yes	No	No
Lay judges rule both on verdict and sentence?	No	Yes	Yes	Yes
Professional judges must agree with majority?	Not applicable ("pure" jury)	Yes; at least 1 out of 3	Not applicable for verdict; No on sentence	No
Transfer of power from professional judges	Most extensive	Extensive	Less extensive	Least extensive

saiban-in trial if they determine that holding a *saiban-in* trial may jeopardize the safety of the lay judges or their families (Article 3, Clause 1, *Act on Criminal Trials with Participation of Saiban-in*). In practice, this authority has rarely been exercised; during the first three years after the introduction of the lay judge system, only two cases were excluded from *saiban-in* trial for this reason (Saiko Saibansho Jimu Sokyoku 2012[c]: 1). Six lay judges (*saiban-in*) deliberate collectively alongside three professional judges to reach both verdict and sentence. This aspect of the Japanese system makes it similar to a European mixed jury system. But in contrast to the German mixed tribunal, Japan's lay judges only serve on single cases rather than for a fixed term, and in this respect, the Japanese system resembles the French mixed jury system more than the German model. The decision is by simple majority vote of the nine lay and professional judges, provided that at least one professional judge agrees with the majority. The collective decision of lay and professional judges is binding for both verdict and sentence, although decisions may be appealed to a higher court.

South Korea's system, introduced in 2008, imposes weaker constraints on professional judges than either Spain's or Japan's. Upon petition of the defendant, South Korea's professional judges are given the power to decide for or against holding a jury trial for a set list of offenses. The list is shorter than Spain's but longer than Japan's. For instance, unlike in Japan, cases of bribery may be tried by jury trial in Korea. If the judges decide to grant the petition, then five, seven, or nine lay judges preside alongside three professional judges, depending on the severity of the crime (Park 2010).[10] South Korea's jurors deliberate separately from professional judges to reach a verdict, but professional judges may enter into the discussion if a majority of the jurors concur, or if the jury cannot agree on a unanimous verdict (ibid). If the jury finds the defendant guilty, it then deliberates together with professional judges to determine the appropriate sentence. Thus, the Korean lay judge system has aspects of both "pure" and "mixed" juries (Cho 2008). Verdict is determined by unanimity, while sentence is decided by majority rule. Unlike in the Japanese system, there is no

---

[10] The more serious felony cases that may result in capital punishment or life imprisonment have nine jurors; other felony cases are run with seven jurors; and cases in which the defendant plead guilty are presided by five jurors (Park 2010: 554).

formal provision as to whether any of the three professional judges must agree with the majority (Lee 2009). This is not surprising, given that the jurors' decisions on verdict and sentence do not formally constrain the professional judges. In other words, the professional judges may simply reject the jury's decision and replace it with their own. Judges are required to inform the defendant of the jury's verdict, and, if the judges choose to differ from the jury, to offer an explanation (ibid).

Taiwan requires a separate discussion. As noted earlier, Taiwan has not formally introduced a lay judge system as of late 2016. This means that Taiwan has made the least transfer of power, indeed no transfer of power, from professional judges to juries/lay judges. But the Ma Ying-jeou Administration (2008–16) did submit a bill to the legislature to introduce a system known as the "lay observer" system in 2012 and launched a pilot program for the same system as well. Under this proposed system, the scope of cases to be heard by lay judges is relatively narrow; only offenses that are punishable by death penalty or life sentence may utilize a lay judge court. Moreover, as in South Korea, professional judges have the authority to rule on whether or not a case should be tried by lay judges. If they do decide to include lay judges, five lay judges then serve alongside three professional judges (Huang and Lin 2013). Deliberation is somewhere in between a "pure" Anglo-American jury and a continental "mixed" jury in that professional judges participate in discussion with the lay judges, but the professional judges are not allowed to express their opinions until the lay judges have deliberated on the facts and application of laws (Judicial Yuan 2014). Professional judges may, however, at any time in the lay judges' deliberations, offer information on admissibility of evidence, interpretation of laws, and other technical issues (ibid). Lay and professional judges collectively decide on verdict and sentence by majority, and there is no requirement that any of the three professional judges must be part of the majority. However, as in South Korea, the decision of the lay judges is not binding on the professional judges. Professional judges are merely required to offer a reason to the defendant if they choose to depart from the lay observer's rulings (ibid). As of late 2016, none of the bills that have been submitted to institutionalize this system have passed, and with the defeat of Ma's Kuomintang in the 2016 elections, this particular design of lay judge system is unlikely to become institutionalized in the near future.

In sum, there is great variation in the systems adopted or proposed by the four countries. Spain's jury system transfers the greatest powers from professional judges to jurors. In the Spanish system, a jury trial is required for a broad range of cases and the jury's decision is final. Taiwan has failed formally to introduce a new system and therefore has made no transfer of power thus far. Among systems that have been adopted, South Korea's new system imposes the weakest constraints on the power of professional judges. In both the Korean system and the Taiwanese pilot system, the rulings by the jury/lay judges are merely advisory and do not formally constrain professional judges. Finally, Japan's lay judge system falls somewhere in between the Spanish case, on the one hand, and the Korean jury and the Taiwanese pilot system, on the other. In Japan, lay judges must be empaneled, and the collective decision of the lay and professional judges is binding.

This broad variation in the design of new jury systems is especially puzzling in view of the fact that all four countries belong to the family of "civil law," rather than "common law," systems. Legal systems around the world are typically categorized as belonging to either the "common law" or the "civil law" tradition. At the broadest level, civil law traditions, which typically stem from continental European legal systems such as those of Germany or France, generally rely more heavily on a codified set of laws, whereas common law traditions, which mostly stem from British precedents, view judicial decisions, or case laws, as the main source of judicial decision-making (Dainow 1967). In civil law systems, legal interpretations are typically developed through scholarly analysis, giving high prestige to legal scholars. In contrast, in common law systems, legal interpretations (notably of precedents) are largely developed by practitioners (Dammer and Albanese 2013: Chapter 3).[11] As noted earlier, most common law systems have adopted "pure" jury systems, while most civil law systems have adopted "mixed" jury systems. This pattern might lead one to suspect that the design of new jury/lay judge systems is largely "path-dependent" (Pierson 2004), i.e. to a substantial degree

---

[11] It is important not to overemphasize the difference between civil and common law systems. Scholars of comparative law have noted the growing convergence between civil and common law systems, with codified law playing a growing role in common law countries such as Britain and the United States, while the importance of case law has grown in countries with civil law traditions (Husa 2004).

shaped by the historical configuration of the existing legal system of the country in question. The distinction between civil and common law systems does certainly constrain the possibilities of judicial reform in important ways. However, as it happens, the four countries that this study focuses on are all typically categorized as "civil law systems," yet they adopted quite different designs of lay judge systems. Differences in legal traditions thus fail to offer a convincing explanation for why these countries adopted different jury/lay judge systems, with Spain and South Korea adopting systems closer to the Anglo-American tradition, i.e. with juries deliberating separately from professional judges, versus Japan adopting and Taiwan proposing a "mixed" system that is closer to the continental legal tradition. In fact, Japan's basic criminal procedures law is actually closer to the American tradition than its homologues in Korea and Taiwan, because Japan's system underwent extensive reforms under the US occupation (e.g. Shiomi 1975). Given this background, from a path-dependency perspective it would not have been surprising if Japan had adopted a system that was closer to the American jury system. Yet this was not what happened. Thus, the institutional configuration of the existing legal system does not appear to determine the extent to which countries transfer powers from professional judges to jurors/lay judges. A separate explanation is required to account for the specific choices that each country made in designing its new system.

The variation in the design of new lay judge systems across the four countries is also puzzling in light of recent theories of international diffusion, or "legal transplantation," to use the term more commonly used in the field of comparative law (e.g. Watson 1974; Langer 2004). At the broadest level, the new jury/lay judge systems introduced around the world since the 1990s may be understood as cases of international policy diffusion. According to this perspective, the tradition of citizen participation in criminal trials that originated in Western Europe has now spread to many other states, whether by processes of competition, learning, or emulation (Simmons et al. 2006). But the mere fact of diffusion does not account for the variations in the systems adopted. Moreover, studies of international diffusion by Schofer and Meyer (2005) as well as Schofer and Hironaka (2005) find that norm diffusion often occurs more rapidly in countries that are more closely integrated into "world society," and especially "small states." This pattern does not explain the puzzle that motivates this study.

Ceteris paribus, smaller states such as Taiwan should have adopted more extensive reforms than a larger state such as Japan, with South Korea and Spain falling somewhere in between. But this is not the pattern that we observe. Indeed, Taiwan has yet to legislate any lay participation at all. These variations in the institutional design of lay judge systems require a separate explanation.

Explaining the Reforms

Judicial Politics and the Jury/Lay Judge System

How might we explain the different reforms instituted in the four countries under study? Judicial politics is a growing area of research in political science. The bulk of studies in this area have been conducted in the subfield of American politics. American politics scholars have debated whether courts make decisions based more on "legal," "attitudinal," or "strategic" considerations (e.g. Segal and Spaeth 1993, 2002); how courts set the policy agenda (e.g. Perry 1991; McGwire and Caldeira 1993; Black and Owens 2009); the relationship between lower and higher courts (e.g. Songer et al. 1994); and inter-branch relations (e.g. Bergara et al. 2003; Harvey and Friedman 2006; Clark 2009), among other issues. These are undoubtedly important topics, but they are quite far afield from the question that is being posed in this study.

On the jury more specifically, there is a small American politics literature on the effects of jury service on political participation and civic-mindedness (e.g. Gastil et al. 2002, 2008, 2010; Gastil and Weiser 2006; Bloeser et al. 2012). A recent study by Bowler et al. (2014) explores the determinants of jury summons response rates. But the question of how to design a new jury system is a non-issue in the United States, which has a tradition of trial by jury that goes back for centuries and is taken largely for granted.

There also exists a small but rapidly growing body of political science research on judicial politics in the subfield of comparative politics. Thus far, this research has focused primarily on judicial independence, both its determinants and consequences (e.g. Ramseyer 2001; Helmke 2002, 2005; Iaryczower et al. 2002; Herron and Randazzo 2003; Vanberg 2005; Helmke and Rosenbluth 2009; Popova 2010, 2012; Gee 2015). A smaller literature examines the lobbying of courts (e.g. Giles and Lancaster 1989; Hoover and den Dulk 2004; Iaryczower et al. 2006; Arrington 2014). However, political science research on juries/lay judge systems outside the United States has been exceedingly rare (for an exception see Doheny and O'Neill 2010). Despite the growing importance and broad international diffusion of these institutions in recent decades, comparative politics scholars have largely overlooked the trend. This book seeks to fill this gap in the political science literature.

Beyond the field of political science, there does exist a vibrant and growing literature on the rapid diffusion of jury/lay judge systems across international borders in the fields of sociology of law and comparative law. A large body of English-language work examines the new lay judge systems in East Asia, including single-country studies of Japan (e.g. Weber 2009; Corey and Hans 2010; Fukurai 2011; Vanoverbeke 2015; Wilson et al. 2015; Dobrovolskaia 2016), South Korea (e.g. Cho 2008; Lee 2009; Park 2010; Choi 2013a; Lee 2016), and Taiwan (Huang and Lin 2013), as well as comparative studies of China and Japan (e.g. Wang and Fukurai 2010), Korea and Japan (e.g. Fukurai and Hans 2012), and across Asia more broadly (Fukurai et al. 2010). Scholars have also explored the new jury systems in post-Communist Eastern Europe and the former Soviet Union (Thaman 1995; Kutnjak Ivković 1999; Kovalev 2010; Kovalev and Suleymenova 2010; Sheyn 2010) and Spain (Thaman 1997). Scholars have also examined emerging systems in Latin America, such as sub-national efforts in Argentina (Bergoglio 2003; Hendler 2005), on-going efforts to introduce a jury system in Mexico (Fukurai et al. 2009), and the aborted effort in Venezuela (Thaman 2002). Scholars have also studied the suspension of lay judge systems in India (Ramnath 2013), and judges' efforts to effectively undermine jury verdicts in Russia (Thaman 2007). These studies provide valuable information on the configuration of different jury/lay judge systems and the contextual factors that led to the introduction, design, and/ or undermining of lay judge systems in each of those countries. They also occasionally provide explicit or implicit causal hypotheses, some of which will be detailed below (see, for instance, Hans 2008). But since these studies have not been undertaken by political scientists, they have not systematically assessed the political factors that promote or delay the introduction lay judge systems and shape the configuration of those systems, let alone doing so via a cross-national comparative study. The aim of this book is to take some first steps toward filling this gap.

The Lay Judge System as Public Policy

To begin to gain a handle on this question, it is useful to view the policy of launching new lay judge systems in the context of other comparable institutional reforms: the introduction of suffrage, military conscription, regressive taxation, as well as delegation. Examining the introduction of new lay judge systems in light of these other issue-areas helps us to generate possible hypotheses for explaining why different countries choose to transfer powers from professional judges to lay judges to varying degrees.

To begin with, the introduction of a jury/lay judge system enables citizens to engage in state decision-making. In this sense, the introduction of a jury/lay judge system is analogous to the extension of the suffrage, which expands the opportunities for citizens to participate in public affairs and to offer input. Studies of democratization may thus yield important insights into the question of why, and to what extent, different countries may choose to allow citizens to take part in state criminal decision-making. Of course, as noted earlier, the jury/lay judge system goes well beyond voting in that it provides citizens the opportunity to directly take part in state decision-making, not merely to choose policymakers who in turn make policy. The cost of participation is also higher for jury/lay judges than for voters. While the act of voting may at most require just a few minutes (plus the time required to get to the voting booth), serving as a juror/lay judge typically requires at least a few hours and, in some instances, it may extend to several months. Nevertheless, there are fundamental similarities between the extension of the suffrage and the introduction of a jury/lay judge system in that both expand the opportunities for citizens to shape policy outcomes, whether directly or indirectly, and, in turn, constrain the power of elites.

Second, it is also possible to compare the jury/lay judge system to military conscription. Serving as a juror/lay judge is typically construed as a civic duty. The term "jury duty" aptly captures this conscriptive dimension. Indeed, most countries impose a fine for citizens who fail to appear for jury duty, just as they punish citizens for avoiding conscription, further underscoring the point that jury duty is more costly than voting, which is often viewed as a right and usually does not carry a penalty for no-shows.[12] Of course, an important difference between the jury/lay judge system and conscription is that in the former, citizens are simply asked to offer their time and best judgment, while in the latter, citizens are required to engage in physical labor, and possibly to sacrifice their lives. For this reason, the introduction of conscription has historically been met with much uproar from the public (Levi 1997). This is usually not the case for the introduction of the jury/lay judge system. Nevertheless, both conscription and the jury/lay judge system involve the introduction of a new civic obligation. Moreover, many thinkers have applauded military conscription as an institution that democratizes the composition of the military and symbolizes the "citizen-soldier" (Janowitz 1983). Thus, existing studies of conscription may yield useful insights for understanding the extent to which different countries choose to introduce varying degrees of constraints upon the powers of professional judges.

Third, a jury/lay judge system may also be viewed as a form of tax policy. Jury duty imposes a tax on citizens' time that could be used for other purposes, such as work, leisure, or otherwise. Unlike the income or sales tax, this particular tax is typically imposed on a fairly small segment of the population at any one point in time. For instance, a 2001 survey shows that in Australia, which has had a jury system since British colonial rule, only 14.5% of respondents had *ever* served on a jury (Horan 2005: 134). In the United States, a study estimates that 37.6% of citizens are likely to serve on juries at some point in their lives (Center for Jury Studies n.d.). So this is a tax that is unevenly applied. Moreover, the severity of the tax is *ex ante* unknown; at the beginning of a trial, it is impossible to predict whether a juror will have to serve for a day, a week, or over several months. There is also uncertainty regarding the timing at which the tax will be imposed. Jurors/lay judges are often randomly selected, and it is usually impossible for citizens to know *ex ante* when they will be summoned to serve. In addition, whereas observers have often noted the progressive nature of military conscription, which often offers the poor opportunities for jobs, incomes, and acquisition of skills (e.g. Leal 1999), it is unlikely that jury service will yield long-term material benefits for those who serve.

---

[12] Some countries, including Australia, Luxembourg, and in the Latin American region, have adopted compulsory voting and impose a fine for abstention (Mackerras and McAllister 1999).

Fourth, new jury/lay judge systems can also be viewed as a legislative decision to introduce new constraints upon the powers of professional judges. Whereas the other three literatures focus on the empowerment and/or coercion of ordinary citizens, this literature focuses on the balance of power between politicians and professionals. The principal-agent literature on the relationship between legislatures and bureaucracies has examined why legislatures delegate discretionary powers to bureaucracies to varying degrees, in what way, and why (e.g. McCubbins and Schwartz 1984; Epstein and O'Halloran 1999; Huber and Shipan 2002). In the field of judicial politics more specifically, some scholars have applied this framework to explain why legislatures may allow courts to conduct judicial review (Rogers 2001; Stephenson 2003). The principal-agent literature may thus also offer useful insights for explaining why, and to what extent, legislatures may transfer powers away from the courts and delegate new powers to jurors/lay judges.

The literatures on the introduction of suffrage, conscription, taxation, and delegation suggest several hypotheses that may explain why different countries transferred varying degrees of powers from professional judges to jurors/lay judges. First, the literature on democratization and the introduction of the suffrage, as well as studies of conscription, potentially point to a bottom-up explanation for the introduction of new channels of citizen input that stresses the importance of *public opinion*. Second, the principal-agent literature on judicial delegation points to *partisan competition* as a determinant of levels of judicial independence. Third, studies of democratization, conscription, and taxation suggest that the *relative strength and ideologies of particular parties*, either leftist or conservative, may be crucial. Each of these hypotheses will be considered in turn below.

Public Discontent toward the Judicial System
An influential line of reasoning among studies of democratization stresses the role of the working class in bringing about the expansion of suffrage in Western Europe (Rueschemeyer et al. 1992; Tilly 1997; Przeworski 2009). As Rueschemeyer et al. (1992: 57) argued, "[t]hose who have only to gain from democracy will be its most reliable promoters and defenders, those who have the most to lose will resist it." In a similar vein, rising public discontent against professional judges offers a possible explanation for the variations in the extent

to which countries transfer powers away from professional judges to juries/lay judges. For instance, if the majority of the public comes to feel that the decisions of professional judges are out of touch with its values, it may push policymakers to introduce a jury/lay judge system that transfers more powers away from professional judges in order to restore confidence and legitimacy in the judicial system.

Scholars have indeed pointed to public discontent with the judicial system as an important determinant for the introduction of jury system in South Korea, and also for the emergence of the issue onto the policy agenda in Taiwan (Cho 2008; Lee 2009; Huang and Lin 2013). Cho (2008) argues that public disgust about judicial corruption was the main factor driving the introduction of the jury system in South Korea. As will be shown in Chapter 6, a series of judicial scandals also led the Ma administration in Taiwan to launch efforts to introduce the "lay observer system" (Huang and Lin 2013). In some cases, there may be actual popular movements that demand reform, as in the case of Taiwan; in other cases, elites may introduce reforms in order to pre-empt such popular movements from growing.

However, beyond pushing the issue of introducing a jury/lay judge system onto the policy agenda, public distrust in the justice system fails to account for the cross-national variations in the actual configuration of the systems that were ultimately adopted in the four cases under study. The World Values Surveys provide useful cross-national data on levels of trust in the justice system, and the figures for the four countries are shown in Table 1.3. The figures reported here are for the survey years closest to the period when the introduction of a jury/lay judge system was under debate in each of the countries.

Table 1.3 shows considerable variation in levels of public trust toward the justice system in the four countries. In no country was the public overwhelmingly distrustful. The Japanese public exhibited by far the highest levels of confidence in the justice system among the four countries, with 77.0% of respondents expressing "a great deal" or "quite a lot" of confidence, and 17.0% expressing "not very much" confidence or "not at all."[13] Table 1.3 also shows that levels of

---

[13] Other existing surveys also confirm Japan's high levels of trust in the courts; although the question wording is somewhat different, the Japanese General Social Surveys find that trust in the courts consistently exceeded 90% during the early- to mid-2000s, when the introduction of the lay judge system was under debate (Shishido and Iwai 2010).

Table 1.3 *Levels of public confidence in the courts/justice system*

	"A great deal" or "quite a lot" of confidence (%)	"Not very much" or "Not at all" (%)
Spain (1995)	44.6	50.9
Japan (2005)	77.0	17.0
South Korea (2006)	50.8	49.1
Taiwan (2012)	47.5	45.7

Source: World Values Surveys (various years). Survey years in parentheses. The question wording was as follows: "I am going to name a number of organizations. For each one, could you tell me how much confidence you have in them: is it a great deal of confidence, quite a lot of confidence, not very much confidence or none at all?" The Spanish survey asked for levels of confidence in "the legal system"; the Japanese and South Korean surveys asked for levels of confidence in "the justice system"; the Taiwanese survey asked for levels of confidence in "the courts."

confidence in the judiciary were much lower in the remaining three countries of Spain, South Korea, and Taiwan around the time that the issue of introducing a jury/lay judge system was being debated in each of these countries. It should be noted that these levels of trust in the justice system in Spain, South Korea, and Taiwan are generally lower than those seen in other developed democracies. The 2005–9 wave of the World Values Surveys shows that the mean percentage of respondents who expressed "a great deal" or "quite a lot" of confidence in the justice system among twelve developed democracies (Australia, Canada, Finland, France, Germany, Italy, Netherlands, Norway, Sweden, Switzerland, the United Kingdom, and the United States) was 60.7%, while the mean percentage of those who indicated "not very much" confidence or "not at all" was 36.9%. Among the twelve countries, only in France and the Netherlands did fewer than 50% of respondents indicate that they had "a great deal" or "quite a lot" of confidence in the justice system. It is interesting that the Netherlands has resisted adopting a lay judge system despite relatively high levels of public distrust in the judiciary. The 1995 Spanish survey shows that 44.6% of respondents expressed confidence in the legal system, while 50.9% did not.[14] In the 2006 South Korean survey, 50.8% of

[14] The Spanish survey asked about the "legal system" rather than the justice system, so the results are not directly comparable with the results for Japan

respondents indicated that they had "quite a lot" or "a great deal" of confidence in the justice system, while 49.1% replied that they had "not very much" confidence or "none at all." According to the 2012 Taiwanese survey, 47.5% of respondents expressed "quite a lot" or "a great deal" of confidence in the courts and 45.7% expressed "not very much" confidence or "none at all."[15]

If higher levels of public distrust in the justice system lead countries to introduce jury/lay judge systems that undermine the power of professional judges to a greater extent, then Spain, South Korea, and Taiwan should have adopted jury/lay judge systems that impose similarly strong constraints upon professional judges, whereas Japan should have introduced weaker constraints. But this is not at all what we see. Spain did introduce strong constraints, but South Korea and Taiwan chose not to seriously undermine the powers of professional judges. By contrast, the Japanese judiciary was subjected to extensive reforms despite high levels of public trust.

Thus, while low levels of public trust in the judiciary may sometimes help to propel the issue of introducing of jury/lay judge systems onto the policy agenda, it does not account for the variations in the extent to which these new systems transfer powers from professional judges to jurors/lay judges.

Delegation and Judicial Independence

If public opinion fails to explain why some countries choose to transfer more powers to jurors/lay judges than others, we must turn to elite-level dynamics. One such perspective is offered by the principal-agent literature on delegation. This literature has explored why legislatures should ever grant discretion to bureaucracies, as well as the conditions

---

and South Korea (below), although the 1990 version of the Spanish survey that asked for levels of confidence in the Spanish justice system yielded largely similar results; 48.5% of respondents indicated "a great deal" or "a lot" of confidence, while 50.4% responded that they had "not very much" confidence or "not at all."

[15] The 2012 Taiwanese survey asked about levels of confidence in the "courts" as opposed to the justice system, although the 2006 Taiwanese survey, which was conducted some years before the issue emerged onto the agenda in Taiwan in early 2011, did ask about the justice system. This latter survey reports slightly lower levels of confidence than the 2012 survey, with 39.0% of respondents indicating "a great deal" or "quite a lot" of confidence, and 50.3% choosing "not very much" confidence or "not at all."

under which legislatures should delegate more or less discretion to bureaucracies (e.g. McCubbins and Schwartz 1984; Epstein and O'Halloran 1999).

From the perspective of this literature, a new jury/lay judge system removes discretionary powers vested in professional judges and transfers them over to citizens. The "fire alarm" view of bureaucratic oversight suggests that legislators may often prefer to design systems that would enable the public to report on bureaucratic abuses. Fire alarm systems are often less costly and they also enable legislators to claim credit more efficiently than so-called "police patrol"-type oversight, which requires much more labor on their part (McCubbins and Schwartz 1984).

Huber and Shipan (2002) argue that legislatures may impose greater limits on bureaucratic autonomy when policy conflict between legislature and bureaucracies is greater, and this perspective may be applied to the relationship between legislatures and the judicial branch as well. The greater the policy conflict between the legislative and judicial branches, the greater the constraints that the legislature may impose on the power of the courts, e.g. by transferring extensive powers to juries/lay judges.

It is important to note, however, that introducing a jury/lay judge system goes far beyond the installation of "fire alarms." As noted earlier, jury/lay judge systems enable citizens to *themselves* take part in policymaking. Thus, far beyond merely installing a "fire alarm," the introduction of such a system is more like installing a "sprinkler." That is, rather than simply improving the monitoring of judicial decision-making, introducing a jury/lay judge system represents a fundamental change in the decision-making apparatus itself. A different framework is necessary to account for the variations in the extent to which different countries take decision-making powers away from professional judges and put them directly into the hands of citizens.

The principal-agent literature has also specifically examined why legislatures would grant courts more or less independence from political interference (e.g. Rogers 2001; Ginsburg 2003; Stephenson 2003). The decision to transfer powers from professional judges to juries/lay judges may be viewed as a curtailment of judicial independence.[16] As noted earlier, judicial independence is typically understood as

---

[16] For an excellent review of the literature on judicial independence, see Helmke and Rosenbluth (2009).

placing professionalism over politics (e.g. Helmke and Rosenbluth 2009). It can thus be argued that jury/lay judge systems undermine judicial independence and the autonomy of professional judges, because some of their powers are handed over to the unprofessional public. Do existing theories of the determinants of judicial independence offer useful perspectives for understanding the variations in the extent to which different countries choose to erode the power of professional judges in this particular way?

One influential line of reasoning suggests that competitive party systems are likely to enhance judicial independence (e.g. Ginsburg 2003; Stephenson 2003; Finkel 2005, 2008). Also known as political insurance theory, this view argues that ruling parties that face being ousted from power are likely to strengthen judicial independence in order to ensure that the courts will not overturn their policies after they leave office.

While this argument was advanced as an explanation of why ruling parties would seek to enhance judicial independence from politics, the argument could also be applied to explaining variations in judicial independence vis-à-vis the public. That is, ruling parties that face greater threat of defeat may seek to strengthen judicial independence to a greater extent, not only vis-à-vis politicians but also vis-à-vis the public that has turned against the ruling party. Conceivably, limiting the power of juries/lay judges may help outgoing parties to shield their policies or themselves from future changes in public opinion. Conversely, ruling parties that are more secure in power may be more willing to cede power to the juries/lay judges, since they may believe that the public is on their side.

This hypothesis, however, does not stand up to the empirical evidence. For instance, Spain's PSOE faced a strong prospect of defeat in the upcoming elections around the time that it introduced the jury system in 1995, but that did not deter them from delegating substantial powers from the professional judges to the jurors. Moreover, while Japan's LDP enjoyed a relatively strong electoral base in 2004, it tried to limit the transfer of power from the professional to the lay judges, while opposition parties, which at the time saw little prospect of forming a government, pushed for a more extensive transfer of power to the citizens. Thus, there appears to be no systematic correlation between the electoral prospects of ruling parties and the extent to which those parties seek to undermine the autonomy of the professional judges by introducing jury/lay judge systems. While political insurance theory may offer a persuasive account for when governments may seek to enhance judicial independence vis-à-vis political interference, it does not explain the variations in the extent to which governments choose to undermine the independence of judiciaries vis-à-vis the public.

At a theoretical level, there could also conceivably be an *inverse* correlation between judicial independence from politicians and the extent to which legislatures are likely to transfer powers away from professional judges to citizens. More independent judiciaries may paradoxically have less leverage for bargaining vis-à-vis legislatures compared to less independent judiciaries. For instance, more independent judiciaries cannot promise the legislature that they would rule in favor of the government on an issue as a quid pro quo for the legislature accommodating the judiciary on other issues because to offer such a promise would compromise their independence. Thus, *ceteris paribus*, judiciaries that are more independent from politics, may be more politically vulnerable to the introduction of jury/lay judge systems than those that are less independent from politics. This vulnerability may lead to greater transfers of power away from professional judges to citizens in countries with higher judicial independence compared to countries with less.

However, the empirical evidence suggests that judicial independence also fails to offer a persuasive account for the variations in the extent to which states chose to transfer powers away from professional judges. Scholars have developed a number of different measures of judicial independence from politics in recent years. These studies generally rank Japan highest among the four countries in *de facto* judicial independence (e.g. Feld and Voigt 2003; Linzer and Staton 2015). But as seen earlier, Japan did not transfer the most powers away from professional judges. Moreover, measures of judicial independence are highly sensitive to specification, and, while scholars generally agree that Japan ranks the highest, they disagree as to whether Spain, Taiwan, or South Korea ranks higher or lower than each other. For instance, Feld and Voigt (2003) rank South Korea higher than Taiwan and Taiwan higher than Spain, but Linzer and Staton (2015) rank Spain higher than Taiwan and Taiwan higher than South Korea. In both studies, the differences among the four countries are not exceedingly large, however. The bottom line is that it is difficult to claim that such small differences in degrees of judicial independence could have produced the significant differences that we observe in the extent to which the four countries have transferred powers away from professional judges. A different explanation is thus necessary.

Partisan Politics

Studies of democratization, conscription, and taxation have all pointed to the importance of partisan politics in shaping those policies, although in different ways in different issue-areas. Most studies of democratization concur that the traditional leftist parties have historically spearheaded the expansion of the suffrage, while parties of the right have generally resisted it (Rueschemeyer et al. 1992; Tilly 1997; Przeworski 2009). Studies of regressive taxation have also stressed the importance of the left-right divide. Scholars of tax policy find, surprisingly, that social democratic governments are more likely to impose regressive taxation than conservative governments (Kato 2003; Beramendi and Rueda 2007). Existing work on conscription also points to the importance of partisan dynamics. During World War I, when many Anglo-Saxon countries began to introduce mass conscription for the first time, the right often favored conscription, while the traditional left, especially organized labor, often opposed it (Adams and Poirier 1987; Levi 1996).[17] Extrapolating from these studies, it is possible to hypothesize either that the left will serve as the main proponent of introducing jury/lay judge systems that transfer extensive powers away from professional judges, just as it supported the extension of the suffrage, or that the right will be the main proponent of reforms, just as it supported the institution of military conscription.

This book agrees with these existing studies on the importance of the relative strength and ideological orientations of particular parties. But traditional left-right dynamics fail to account for the extent to which different countries have transferred powers from professional judges to juries/lay judges. For instance, as will be shown in Chapters 5 and 6, while Japan's Liberal Democratic Party (LDP) and Democratic Party of Japan (DPJ) differed almost not at all on the "taxes versus

---

[17] The left did not oppose mass conscription in all countries. As Kier (1999) notes, the French left, for instance, supported mass conscription because it viewed a standing army as a threat to democracy. But as Flynn (2002) argues, the French left, as with the left in other countries, became increasingly wary of conscription in the twentieth century and successfully fought to shorten the duration of required service.

spending" policy dimension that is one of the classic cleavages between the left and the right (Benoit and Laver 2006), they took markedly different positions on the design of the new Japanese lay judge system.

In sum, none of the existing hypotheses sufficiently accounts for the puzzle that motivates this book. Rising public distrust of the justice system may propel the issue of judicial reform onto the policy agenda, but it does not account for the variations in the extent to which countries transfer powers from professional judges to jury/lay judges. Neither the desire to boost judicial independence, nor judicial independence itself, nor the strength of the traditional left or the right offers a cross-nationally valid account for the variations in the configuration of new jury/lay judge systems. The book thus develops an alternative theoretical argument.

Overview of Argument

This book advances a two-step framework that stresses the role of partisan dynamics in shaping the extent to which the new jury/lay judge systems of different countries transfer powers from professional judges to juries/lay judges. The book builds on the basic insights from studies of democratization, conscription, taxation, and delegation that stress the crucial role of partisan politics, but it argues that partisan politics mattered in a different way than has been conceptualized in those existing studies. First, the book argues that the introduction of jury/lay judge systems is typically promoted most vigorously by "new left"-oriented parties, or what Herbert Kitschelt terms "left-libertarian" parties. These parties first emerged in Western Europe and North America during the 1970s and exhibit a particular concern over issues relating to the environment, minorities, and the values of creative self-fulfillment, self-determination, and participation. Kitschelt (1994: 10) stresses that the new left aims not only to achieve substantive policy outcomes, but also to improve the "quality of the process" through which those outcomes are brought about. New left-oriented parties are thus likely to be more eager to introduce measures for direct participation, like the jury, into decision-making processes, than *either* "old left"-oriented parties *or* conservative parties. Therefore, the more that parties in any given country adopt new left issues, the more likely they are to push for greater citizen participation, such as the introduction of a jury/lay judge system. Both rightist and leftist parties that shun new left concerns should be ideologically uninterested in, or even hostile to, such progressive reforms of the judiciary, although they may be willing to contemplate introducing more cosmetic forms of lay participation.

Second, the configuration of new jury/lay judge systems is contingent on the relative power of new left-oriented parties within the political system. *Ceteris paribus*, the stronger the new left-oriented parties vis-à-vis conservative parties or old left parties, the more new jury/lay judge systems should transfer powers from professional judges to jury/lay judges. Conversely, the weaker that new left-oriented parties are within the overall political system, the more the professional judges should be able to retain their powers. The theoretical basis for this hypothesis will be fleshed out in further detail in Chapter 2.

The view that the strength of new left-oriented parties crucially shapes the configuration of new jury/lay judge systems underscores the point that lay judge systems come about as a result of bargaining among key political actors. The book's focus on both partisan preferences and partisan dynamics as key to understanding the design of new jury/lay judge systems yields several broader insights for the field of comparative politics.

First, the book underscores the point made by O'Donnell and Schmitter (1986) and Luebbert (1991) in their studies of democratization, that decisions to open up channels for public participation are often fundamentally elite-driven and come about as a result of bargaining among elites. The influence of the public over the extent to which it becomes empowered is at best indirect. Thus, for instance, high levels of public distrust vis-à-vis professional judges do not necessarily lead to the introduction of lay judge systems that undermine the powers of professional judges to a greater degree, and vice versa. But high levels of certain *parties'* distrust vis-à-vis professional judges may have a much greater impact over the design of new systems, especially if those parties are relatively influential within the overall party system. This point also dovetails with the argument advanced by recent studies of democratization that partisan dynamics crucially shaped the trajectory of democratization in nineteenth-century Europe (Capoccia and Ziblatt 2010; Ertman 2010). The basic insight that elite-level dynamics play a key role in designing systems of public participation also has implications for the *implementation* of lay judge systems once these systems are introduced. Since they are often not a response to concrete mass public demand, nascent jury/lay judge systems may encounter difficulties in mobilizing people to serve.

Second, the book's focus on partisan dynamics reaffirms the value of the "political insurance" approach adopted by recent studies of judicial independence. But while new jury/lay judge systems undermine the independence of judges vis-à-vis the public, neither theories of judicial independence nor judicial independence itself can account for the extent to which states transfer powers from professional judges to jurors/lay judges. Ruling parties faced electoral defeat in Spain, South Korea, and Taiwan at the time that each of these countries considered introducing a new jury/lay judge system, but the three countries transferred powers to jurors/lay judges to very different degrees. By contrast, Japan, where the ruling party was relatively secure in power, chose to undermine the independence of professional judges to a considerable degree, indeed to a greater extent than in South Korea or Taiwan, where ruling parties' hold on power was more tenuous. In addition, there is little correlation between countries' scores on measures of judicial independence and the extent to which states transferred powers away from professional judges to juries/lay judges. The study thus suggests that the conditions that promote judicial independence from *politics* are quite different than those that promote judicial independence from the *public*.

Third, this book finds that the extent to which states transfer powers away from the professional judges to citizens, thereby allowing citizens to take part in judicial decision-making but concomitantly imposing a new obligation on citizens, is shaped neither by the traditional left nor the right, but by the relative strength of the *new* left. Recall that opposition to the draft was one of the core political agendas for the nascent new left, not only in the United States during the Vietnam War but also in other developed democracies as well (Foley 2003; Symons and Cahill 2005). The present study shows that the new left, which had staunchly opposed conscription during its earlier years, has paradoxically been an eager advocate of introducing the jury/lay judge system, which is another form of civic obligation. This implies that although new left ideas have also sometimes been referred to as "left-libertarian" (e.g. Kitschelt 1994), the "libertarianism" of the new left is contingent on the nature of the issue in question.

Plan of the Book

The book draws on both mixed-method analysis of the Japanese case and comparative case studies of Taiwan, South Korea, and Spain to support the hypotheses offered above. A substantial portion of the empirical material presented in this book thus focuses on Japan. As noted earlier, Japan is an especially useful case for illuminating the conditions that shape the design of new jury systems, because among the four cases under study, Japan represents the most established political system. Whereas the Spanish democratic system only came into being in the late 1970s, the Korean system in the late 1980s, and the Taiwanese democracy in the 1990s, the current Japanese democratic system has been in existence since the late 1940s. Its political system, including the judicial system, is therefore the most entrenched and the most institutionalized among the four countries. One could thus have expected Japan to make the least dramatic break from the existing system compared to the newer democracies, where institutions are less well entrenched and more fluid. Nevertheless, Japan made a relatively clean break from the past, transferring greater powers to the broader public than the newer democracies of Korea and Taiwan. This makes it a particularly useful "crucial case" through which to illuminate the political dynamics that shape the design of new jury systems. The study presents quantitative content analyses of a new dataset of over fifty years of postwar parliamentary debates over the jury/lay judge system in Japan, as well as careful process-tracing of the precise mechanisms through which partisan dynamics shaped the design of the Japanese *saiban-in* system.

The book also reports the results of in-depth original field research on the case of Taiwan. As Taiwan has not yet introduced a new jury/lay judge system, it offers an especially useful case for this book. Not only do the reform proposals advanced by different Taiwanese parties provide additional opportunities to test the validity of the hypothesis presented in this study, but the case also illuminates the conditions under which no transfer of powers from professional judges to jurors/lay judges may occur. The book also features shadow case studies of Spain and South Korea.

The book will proceed as follows. Chapter 2 elaborates on the novel theoretical framework that was sketched above: the importance of partisan dynamics to explain the configuration of new lay judge systems in developed democracies. Chapter 3 begins the empirical section of the book with extensive discussion of the partisan ideological spectrum in the four countries under study. Chapter 4 offers some historical background to the issue of introducing a jury/lay judge system in Japan, including quantitative content analysis of parliamentary discussions of the issue up to 1996. Chapter 5 tests the empirical validity of the theoretical argument presented in Chapter 2 by conducting detailed process-tracing of the introduction of the *saiban-in* system in Japan. Chapter 6 further tests the theory through content analysis of deliberations over the reform in the Japanese national Diet after 1996. Chapter 7 offers in-depth process-tracing of the case of Taiwan based on original field research. Chapter 8 presents the case studies of Spain and South Korea. Chapter 9 lays out some data on the impact that new jury/lay judge systems have had on verdict and sentencing patterns, focusing primarily on the case of Japan but also with data from South Korea and Spain. Chapter 10 summarizes and concludes.

2 | *Theoretical Framework: Participation and Partisan Politics*

Overview

As outlined in Chapter 1, there exists considerable variation in the configuration of new jury/lay judge systems that developed democracies have adopted since the early 1990s. Spain and Japan introduced systems that impose stronger constraints on the power of professional judges, while Korea's new system and Taiwan's pilot system preserved the power of professional judges to a much greater extent.

What accounts for this cross-national variation in the newly introduced jury/lay judge systems of developed democracies? Chapter 1 showed the limitations of a number of plausible hypotheses: public distrust of the judiciary, the desire to boost judicial independence, and traditional left-right partisan ideology. This chapter lays out an alternative theoretical framework that elucidates why different countries have transferred powers from professional judges to lay judges/juries to markedly different degrees.

The chapter advances a two-step theoretical framework that focuses on partisan dynamics. First, regarding partisan preferences toward jury/lay judge systems, parties that embrace so-called "new left" issues to a greater extent are more likely to favor a greater transfer of powers to juries or lay judges. The more that parties adopt "new left" causes, the more likely they are to push for systems that significantly undermine the powers of professional judges. Conversely, conservative parties and leftist parties that are more reluctant to adopt "new left" issues should want professional judges to retain more of their powers.

Second, the actual impact of new left-oriented parties on the design of new jury/lay judge systems should be contingent on the relative influence of those parties within the overall party system. The greater the political power of new left-oriented parties vis-à-vis other parties, the greater the likelihood that a more extensive transfer of powers from professional judges to juries/lay judges will occur. Conversely,

Table 2.1 *Expected transfer of powers from professional judges to jury/lay judges*

	Relative power of new left-oriented parties	
	Weaker	Stronger
Parties' adoption of new left issues: Less extensive	Limited transfer	Moderate transfer
More extensive	Moderate transfer	Extensive transfer

the more limited the political power of new left-oriented parties, the more likely that professional judges will retain more of their powers.

This basic theoretical argument of this study can be illustrated as shown in Table 2.1.

The remainder of this chapter will delineate in greater detail the precise mechanisms that drive these hypothesized expectations. The following section sketches how the left and the right have traditionally viewed the broad issue of citizen participation, and how the left's views have changed with the rise of the new left. The third section discusses how the new left, and in particular new left proponents of "deliberative democracy," has viewed the institution of the jury more specifically. The fourth section discusses how the left-right dimension may take on distinctive characteristics in "post-developmental" states, making leftist parties in these countries particularly likely to embrace new left causes. The fifth section moves from explaining parties' preferences to explaining policy outcomes, i.e. the configuration of new jury/lay judge systems, by examining the factors that shape the relative power of new left-oriented parties over the design of those systems. The sixth section summarizes and concludes.

Participation and the New Left

Until recent decades, neither the left nor the right had been particularly keen to expand the direct participation of citizens in policymaking in most developed democracies. Of course, as noted in Chapter 1, the left had historically spearheaded the expansion of suffrage (Rueschemeyer et al. 1992; Tilly 1997; Przeworski 2009), but the expansion of suffrage had been viewed as a means of fostering public input into *representative* democracy, rather than in policymaking per se. In terms of policymaking, the left's ideal was centralized state planning. Moreover, as Robert Michels (1911 [1999]) famously noted, labor parties actually pioneered the top-down, hierarchical, bureaucratic political party structure that was subsequently also adopted by the right. Corporatism, which is also often associated with traditional left-labor parties, also assumes a hierarchical structure whereby top union leaders negotiate with state and business elites, and union members vote in accordance with the union leaders' orders (Schmitter 1974; Katzenstein 1985). Meanwhile, right parties tended to view proposals for direct citizen input as opening the door to "mob rule" (Burke 2008). In short, the left and the right had both traditionally favored hierarchical, top-down decision-making, not direct popular input in policymaking.

The left's comfortable acceptance of hierarchy began to fade during the 1960s and 1970s with the rise of the new left. As is well known, the new left began to emerge in the 1950s and 1960s as a reaction against the old left, which traditionally stood not only for income redistribution and state intervention in the economy, but also planning, hierarchy, and control (e.g. Kitschelt 1994). The new left is characterized by a concern over issues relating to the environment and minorities, and perhaps above all, the values of creative self-fulfillment, self-determination, and participation. As Kitschelt (1994: 10) notes, the new left stresses not only the achievement of substantive policy outcomes, but also much more the "quality of the process" through which those outcomes are brought about. This strong attention to the "how" of the political process sets the new left apart from both the old left and the right.

Scholars have pointed to a number of different factors that have led to the rise and expansion of the new left. Inglehart (1988) points to the growing number of "postmaterialist" citizens in advanced industrialized societies who have spent their "formative years" in conditions of affluence. Duch and Taylor (1993) find that educational attainment and economic conditions both influence levels of postmaterialism. Kitschelt (1994) argues that a more educated citizenry, rising numbers of professional workers, and the expansion of the welfare state have propelled the rise of what he terms "left-libertarian" citizens with high levels of political self-efficacy.

The new left has made its mark on partisan politics in developed democracies. The rise of "left-libertarian" *citizens* who value new left issues has spawned *parties* that value those issues, and vice versa. In some cases, new left parties have taken the form of entirely new parties, as in the case of the Green Party in Germany. In others, "old left" parties in many European countries adopted what Meguid (2005) has termed an "accommodative strategy," co-opting the positions of green parties and transforming themselves into champions of issues relating to the environment, minorities, and participation. For instance, the website of the German Social Democratic Party, a once-prototypical "old left" party, now proudly proclaims the slogan: "Clean Environment, Healthy Climate."[1] The French Socialist website also reads: "Le développement durable est au coeur de notre projet politique (sustainable development is at the heart of our political project)."[2] The Democratic Party in the United States has also come to embrace pro-environment and pro-choice positions. In fact, as Jennings (1987, 2002) shows, former 1960s new left student activists in the United States overwhelmingly support the Democratic Party, several decades since the protest era.

The general trend of leftist parties has thus certainly been in the new left direction. But the extent to which cleavages over emerging new left issues overlap with the traditional left-right policy cleavage has varied considerably across different countries. Scholars have in fact often conceptualized the new left as comprising an entirely new issue dimension that cross-cuts the old left-right policy cleavage. For instance, Inglehart (1988) speaks of a materialist-postmaterialist issue dimension, and Kitschelt (1994) refers to an authoritarian-libertarian issue dimension that is distinct from, and cross-cuts, the traditional cleavage over redistribution and state control.

A voluminous body of work has sought to establish empirically the extent to which a new political cleavage has in fact emerged among parties of developed democracies (e.g. Laver and Hunt 1992; Huber and Inglehart 1995; Knutsen 1998; Budge et al. 2001; Klingemann et al. 2006). These studies have employed various ways to estimate the policy positions of political parties across time and across different countries. Some have relied on expert surveys (Laver and Hunt 1992;

---

[1] German Social Democratic Party, "Saubere Umwelt, gesundes Klima," www .spd.de/standpunkte/saubere-umwelt-gesundes-klima/, accessed February 26, 2016.

[2] French Socialist Party, "Développement durable et ruralité," www.parti-socialiste.fr/nos-idees/developpement-durable-et-ruralite, accessed January 18, 2015.

Huber and Inglehart 1995; Knutsen 1998), while others, most notably the Comparative Manifesto Project (CMP), have drawn on content analyses of party manifestoes (e.g. Budge et al. 2001; Klingemann et al. 2006). In either vein, scholars generally concur that claims of an entirely new issue cleavage are exaggerated. While issues of redistribution and state intervention in the economy continue to serve as the main issues that divide the "left" and the "right," more recently, "new left" issues relating to the environment, minorities, and participation have *also* come to separate the left from the right in most developed democracies (Spoon et al. 2014). Thus, leftist parties have typically added new left issues as further differentiation from the right. But there also exists a great deal of variation across different countries.

For instance, expert surveys conducted by Laver and Hunt (1992) on twenty-four countries find that environmental issues – a prototypical "new left" issue – comprised the same policy dimension as "public ownership" – a prototypical "old left" issue – to a much greater extent in countries such as Australia, Austria, Japan, and Spain, than in Belgium, Denmark, and Ireland. Similarly, based on a survey of 800 experts in forty-two countries, Huber and Inglehart (1995) reported that "economic or class conflict" continued to be the issue most often cited as dividing the left from the right in most developed democracies. The "traditional vs. new culture" cleavage, which consists of issues relating to the environment, moral order, and participation, among others, was the second most frequently cited as separating the left from the right in some countries – such as Spain, the United States, and the Netherlands – but less so in others, such as Sweden and Britain (ibid). Using more recent expert survey data, Bakker et al. (2015) also confirm that parties' positions on economic left-right dimension are strongly correlated with their positions on what they term the "green/ alternative/libertarian (GAL) – traditional/authoritarian/nationalist (TAN)" dimension in the fourteen initial EU member countries, but again with considerable cross-national variation in the strength of the correlation.

These findings from expert surveys have been corroborated through party manifesto research as well. For instance, drawing on CMP data, Laver and Budge (1992) find, using an inductive approach based on twenty policy dimensions, that parties' positions on the "taxes versus services" issue were more closely associated with their positions on environmental issues in some countries – such as Australia and

Germany – than in others, such as Greece, Ireland, and New Zealand. Also drawing on CMP data on twelve European countries, Klingemann (1995) reports that parties' positions on issues of decentralization, environmental protection, democracy, and multiculturalism are more closely correlated with their positions on the capitalist/socialist economy or expansion/limitation of the welfare state in some countries than in others. Drawing on a longer time-series of CMP data that spans five decades, Franzmann and Kaiser (2006) find a close affinity among manifestoes of the "left" with favorable attitudes toward not only regulation of the economy but also "environmental protection," "democracy," "social justice," and "underprivileged minority groups" in some countries, such as Germany, Italy and Sweden, but not in others, notably the United Kingdom. The same study reports the "right" to be associated not only with issues such as "enterprise" and "efficiency" but also "social harmony" and "traditional morality," again to differing degrees in different countries. Dalton (2009) also finds, drawing on both expert surveys and CMP data, that while the correlation between parties' positions on environmental issues, the prototypical new left issue, and their positions on economic issues strengthened between 1989 and the early 2000s from 0.64 to 0.76, the correlation still was not perfect.

Studies that have examined the policy positions of individual parties have lent support to the findings from the cross-national studies. Drawing on expert surveys, Laver and Hunt (1992) find the correlation in leftist parties' policy positions between the "tax vs. spend" dimension and the environmental policy dimension to be weaker for New Zealand's Labor Party and Sweden's Social Democratic Party than for the Austrian Socialist Party and the German Social Democratic Party. Also drawing on expert surveys, Kitschelt (1994) finds that leftist parties in different countries have adopted "new left" issues to varying degrees. He reports that leftist parties in Spain, Denmark, and Germany have embraced new left issues to a greater extent than their counterparts in Sweden or Britain. Drawing on more recent expert survey data, Benoit and Laver (2006) also find that leftist parties have more thoroughly adopted new left positions in countries such as Australia, Austria, France, Germany, Japan, and Spain, while in countries such as Cyprus, Iceland, and Luxembourg, leftist parties have taken up new left positions to a much more limited degree.

Thus, while the cleavage over new left issues could in theory cross-cut the traditional left-right cleavage or converge with it, in fact the patterns are different in different countries. The two issue cleavages have converged in many countries, while they still constitute separate issue cleavages in others. The old left/right cleavage has thus increasingly morphed into a left-libertarian/right-authoritarian cleavage in many developed democracies, but the correlation is not perfect. It is possible that the two issue dimensions may eventually converge completely in future decades, but this cannot be predicted with certainty.

Scholars have pointed to several different factors that affect why different "old left" parties may adopt new left issues to different degrees. Adams et al. (2006) stress the differences in the extent to which public opinion has embraced new left causes in different countries. Kitschelt (1994) and, more recently, Schumacher et al. (2013) point to an interactive effect between broad societal factors, including public opinion, and party-organizational factors. Meguid (2005) contends that a combination of electoral threat posed by new parties and the configuration of electoral rules shapes the likelihood that old left parties adopt new left issues (also Spoon et al. 2014).

Leftist parties that embrace new left issues to a greater extent should be more likely to push for new left policy measures, such as environmental protection, transparency, and greater citizen participation. Theoretically, the idea of introducing a jury/lay judge system should fit precisely into this cluster of issues. But how has the new left actually viewed jury/lay judge systems more specifically? The next section explores this question in detail.

Deliberative Democracy and the Jury

In recent years, many social theorists have embraced the idea of lay participation in court trials as one of the few available avenues for "deliberative democracy" in contemporary society. The theorists' intellectual labor has been highly appreciated and to some extent put into practice by many new left activists and politicians.

Building on Jürgen Habermas's view of the "public sphere," theorists of "deliberative democracy" argue that "when citizens or their representatives disagree morally, they should continue to reason together to reach mutually acceptable decisions" (Gutmann and Thompson 1996: 1). Deliberation among citizens is argued to be important because "[t]he moral authority of collective judgments about policy depends in part on the moral quality of the process by which citizens collectively reach those judgments" (ibid: 4). In this view, the *process* by which policy decisions come about is an integral part of the authority and legitimacy of the policy itself. Deliberative democracy is not viewed by these theorists as a replacement for representative democracy but is usually seen to augment and to strengthen it (Delli Carpini et al. 2004).

As with much new left thinking, the idea of "deliberative democracy" is rooted in a critique of the modern bureaucratic system. Kelly (2004: 42–3) argues:

Habermas sometimes characterized the welfare state as halfway successful. On one hand, the welfare state gives institutional flesh to the social rights of citizens, that is, those that aim to secure their well-being. However, the further the state becomes involved in the everyday well-being of its citizens, the more it tends to bring systematic power into the lifeworld. The resulting juridification of the lifeworld replaces the spontaneous, communicative organization of everyday life with legal and administrative relations. The encroachment of bureaucratic power on the communicative forms of interaction in the lifeworld naturally gives rise to alienation.

Kelly (2004: 48) goes on to point out:

Habermas . . . proposed an account of deliberative democracy that fashions a connection between the public and the administrative state in a way that respects individual rights but also creates procedures by which communicatively generated power can steer (or counter-steer) administrative power. As Habermas . . . put it, the idea is that the public sphere assumes responsibility for the "pool of reasons from which administrative decisions must draw their rationalizations" . . . [W]hen popular sovereignty is realized, the political system is structured in such a way as to create procedures by which the free and open public sphere can generate and communicate ideas that mark the range of appropriate administrative discretion.

In Habermas's view, then, deliberation in the public sphere is a means for citizens to not only constrain, but also legitimate, bureaucratic action.

Deliberative democracy is not just a critique of modern bureaucracy. Theorists of deliberative democracy also question the fundamental premises of the aggregative view of democracy based on voting and bargaining (Chambers 2003). Both in voting and bargaining, preferences are viewed as being fixed, and democracy serves as the mechanism via which those fixed preferences are aggregated. Deliberative democracy theorists, on the other hand, see preferences themselves as requiring justification and also to be malleable, typically via discussion (e.g. Gutmann and Thompson 2004, esp. Chapter 1; Fishkin 2009). While discussion may not necessarily lead to consensus, agreements reached via discussion are viewed to be more legitimate than those reached solely through bargaining or aggregation (Bohman and Rehg 1997; Thompson 2008).

Huckfeldt et al. (2004) summarize three key elements of deliberation: that it occurs in small groups; that it "involves the egalitarian and open-minded exchange" of perspectives; and that it has the potential to stimulate learning from each other, and, in turn, "higher levels of political engagement, tolerance, and compromise among competing viewpoints" (3). Indeed, theorists of deliberative democracy concur that the benefits of deliberation lie precisely in its educational effects on citizens. Mendelberg (2002: 153–4) also argues that as a result of deliberation,

[C]itizens are more enlightened about their own and others' needs and experiences, can better resolve deep conflict, are more engaged in politics, place their faith in the basic tenets of democracy, perceive their political system as legitimate, and lead a healthier civic life.

These theorists concur, then, that deliberation induces learning and enlightenment. Even without assuming that deliberation will transform individuals into enlightened, public-spirited citizens, Gutmann and Thompson (1996: 42) argue that:

[C]itizens and their representatives are more likely to take a broader view of issues, and to consider the claims of more of their fellow citizens, in a process in which moral arguments are taken seriously than in a process in which assertions of political power prevail.

Further, in this process:

Through the give-and-take of argument, citizens and their accountable representatives can learn from one another, come to recognize their individual and collective mistakes, and develop new views and policies that are more widely justifiable. When individuals and groups bargain and negotiate, they may learn how better to get what they want. But unless they also deliberate with one another, they are not likely to learn that they should not try to get what they want. (43)

Thus, deliberation provides opportunities for civic learning. This transformative aspect of deliberation distinguishes it from bargaining, which leaves preferences unchanged (Dryzek 2000).

Given these goals, it is perhaps not surprising that theorists of "deliberative democracy" have often looked to the jury as a one of the few institutionalized opportunities for reasoned public deliberation in contemporary society. Gastil and Weiser (2006: 607) argue:

The ideal deliberative setting would involve a broad cross-section of the public in an experience that concluded with real legal or policy outcomes. As it happens, there is only one such research setting in the United States at this time – the trial jury.

Abramson (1994: 8) also notes:

Deliberation is a lost virtue in modern democracies; only the jury still regularly calls upon ordinary citizens to engage each other in a face-to-face process of debate. No group can win that debate simply by outvoting others; under the traditional requirement of unanimity, power flows to arguments that persuade across group lines and speak to a justice common to persons drawn from different walks of life. By history and design, the jury is centrally about getting persons to bracket or transcend starting loyalties.

Thus, many proponents of deliberative democracy have held the institution of the jury in particularly high regard, often viewing it as the *only* institution in contemporary society that allows citizens to engage in the crucial experience of reasoned deliberation. It is notable that Alexis de Tocqueville's well-known praise of the jury as a "school, free of charges, and always open" for the masses (Tocqueville 1840/2000) and the new left praise of the jury as a forum for deliberative democracy are actually based on similar reasoning. Indeed, proponents of deliberative democracy frequently invoke Tocqueville's view of how the jury promotes public-spiritedness. Both stress the benefits of the jury as a forum for social learning and for broadening one's horizons. Both agree that this learning occurs through small-group deliberation.

Scholars have found ample evidence that deliberation in juries and other settings indeed often does lead to higher levels of voting, heightened political self-efficacy, and greater levels of political trust (e.g. Wuthnow 1994; Fishkin 2009; Gastil et al. 2010). But empirical scholars of communication have noted that the political theorists' view of the benefits of deliberation is somewhat optimistic, for at least two reasons. First, a long line of social-psychological studies of the jury has revealed that even within juries, status differences among jurors lead to different levels of participation in discussion (e.g. Strodbeck et al. 1957; Berger et al. 1972; Levine et al. 2001). In practice, deliberations among jurors do not necessarily occur among "equals"; instead, some members of the jury are able to exert more influence over their peers by virtue of their social prestige and/or expertise. Thus, the idea that jurors may deliberate with each other on an equal footing is largely a myth. This point is also underscored in studies of the "mixed" juries that are common in continental Europe, in which professional and lay judges deliberate collectively to reach both sentence and verdict. These studies typically find that lay jurors are often reluctant to voice their opinions in front of professional judges, especially when they disagree with the professional judges (e.g. Bliesener 2006). For instance, a survey of German lay judges in the cities of Bochum and Frankfurt found that only 19% of lay judges indicated that they "very often" or "quite often" expressed views that were different from the presiding judge (Machura 2001: 462). Diesen's (2001: 314) study of the Swedish lay judge system also reports that lay judges outvote professional judges in only 1–3% of cases.

In contrast to most theorists of deliberative democracy, Tocqueville was well aware that deliberating as a jury would involve interaction among unequals. Indeed, this is a crucial point on which Tocqueville and most theorists of deliberative democracy diverge. Tocqueville expresses his hope that by serving on juries, the average citizen will learn from the "most learned and enlightened members of the upper classes" (Tocqueville 1840/2000: 262). Thus, in Tocqueville's view, juries serve as "schools" precisely because members of juries are unequal. This view stands in stark contrast to that offered by proponents of deliberative democracy, who typically view the jury as a valuable forum because it enables the exchange of views among equals.

Second, even when individuals are of relatively similar social status, the empirical evidence for the view that individuals who engage in deliberation with others with different opinions are able to reflect upon their assumptions and ultimately reach compromise has been mixed. While the idea of deliberative democracy assumes that individuals are able to weigh different arguments, reach compromise, and become further motivated to participate in public life, Mutz (2002) finds that when faced with competing arguments, individuals often become "ambivalent" and withdraw from public life rather than being energized to participate. Furthermore, studies of small-group deliberation have often found that instead of reaching consensus, groups may become polarized (Brown 2000; Price 2009). Indeed, juries have not infrequently been known to "hang," that is, to fail to reach a consensus.

These empirical findings notwithstanding theorists of "deliberative democracy" still have especially high hopes for the jury as a forum for civic education. As Gastil et al. (2010: 19) argue:

[T]he jury acts in a way that draws private citizens into political society to exercise official state power. By connecting each of these three spheres in democratic society, the jury provides an exceptional opportunity to educate jurors in the roles and responsibilities of democratic citizenship.

Gastil et al. (2010: 23) go on to list a broad array of "radiant" educational effects that may be expected from serving on juries:

Specifically, after a stint of rewarding, enlightening jury service, one might seek out more contact with fellow citizens through everyday conversations about community life – the same community, most often, to which the civil or criminal trial pertained. This might start as talking about the jury service experience, but it could also blossom into a more general interest in community and political affairs and a desire to have a smaller-scale deliberative conversation about such matters with fellow citizens.

Juries, then, offer "educational opportunities" for civic learning (ibid: 5). Here again, the view advanced here is remarkably similar to that offered almost 200 years ago by Tocqueville, but without Tocqueville's realism about status differences within societies.

Note that another key difference between Tocqueville and proponents of deliberative democracy is that the former acknowledges, and is comfortable with, the coercive aspect of jury service, while the "deliberative democracy" defense of the jury downplays it. Unlike voting, which is not mandatory in most countries, failing to appear for a jury summons can lead to penalties in many countries. For instance, the US federal courts recently increased the fine for failure to appear from $100 to $1,000 (United States Courts n.d.). Similarly, Japanese citizens who fail to appear may be fined up to 100,000 yen (roughly $1,000; *Act on Criminal Trials with the Participation of Saiban-in* 2004, Article 102). Nevertheless, "deliberative democracy" proponents of the jury typically tend to downplay the coercive element in jury duty and stress the benefits of the experience of deliberation itself.

In sum, new left-oriented theorists have had high hopes for popular deliberation, and for the jury more specifically. They have promoted the jury trial as an ideal, despite the mixed empirical evidence for the enlightening effects of deliberation, and despite the uneasy marriage between coercion and participation that jury systems typically entail.

The positions of right-leaning thinkers vis-à-vis the jury have been more varied. On the one hand, some thinkers on the right have become increasingly uneasy with the coercive dimension of the jury. Unlike in Tocqueville's day, it is increasingly difficult for theorists of any stripe to openly advocate for adult citizens to be required to do something because "it is good for them." Some thinkers do advocate mandatory public service for young people on the basis that they need proper education and discipline (see Krebs 2006), but it is something else entirely to advocate forced mobilization of the general adult population. Thus, while some on the right continue to favor mandatory military service (Holsti 1998/9), a paternalistic defense of jury service is much less common.

Another very different strand of the right that has become prominent in a few countries, notably the United States, is right-wing libertarianism. Indeed, in the United States, the libertarian right, even more than the left, has spearheaded the attack on professionals across a broad spectrum of organizational fields (e.g. Shogan 2007). In the US context, the "right" stands increasingly for a revolt against the authority of professionals, and thus typically supports jury service. This line of thinking echoes Tocqueville's second defense of the jury.

But the United States is an outlier among developed democracies in the predominance of this kind of right-wing ideology. Most mainstream right thinkers in Europe and East Asia are very comfortable with technocracy. This is especially true in post-developmental states, where the new left-new right cleavage is clearly also an anti-professional vs. pro-professional cleavage. This point will be explored in more detail in the next section.

The New Left in Post-Developmental States

The partisan dynamic regarding the issue of lay judge participation takes on distinctive characteristics in post-developmental states. All four countries studied in this book, namely Japan, South Korea, Spain, and Taiwan, can be characterized as such. Of course, in many developed countries, such as the United Kingdom, where lay participation systems have been in place for centuries, lay participation long predates the rise of the modern state and may simply be taken for granted. But in post-developmental states such as Japan, South Korea, Spain, and Taiwan, the issue becomes part of the broader new left attack on developmentalism.

While there exists a lively debate over whether rapid industrialization in these four countries transpired because of, or in spite of, their "developmental states" (for influential views see Johnson 1982; Samuels 1987; Okimoto 1989; Woo-Cumings 1999), observers concur that developmental states share a strong centralized bureaucracy, weak unions, and weak public input into the policymaking structure. The ruling parties and bureaucracies of these "developmental states" typically also have strong ties to the big business community (e.g. Samuels 1987; Amsden 1989; Okimoto 1989; Calder 1993). The bureaucracies of these countries enjoy broad discretion in policymaking with little judicial oversight, and the judicial branches of developmental states tend to be relatively weak and to rarely rule against the government (Ginsburg 2001). These were clearly the patterns seen in Spain, South Korea, and Taiwan under authoritarian rule, and also post-1945 Japan, although as a democracy, it developed these traits to a lesser degree than in the three authoritarian states.[3]

Developmental states are likely to be governed by parties on the right because suppressing labor demands for greater redistribution, if not outright repression of the labor movement itself, is typically a major part of their rapid industrialization programs. Developmental states

---

[3] Scholars of Japan have often noted the timidity of the Japanese Supreme Court in ruling against the government (e.g. Ramseyer 2001).

are also typically characterized by, and may even require, extensive networks between the state and big business (Samuels 1987; Amsden 1989; Okimoto 1989; Wade 1990). Not surprisingly, parties that enjoy such ties tend to be conservative parties. Among the developmentalist states covered in this book, Japan has been governed for much of the postwar period by the conservative Liberal Democratic Party, and prewar Japan never saw rule by a left-labor party. Meanwhile, the developmental states of South Korea, Spain, and Taiwan were all governed by conservative parties during their dictatorships, and for a considerable time during their democratic periods as well.

With conservative parties inextricably tied into the developmental state apparatus, opposition parties in developmental states end up adopting political programs that challenge that apparatus. And because developmental states are typically more business-oriented, centralized, and bureaucratic than non-developmental states, opposition parties in developmental states are much more likely to take up new left concerns. Thus, to be a "leftist" in post-developmental states today is almost synonymous with being not only pro-redistribution but also pro-environment, pro-decentralization, and anti-bureaucracy. For instance, Japanese opposition parties focused heavily on redistribution and the expansion of the Japanese welfare state in the early post-war era, but they have become increasingly vocal advocates for "new left" issues since the 1960s as well. This includes issues relating to the environment; Japan's opposition parties enjoyed great success during the late 1960s and early 1970s on an anti-pollution platform (e.g. Upham 1987; Calder 1988).[4] They have also pushed for policies to "open up" the bureaucracy and to improve the quality of governance through legislation on administrative procedures, freedom of information, and greater participation of citizens in the policymaking process, among other measures. Both the Japan Socialist Party and the Japan Communist Party, for instance, separately submitted bills to the Japanese Diet for a freedom-of-information act during the early 1980s, long before the Diet finally passed such a law in 1999. The idea of introducing a jury/lay judge system fits precisely into this category of policies.

---

[4] Indeed, drawing on expert surveys, Laver and Benoit (2005) find that along with social and defense policies, environmental issues also divide the left from the right in Japan, and that the impact of environmental issues is greater than in most developed countries.

Given this broad set of new left policy commitments, opposition parties in post-developmental states should typically be more favorable toward giving extensive powers to juries/lay judges than their conservative party counterparts. The validity of this hypothesis will be tested in the case study chapters that follow.

Of course, even in developmental states, we should expect leftist parties in some countries to adopt new left issues to a greater extent than their counterparts in others, and some leftist parties in other developmental states to adopt new left issues to a greater extent than other leftist parties in the same country. Thus, *ceteris paribus*, we may expect leftist parties that adopt new left issues to a greater extent to favor a greater transfer of powers from professional to lay judges.

From Preferences to Outcomes: Partisan Dynamics

Thus far, this chapter has argued that *ceteris paribus*, parties that adopt new left issues to a greater extent are more likely than other parties to favor lay judge systems that impose greater constraints upon the power of professional judges. Conversely, both conservative parties and leftist parties that have resisted new left causes should prefer jury/lay judge systems that enable professional judges to retain more of their powers over verdict and sentencing. The chapter has also argued that opposition parties in post-developmental states are particularly likely to spawn leftist parties that embrace new left issues, due to their opposition to the ruling conservative party's development agenda and alliance with the bureaucracy.

But the emergence of new left-oriented leftist parties is not a sufficient condition for an extensive transfer of power from professional judges to jury/lay judges to materialize. This is because the political influence of those parties varies considerably across different countries and over time. The impact of new left-oriented parties over the configuration of new jury/lay judge systems is contingent upon the relative power of those parties within the overall party system. *Ceteris paribus*, the stronger the power of new left-oriented parties at the time that the question of introducing a jury/lay judge system emerges onto the policy agenda, the greater the transfer of powers from professional judges to juries/lay judges. Conversely, the stronger the power of conservative or old left parties within the party system at the time that the introduction of a jury/lay judge system rises onto the policy agenda, the more powers professional judges should be able to retain.

This hypothesis suggests that new jury/lay judge systems should impose the strongest constraints upon the power of professional judges in countries where new left-oriented leftist parties govern alone, while they should introduce the weakest constraints, if any, where conservative parties rule alone.

But there are a number of possible constellations of power that lie in between these extreme cases. First, parties in parliamentary systems often rule in coalition with other parties. In such contexts, the parties in coalition must negotiate the configuration of new jury/lay judge systems. Studies have found that junior coalition partners often wield considerable influence over policymaking (e.g. Hofferbert and Klingemann 1990; Kaarbo 1996, 2008; Oppermann and Brummer 2014). If this is the case, then even smaller new left-oriented parties that govern in coalition with larger conservative parties may successfully push for new jury/lay judge systems that impose substantial constraints upon the power of professional judges, although not quite to the extent that they could if they were in power alone. Similarly, if larger new left-oriented parties rule in coalition with smaller conservative parties, the latter may be able to block a major transfer of powers away from professional judges, producing a system that imposes weaker constraints upon the power of professional judges than the larger new left-oriented party may like. Note that coalitions may be formal or informal; minority governments may need to rely on informal coalitions with smaller parties if they do not enter into formal coalitional agreements (e.g. Bouissou 2001).

Second, in presidential and semi-presidential systems there is the possibility of "divided government" (e.g. Bräuninger and König 1999; Coleman 1999; Howell et al. 2000; Manow and Burkhart 2007). This means that a conservative party may control the executive but a leftist party may control the legislature, or vice versa. Divided governments increase the number of veto points; Coleman (1999) and Howell et al. (2000), for instance, report that divided governments produce fewer significant legislative enactments than unified governments. Thus, *ceteris paribus*, divided governments may be less likely to produce major policy shifts like the introduction of a lay judge system. If they do succeed in enacting such a policy change, as with parliamentary coalitions, divided governments should produce a negotiated outcome, with the resulting new system falling somewhere in between the preferences of the party that controls the executive branch and the majority party in the legislature.

Another confounding factor is "divided legislatures," which may occur in countries with bicameral legislatures, whether in parliamentary, presidential, or semi-presidential systems. In this case, the party that controls one of the houses of the legislature differs from the party that controls the other house; a conservative party may control one of the houses while a leftist party controls the other, or vice versa. Bräuninger and König (1999) and Manow and Burkhart (2007) find that legislative productivity is significantly lower under "divided legislatures" than under "unified legislatures." Bräuninger and König (1999) further report that divided legislatures significantly constrain the leadership of the ruling party, especially when the policy preferences of the ruling party and the opposition diverge. Thus, as in the case of divided governments, "divided legislatures" should also diminish the chances for the enactment of major policy reforms such as the introduction of a jury/lay judge system, and if such a reform is achieved at all, the end result should also fall somewhere in between the preferences of the ruling party and the opposition.

A fourth factor has to do with party cohesion. Where party cohesion is weak, party leaders may hope to introduce new jury/lay judge systems but may be undermined by their own party members. The sources of party disunity may be several. For instance, legislators may seek to distance themselves from presidents or prime ministers if the chief executive is unpopular. This may be especially the case in presidential or semi-presidential systems if the executive is in her/his final term and lacks the leverage to rein in legislators (Shugart and Carey 1992; Kasuya 2013b). Alternatively, the sources of party disunity may also be ideological, particularly for new left-oriented parties. Because of their commitment to decentralization and participation, new left-oriented parties are typically more committed to democratic procedures within the party than old left parties, leaving them more averse to imposing party discipline from above. Of course, this is a matter of degree, and green parties across Europe have gradually centralized their organizational structures as they have entered the electoral arena and subsequently government (Poguntke 2002). However, as Poguntke (2002; also Bolleyer 2012) argues, not all green parties have centralized to the same degree. Thus, among new left-oriented parties in general, we may expect to see a range in the extent of centralization, and therefore of party discipline.

A fifth factor is expectations of possible future transfers of power. For instance, conservative parties may wish to enact a weak lay judge system in order to forestall the enactment of a strong lay judge system by a forthcoming leftist government, and vice versa. This may be a form of "preemptive" policymaking (e.g. Kitschelt 1994; Callander and Hummel 2014). Indeed, Callander and Hummel (2014) show how parties that expect to lose power may introduce policies that they would never introduce if their hold on power were more secure.

In theory, several of the above conditions may exist at the same time. For instance, coalition governments or divided governments may also face divided legislatures. A weak president facing a divided legislature and a strong chance of defeat in the next elections may feel compelled to introduce a jury/lay judge system in order to preempt the introduction of a stronger system by the incoming administration. Depending on the configuration of parties, these conditions could enhance or diminish the influence of new left-oriented parties.

One further note is in order. The theoretical framework presented in this chapter focuses on the *design* of new jury/lay judge systems, not on the *fact* of new systems. It takes the emergence of the question of introducing a jury/lay judge system onto the policy agenda as exogenous. It does not predict whether such a reform is more likely to occur under conservative or the rule of new left-oriented parties. New left-oriented parties are likely to favor systems that undermine the powers of professional judges to a *greater extent* than conservative parties, but the issue of introducing some form of lay participation may emerge under conservative party rule as well. While this is fundamentally an empirical question, the four cases under study in this book suggest that this assumption may not be so far-fetched. In two of the four cases, the jury/lay judge system was adopted under leftist party rule (Spain and South Korea), but in Japan, it happened under conservative party rule, and in Taiwan, a conservative government devoted considerable effort to creating one. As will be seen later, among the latter two cases, the question of introducing a jury/lay judge system in Japan emerged during a period of "divided legislature," when new left-oriented parties had the capacity of pushing the issue onto the agenda. But in Taiwan, a series of judicial scandals led the conservative Ma administration to take up the issue as a means of restoring public trust in the judiciary, even though it was not dependent on new left parties in the legislature. Thus, there are multiple channels through which the issue may emerge onto the agenda even when new left-oriented parties are not themselves in power. Of course, since the number of countries examined in this study is small, this question should be examined more closely as more cases become available.

Summary

This chapter has presented a two-step framework that explains the configuration of new jury/lay judge systems in developed democracies. First, *ceteris paribus*, new left-oriented parties are more likely to favor the imposition of stronger constraints upon professional judges than parties that have embraced new left causes to a lesser extent. Second, the political impact of new left-oriented parties, in turn, depends on their relative power within the political system. *Ceteris paribus*, the resulting lay judge system should impose more extensive constraints upon professional judges if new left-oriented parties are stronger relative to other parties within the party system. Conversely, where conservative parties are stronger, professional judges should retain more of their autonomy.

The next chapters will test the validity of these hypotheses, drawing on the cases of Japan, Taiwan, South Korea, and Spain.

3 | *The Distribution of Cases*

Overview

The previous chapter laid out a theoretical framework for understanding the political dynamics that lead countries to adopt different configurations of jury/lay judge systems, and specifically the extent to which they transfer powers from professional judges to juries/lay judges. The chapter pointed to two key factors: (1) the extent to which leftist parties adopt new left causes and (2) the relative power of those new left-oriented parties vis-à-vis other parties in the system.

The remainder of this book tests the hypotheses presented in the previous chapter by drawing on the cases of Japan, Taiwan, South Korea, and Spain. The book tests the hypotheses both via mixed methods and across four country-cases, thus subjecting the theory to a rigorous test. The first step toward testing the hypothesis on the four country-cases is to gain a sense of how the two key independent variables, i.e. the extent to which parties have taken up new left issues and the relative power of those parties, map out empirically in the four countries under study. This is the task of the present chapter.

The chapter will proceed as follows. The following section assesses the policy positions of major parties in the four countries to evaluate the extent to which they have adopted new left concerns during the relevant time period. The third section lays out the relative strength of new left-oriented parties in the four countries. The fourth section combines the assessments made in the second and third sections to generate hypotheses to be tested empirically in the following chapters. The fifth section summarizes and concludes.

Embracing the New Left

To what extent have parties in Japan, South Korea, Spain, and Taiwan adopted new left issues? This study pieces together multiple data sources to gain a sense of the distribution of parties' policy positions on new left issues in the four countries. Note that the debate over the introduction of jury/lay judge systems in Japan, South Korea, Spain, and Taiwan occurred at different time periods, and the data need to correspond to the specific time period of interest: the early- to mid-1990s for Spain, the early 2000s for Japan, the mid-2000s for South Korea, and the early 2010s for Taiwan.

The following discussion of parties' policy positions draws primarily on two main sources that have been used extensively by political scientists: expert surveys and party manifesto data. Both are known to have strengths and weaknesses. Scholars have noted that expert surveys may overstate the differences among parties, and that manifestoes may serve as a better measure of policy salience than of policy positions per se (Budge 2000; Volkens 2007; Bakker and Hobolt 2013). Manifesto measures have also been criticized for lacking a measure of uncertainty (Benoit and Laver 2007). Nevertheless, scholars have also found a high degree of correlation between the expert survey assessments and manifesto coding results, especially the results of the Comparative Manifesto Project (CMP, e.g. Benoit and Laver 2007; König et al. 2013; Bakker et al. 2015). Taken together, the available data reveals a considerable amount of information on where parties in different countries stand on new left issues. This section examines the party positions of Japan, Spain, South Korea, and Taiwan, in turn.

Japan

The issue of introducing a jury/lay judge system emerged in Japan around 1998 and culminated in the passage of the *Act on Criminal Trials with Participation of Saiban-in* in 2004. For Japan around this time period, data on parties' policy positions is available via expert surveys as well as manifestoes. Kato (2014) reports on a series of expert surveys on party positions since 1996. For the purposes of the present study, the 2000, 2003, and 2005 surveys were closest to the time when the issue of introducing a jury/lay judge system was being considered. Among the items in the expert surveys, six of them, specifically social issues, environment, decentralization, national identity, citizens' rights, and immigration are useful for tapping parties' perceived positions on new left issues. Experts were asked to place the parties' positions on these issues along a left-right continuum ranging from

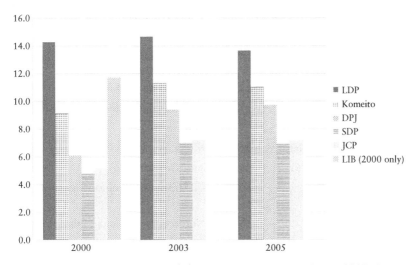

Figure 3.1 Mean scores on new left issues, expert surveys, Japan 2000–5
Source: Kato (2014). Most left-wing position = 1; most right-wing position = 20.

one (most left wing) to twenty (most right wing). The precise wording of the questions is provided in Appendix 3.A at the end of this chapter.

This book takes the mean of the scores for the six issue-areas mentioned above to create an index of parties' positions on new left issues. There were five major parties in existence in Japan around the time: the Liberal Democratic Party (LDP), the Komeito, the Democratic Party of Japan (DPJ), the Social Democratic Party (SDP), and the Japan Communist Party (JCP). In addition, figures for the Liberal Party (LIB) were included for 2000 because it was in coalition with the LDP between late 1998 and early 2000. The LIB merged with the DPJ in 2003 and disbanded. The index for each of the six parties for the years 2000, 2003, and 2005 is shown in Figure 3.1.

Figure 3.1 shows that for all relevant years of survey data, experts consistently viewed the LDP as standing farthest to the right among the major parties in terms of new left issues. The Komeito was somewhat more interested in new left ideas than the LDP. The DPJ, the JCP, and the SDP were the most new left-oriented. In 2000, the Liberal Party stood just to the left of the LDP and to the right of the Komeito. This pattern is remarkably consistent across the three surveys under study.

Table 3.1 *Measures of GAL–TAN, Comparative Manifesto Project*

Authoritarian emphases (TAN)	Libertarian emphases (GAL)
Political authority (305)	Environmental protection (501)
National way of life: Positive (601)	National way of life: Negative (602)
Traditional Morality: Positive (603)	Traditional morality: Negative (604)
Law and Order (605)	Culture (502)
Multiculturalism: Negative (608)	Multiculturalism: Positive (607)
Social harmony (606)	Anti-Growth (416)
	Underprivileged minority groups (705)
	Non-economic demographic groups: Positive (706)
	Freedom and human rights (201)
	Democracy (202)

Source: Bakker and Hobolt (2013: 38). Numbers denote item number in the CMP data.

These results match the findings by Benoit and Laver (2006) that "social liberalism" serves as a key policy dimension that divides the LDP and the opposition parties in Japan. Indeed, Benoit and Laver (2006) note that Japan is distinctive among industrialized democracies in the strength of this new left partisan cleavage, even if, as Kato's (2014) data suggests, the new left issue cleavage may not be as salient as economic issues.

This basic picture of the importance of the new left partisan cleavage in Japan is corroborated by manifesto data compiled by the CMP. Following Bakker and Hobolt (2013), the present study codes parties' new left orientation, or the "green/alternative/libertarian" versus the "traditionalism/authority/nationalism" (GAL–TAN) dimension, using the items shown in Table 3.1.

Following Bakker and Hobolt (2013), we can calculate an index of the GAL–TAN dimension by subtracting the percentage of manifestoes devoted to authoritarian emphases (TAN) from the percentage of manifestoes devoted to libertarian emphases (GAL). The results for Japan are shown in Figure 3.2. As with the expert surveys, the figures

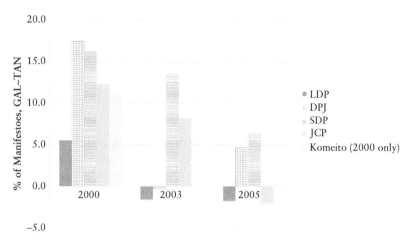

Figure 3.2 GAL–TAN index, Japan, 2000–5
Source: Comparative Manifesto Project (Lehmann et al. 2015, Manifesto Corpus. Version: 2015-5).

show the results for the relevant years for which data is available: 2000, 2003, and 2005. Note that in contrast to the expert surveys, a higher score on the GAL–TAN index denotes greater new left orientation.

Overall, the results shown in Figure 3.2 confirm the findings from the expert surveys. Figure 3.2 shows the LDP's election manifestoes consistently scoring lower on the GAL–TAN index compared to the DPJ, the SDP, or the JCP, with the exception of the JCP in 2005. This pattern confirms the expert surveys' placement of the LDP to the very right of the Japanese political spectrum in terms of new left issues. Unfortunately, the Japanese version of the CMP includes data for the Komeito only for 2000, but the 2000 data confirms the expert surveys' placement of the Komeito moderately to the left of the LDP. The CMP data do indicate more variability among the non-LDP parties than the expert surveys. The DPJ was the most new left-oriented party in 2000 but was second behind the JSP in 2005 and third behind the JSP and the JCP in 2003. Nevertheless, it was consistently more new left-oriented than the LDP. The JCP is found to be more new left-oriented than the LDP in 2000 and 2003 but not in 2005, although the 2005 figures may be an anomaly.[1] Recall that in the expert surveys, the JCP had consistently been placed to the left of the LDP. The SDP is consistently strongly oriented toward new left issues.

Spain

The Spanish jury system was passed in 1995. The policy positions of Spanish political parties from this time period are also available through both expert surveys and CMP data. A 1989 expert survey found that parties' positions on environmental issues were highly correlated with their positions on traditional economic issues such as "taxes versus services" or "public ownership" (Laver and Hunt 1992). In particular, the 1989 surveys placed the socialist Socialist Workers' Party (*Partido Socialista Obrero Español*, PSOE) to the left of the conservative Popular Coalition (*Coalición Popular*, CP), which later became the conservative People's Party (*Partido Popular*, PP), on both environmental and traditional economic issues (ibid). The two regional parties, Convergence and Union (*Convergència e Unió*, CiU), from Catalonia, and the Basque Nationalist Party (*Partido Nacionalista Vasco*, PNV), from the Basque Country, stood roughly in between the CP/PP and the PSOE on environmental issues. The far-left United Left (*Izquierda Unida*, IU) stood farther to the left than the PSOE on environmental issues as well. Huber and Inglehart (1995) confirm these findings in their 1992 expert survey. The study shows that while Spanish experts cited "economic or class conflict" as the primary issue cleavage separating Spain's major political parties, they cited issues relating to "traditional or new culture" as the second most important partisan cleavage. The same pattern is confirmed in Benoit and Laver (2006), which draws on an expert survey conducted in 2002–3.

The CMP data corroborates these results for the most part, although with some minor differences. The results are shown in Figure 3.3. The GAL–TAN index is shown for Spanish political parties for 1993

---

[1] In contrast to other leftist parties, the JCP's 2005 manifesto included no references to the environment (per 501) and no references to "non-economic minority groups" (per 706). Unfortunately, data after 2005 for Japan is not available on the CMP database as of writing, so it is impossible to assess whether or not this trend has continued.

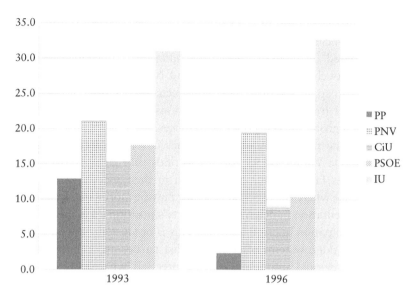

Figure 3.3 GAL–TAN index, Spain, 1993–6
Source: See Figure 3.2.

and 1996, the closest years to the passage of the jury bill for which data was available.

Figure 3.3 shows that in line with the findings from the expert surveys, the CMP data places the conservative PP as scoring the lowest on the GAL–TAN index for both 1993 and 1996. For both years, the far-left IU scored the highest, again confirming the findings from the expert surveys. The CMP data also show the CiU as slightly less new left-oriented than the PSOE, which is less new left oriented than the IU, in line with the expert surveys. Although the expert surveys had placed the Basque PNV in between the PP and the PSOE, the CMP data place the PNV as being more new left-oriented than the PSOE.

In addition to parties' positions on new left issues, the strength of the regional cleavage in Spain may also impact parties' positions on the introduction of a jury system. This point takes us somewhat beyond the basic theory that has been elaborated in this book. As De Winter (1998) notes, there is a range in the policy demands of regionalist parties. Some parties merely push for the recognition of the regional language and/or ending discrimination, while others aspire to greater self-government or even independence. Regionalist parties' support for greater recognition of minorities, as well as decentralization, are typically policies that are also espoused by new left-oriented parties. Indeed, based on analyses of party manifestoes, De Winter (1998: 209) finds twelve Western European and North American regionalist parties to span the entire left-right spectrum in terms of economic issues. Apart from their regionalist positions, regionalist parties are a very mixed group in their policy preferences.

Despite the fact that regionalist parties cover the entire left-right spectrum, De Winter (1998: 209) also finds that eight of twelve of those parties favor greater participation in their manifestoes. Thus, here is a case where the regional cleavage may be more salient than the new left orientation in determining a party's position on an issue such as lay participation in criminal trials. This is because the introduction of jury/lay judge systems offers regionalist parties an opportunity to strengthen regional autonomy, which is precisely what they stand for. *Ceteris paribus*, regionalist parties should support systems that transfer extensive powers from professional judges to the jurors/lay judges, regardless of those parties' more typical positions on "old left" or "new left" issues. Thus, in the Spanish context, we might expect the CiU and the PNV to favor empowering jurors/lay judges to a significant degree.

South Korea

The bill to introduce the Korean jury system was passed in 2007. In contrast to Japan and Spain, Michael Laver and his associates responsible for the Chapel Hill expert surveys have not conducted expert surveys on South Korean party positions. One expert survey that has been conducted that asks for South Korean parties' perceived positions around the time of judicial reforms is the one by the Democratic Accountability and Linkages Project (DALP, 2008–9). Unfortunately, the survey was conducted just after the jury system was passed in 2007. Ideally, it would have been desirable to draw on a survey that was conducted *prior* to the passage of the bill. But the timing of the survey is close enough to the passage of the bill that it may still provide a reasonably good sense of parties' positions around the time that the system was being considered.

The DALP survey includes a question that asks country experts to assess, on a scale of one to ten, parties' positions on "traditional authority, institutions, and customs," or more specifically, issues relating to

Table 3.2 *Positions of South Korean parties on new left issues*

Party	Mean score	Standard error
UDP	4.73	1.67
GNP	7.33	1.45
LFP	8.33	1.23

Source: DALP dataset (2008–9). 1 = most liberal, 10 = most conservative. See text for exact question wording.

"religion, marriage, sexuality, occupation, family life, and social conduct in general" (Kitschelt 2013). As no question that taps experts' assessments of party positions on the environment or participation was included, this item is the closest question that taps party positions on new left issues. Indeed, the responses to this DALP item for Japan, shown in Appendix 3.C at the end of this chapter, track very closely the results from the Chapel Hill expert surveys shown earlier, lending support to this measure. A score of one indicates that the party advocates full individual freedom from state intervention, and a score of ten indicates that the party favors full state enforcement of compliance. Note that as with other expert surveys, the DALP survey is most useful as a measure of relative party positions within a given country, rather than comparing party positions across countries. The distribution of Korean parties' scores on this measure is shown in Table 3.2.

Table 3.2 shows that the United Democratic Party (UDP), which is typically viewed as a leftist party, is indeed rated as embracing new left issues to a greater extent than the Grand National Party (GNP) and the Liberty Forward Party (LFP), both of which are typically seen as conservative parties. The UDP was formed out of the Millennium Democratic Party (MDP), which was in power in South Korea around the time that the jury system was passed. Unfortunately, the DALP survey did not ask respondents to rate the far-left Democratic Labor Party (DLP).

CMP data for South Korea provides perhaps better information. The issue of judicial reforms, including the introduction of a jury, emerged onto the Korean policy agenda around 2003 and the system passed the legislature in 2007. CMP data for Korea is available for the years 2000, 2004, and 2008, and the distribution of the GAL–TAN scores for Korean parties is shown in Figure 3.4.

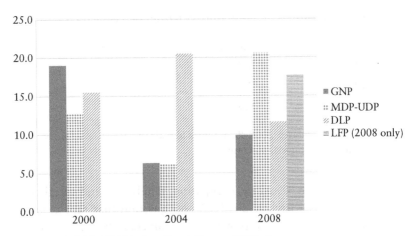

Figure 3.4 GAL–TAN index, South Korea, 2000–8
Source: See Figure 3.2.

Figure 3.4 shows that for 2008, the GAL–TAN coding of Korean parties is mostly consistent with the DALP codings shown in Table 3.2. This is an important reliability test of the DALP data. Both find the UDP to stand to the left of the GNP. There is some disagreement between the GAL–TAN coding of the LFP, which puts it to the left of the GNP but somewhat to the right of the UDP, and the DALP data, which finds the LFP to stand to the right of both the UDP and the GNP.

The striking finding from the CMP data is that parties' relative positions on the GAL–TAN index in South Korea during this period were highly unstable over time, and certainly less stable than either Japan or Spain. The GNP, which is often viewed as the conservative party, surprisingly scored the highest on the GAL–TAN index in 2000. It then scored the second lowest among the three parties in 2004 and was the fourth among four parties rated in 2008. Meanwhile, the MDP, later UDP, which is often viewed as the "leftist" major party of South Korea, actually scored the lowest on the GAL–TAN measure in 2000 and 2004 but then surged ahead of the GNP and even the far-left DLP in 2008.[2]

It is fair to conclude from the wild fluctuations in this data that new left issues did not structure the Korean policy space to the extent that

---

[2] The LFP was only founded in 2008, so data for 2000 and 2004 are not available in the CMP. Unfortunately, expert survey data for the DLP was not available in the DALP survey.

they did in the other three countries. Moreover, a closer examination of the CMP data reveals that changes in Korean parties' GAL–TAN scores over the eight-year period shown in Figure 3.4 were not driven by any single subcategory within the GAL–TAN index, but by changes in parties' scores on many of the subcategories across the board.

What may account for the unstable results in the South Korean case? An important point to note here is that during the period under study, the South Korean party system was undergoing a major realignment, from one based on regional cleavages to one based more on ideological cleavages (Heo and Stockton 2005). Since democratization in the late 1980s, the South Korean party system had been defined by a regional cleavage, in which partisan competition was only weakly defined by ideological divides.[3] This was the case largely into the early 2000s, and thus around 2000, at the beginning of the period shown in Figure 3.4, the new left cleavage only weakly structured the Korean party system. Thereafter, a transformation began to occur, especially with the end of the "Three Kims" era and the ascendance of Roh Moo-hyun, who became president in 2003 and accelerated the decline of the regional cleavage and the rise of the ideological cleavage. According to Asaba (2009), foreign policies toward North Korea (pro-North Korea, anti-North Korea) and the United States (pro-United States, anti-United States) and economic policy have emerged as the main issues of contention among major Korean parties since the mid-2000s, with the GNP as the party of the right and the MDP-UDP as the party of the left. But the process of realignment was gradual and somewhat chaotic. Reflecting this process of realignment, Rich (2014) reports that during the 17th Korean National Assembly (2004–8), 178 legislators made a total of 390 changes in party affiliation.

The CMP data shown in Figure 3.4 captures just this process of realignment at work. Scholars generally concur that by 2008, the Korean party system had realigned itself along an ideological left-right cleavage (Hix and Jun 2009; Onishi 2014), and Figure 3.4 shows that the emerging left-right cleavage also overlaps considerably with the new left cleavage as well. In fact, the CMP results for 2012 (not shown) are largely similar to those for 2008, underscoring the point that by 2008, the process of realignment was largely complete. As in 2008, in 2012

[3] This point is echoed by Jou (2011), who, drawing on 2001 World Values Survey data, finds a weaker association between post-materialism and left-right self-placement among the South Korean public compared to Japan or Taiwan.

the MDP-UDP (renamed the Democratic Party) scored higher on the GAL–TAN index than the GNP (renamed New Frontier Party, NFP). Thus, it appears that the period under study, between 2000 and 2008, was a period of flux, which stabilized after 2008 as the MDP-UDP became more consistently new left-oriented than the GNP.

Thus, at the time that the issue of introducing a jury system was under debate in the early- to mid-2000s, a major shift was underway in Korea's party politics. This instability in parties' relative positions on new left issues should also have repercussions for the debate over introducing the jury/lay judge system. Korea's MDP-UDP should have been less consistently committed to the new left value of participation than its counterparts in other countries, and it certainly should have had less party cohesion on the issue than it did.

Taiwan

The idea of introducing a lay judge system emerged onto the Taiwanese policy agenda around 2010. Neither the Laver group's expert surveys nor CMP data is available for the case of Taiwan. Thus, as a second-best approach, we draw on two alternative sources. First, the DALP expert survey that was used above for South Korea is also available for Taiwan. The timing of the DALP survey was close enough to the period in which the debate occurred to provide a sense of parties' relative positions. Second, Fell (2005, 2007) provides results of content analyses of Taiwanese election campaign advertisements.

First, we again draw on the new left item on the DALP survey to assess the relative positions of Taiwanese parties on new left issues. The results are shown in Table 3.3.

Table 3.3 shows that experts place the Democratic Progressive Party (DPP) to the left of the ruling Kuomintang (KMT) in terms of new left issues. But experts did not see a stark difference between the KMT and the DPP in their positions on new left issues; the difference in experts' assessments for the two major parties was much smaller than in DALP surveys for South Korea or Japan (shown in Appendix 3.C). Indeed, scholars have noted that partisan issue polarization in Taiwan is less pronounced than in many other developed democracies, such as Japan or South Korea (Dalton and Tanaka 2007; Dalton 2008; Lupu 2014).[4]

---

[4] Fell (2011) points to recent re-polarizing trends between the KMT and DPP.

Table 3.3 *Positions of Taiwanese parties on new left issues*

Party	Mean score	Standard error
DPP	3.22	1.77
KMT	4.72	2.63

Source: DALP dataset (2008–2009). 1 = most liberal, 10 = most conservative.
See explanation in Table 3.2 for exact question wording.

The assessment of the DPP as the more new left-oriented party within the Taiwanese party system is corroborated by Dafydd Fell, who, in a series of studies, has measured the policy positions of Taiwan's major parties. For instance, in the most comprehensive analysis of Taiwanese party positions to date, Fell (2005) draws on quantitative and qualitative analyses of parties' campaign advertisements in nine national-level elections between 1991 and 2004. He finds that while national identity issues have often been the most salient issue dividing the KMT from the DPP, the KMT has also tended to stress issues of government competence, economic growth, and law and order, while the DPP has been more committed to the expansion of social policy. These are issue cleavages that map very closely to the traditional right-left cleavage in Western Europe. But in addition, Fell (2005) also finds that the DPP expresses a greater concern than the KMT over new left issues, specifically corruption, women's issues, and freedom and human rights. Fell's (2007) analysis of campaign advertisements in Taiwanese local elections also shows that the DPP candidates stressed women's issues, corruption, and environmental issues, while KMT candidates stressed economic achievements and capacity to govern. Ho (2005) also points to the close link between Taiwanese environmental movements and the DPP.

Summary

In sum, parties in Japan, Spain, South Korea, and Taiwan have embraced new left issues to varying degrees, and some leftist parties in the same country have been more eager to take up new left concerns than others. The existing data suggest that the DPJ and SDP in Japan, and to some extent the JCP, as well as the Spanish PSOE and the Taiwanese DPP, have consistently adopted new left issues.

Meanwhile, the LDP in Japan, the PP in Spain, and the KMT in Taiwan have consistently been much less receptive to new left issues. In these cases, new left concerns tended to reinforce left-right cleavages. The expert surveys suggest that Japan's Komeito appears to fall somewhere in between the LDP and the DPJ. Thus it is not surprising that the LDP chose to enter into coalition with the Komeito in 1999 and has remained in coalition with it to the present, with the exception of the period that the LDP was out of power (2009–12). In South Korea, by contrast, there was much instability in party positions on new left issues during the crucial time period for this study. The new left issue dimension did not consistently separate the left from the right, at least for the period under study. In some years, conservative parties appear to highlight new left issues to a greater extent than leftist parties, and vice versa. Whatever tendencies there were did not represent a major cleavage between the parties.

The Strength of New Left-Oriented Parties

There existed considerable variation across Japan, South Korea, Spain, and Taiwan in the strength of new left-oriented parties around the time that the issue of introducing a jury/lay judge system was high on the policy agenda in the respective countries. The strength of new left-oriented parties vis-à-vis other parties in the party system is provided in Table 3.4.

As shown in Table 3.4, the new left was strongest in Spain, where a new left-oriented party (PSOE) ruled as a minority government with cooperation from far-left and regionalist parties. In Japan, the conservative LDP was in power with the conservative Liberal Party during the early stages of the debate over the introduction of a jury/lay judge system, but it faced a situation of "divided legislature" as the ruling coalition did not control the upper House of Councillors, which was held by new left-oriented parties. The new left-oriented opposition parties later lost their majority in the House of Councillors, but this was the result of the moderately new left-leaning Komeito entering into coalition with the LDP, so the new left perspective actually retained considerable leverage over policy outcomes. In South Korea, the leftist President Roh Moo-hyun came into power in 2003 with the new left-tinged slogan, "Government of Participation," but he lacked a majority in the legislature for most of his term, greatly undermining

Table 3.4. *Strength of new left-oriented parties within party system at the time of enactment of lay judge systems, Spain, Japan, South Korea, and Taiwan*

Taiwan (proposal, 2011–16)	South Korea (2007)	Japan (2004)	Spain (1995)
New left-oriented DPP controls neither executive nor legislature (both held by conservative KMT)	Weakly new left-oriented MDP-UDP controls executive, but conservative GNP controls legislature	Conservative LDP in power with conservative LIB but new left-oriented DPJ, SDP, JCP initially control Upper House; later, conservative LDP enters into coalition with moderately new left-oriented Komeito	New left-oriented PSOE in power as minority government with cooperation with far-left and regional parties (IU, PNV, CiU)

Weaker ←——— Strength of New Left-Oriented Party ———→ Stronger

his influence over legislation. Moreover, the partisan realignment in progress at the time, combined with Roh's low popularity ratings and his "lame duck" status, severely undermined party cohesion and, in turn, the MDP-UDP's new left orientation. In Taiwan, the conservative KMT under President Ma Ying-jeou controlled both the executive and legislature, effectively shutting the new left-oriented DPP out of legislative influence between 2008 and 2016. However, as in South Korea, Ma's low approval ratings, as well as his lame-duck status in his second term, also undermined the KMT's party cohesion, so Taiwan in this period cannot be said to have been *solidly* anti-new left either. The bases for these assessments will be elaborated more fully in the case study chapters.

What can we predict on the basis of these constellations of factors, both in terms of the extent to which parties adopt new left concerns and the relative power of such parties? The model presented in this book predicts the strongest constraints upon professional judges' powers to materialize in Spain, and this is in fact what happened, as will be detailed in Chapter 8. The Spanish case exhibits a combination of leftist parties that are strongly oriented toward new left issues and those parties' control of the legislature. Spain thus adopted a jury system in which professional judges had little discretion over which cases would be tried by a jury and in which the juries' verdicts were binding on professional judges.

Second, the model expects Japan to introduce significant constraints on the power of professional judges, but less so than Spain. As noted earlier, in the initial stages of Japan's judicial reforms, the conservative LDP faced a "divided legislature" in which the opposition controlled the House of Councillors. Within the opposition, the new left-oriented DPJ enjoyed a plurality. This would lead us to expect considerable influence on the part of the opposition parties, in particular the DPJ, to set the terms of the debate over introducing a jury/lay judge system. In fact, as will be elaborated in the case study, the situation of "divided legislature" enabled the new left-oriented opposition parties to force the issue of introducing a jury/lay judge system onto the policy agenda. Over the course of the debate, the Komeito joined the LDP in a ruling coalition, and the opposition lost control of the House of Councillors. But this was not a complete loss for the new left perspective, as the Komeito itself has some new left leanings. The hypothesis advanced in this book leads us to expect the Komeito to push for greater constraints on professional judges than the LDP, although not quite to the extent that the more new left-oriented parties would do. In fact, the Komeito did succeed in pushing the LDP to adopt stronger constraints on professional judges than the LDP had proposed, although not as strong as would have been the case if the more new left-oriented DPJ, SDP, or the JCP had been able to exert greater influence. This history will be reviewed in detail in Chapters 4 through 6.

Third, in South Korea, the model predicts only a modest transfer of power from professional judges, and again, this was what transpired. President Roh himself was elected on a new left-sounding platform of "Government of Participation," but the president was hampered by divided government and ongoing partisan realignment during most of his term. Moreover, the low popularity of President Roh precipitated a decline in his own party's cohesion. The result was a new jury system that imposed only very limited constraints on the power of professional judges. The Korean case will be laid out in Chapter 8.

The power of the new left was most limited in Taiwan, where the conservative KMT controlled both the executive and the legislature. The model would therefore expect a limited transfer of power from professional judges, even though the opposition parties are expected to demand strongly an extensive transfer of power. This is in fact what happened. The new left-oriented DPP pushed for an American-style jury system that would transfer considerable powers away from professional judges, but during Ma's term, it had very limited leverage to impose its will on policy. On the other hand, Ma's low popularity also undermined party cohesion within the KMT, crippling even Ma's weak lay judge system proposal within the Legislative Yuan. This story will be detailed in Chapter 7.

APPENDIX 3.A

Measurement of New Left Issues, Expert Survey (Japan) 2000–2005

The index of parties' positions on new left issues was created using the following items in the expert surveys (Kato 2014).

Table 3A.1 *2000 Survey*

	"Left" end point	"Right" end point
Social	Promote policies aimed at creating greater equality for women	Oppose policies aimed at creating greater equality for women
Environment	Promote environmental protection, even if this slows economic growth	Promote economic growth, even if this damages environment
Decentralization	Promote decentralization of decision-making to local bodies	Oppose decentralization of decision-making to local bodies
Citizens' Right	Promote policies increasing public access to information	Oppose policies increasing public access to information
National Identity	Do not encourage increased respect for Emperor	Encourage increased respect for Emperor

Source: Kato (2014).

Table 3A.2 *2003 Survey*

	"Left" end point	"Right" end point
Social	Favor liberal policies on matters such as abortion, homosexuality, and euthanasia	Oppose liberal policies on matters such as abortion, homosexuality, and euthanasia
Environment	Support protection of the environment, even at the cost of economic growth	Support economic growth, even at the cost of damage to the environment
Decentralization	Promote decentralization of all administration and decision-making	Oppose any decentralization of administration and decision-making
Immigration	Favor policies designed to help immigrants integrate into Japanese society	Favor policies designed to help immigrants return to their country of origin
National Identity	Do not encourage increased respect for Emperor	Encourage increased respect for Emperor

Source: Kato (2014).

Table 3A.3 *2005 Survey*

	"Left" end point	"Right" end point
Social	Favor liberal policies on matters such as abortion, homosexuality, and euthanasia	Oppose liberal policies on matters such as abortion, homosexuality, and euthanasia
Environment	Support protection of the environment, even at the cost of economic growth	Support economic growth, even at the cost of damage to the environment
Decentralization	Promote decentralization of all administration and decision-making	Oppose any decentralization of administration and decision-making
Immigration	Favor policies designed to help immigrants integrate into Japanese society	Favor policies designed to help immigrants return to their country of origin
National Identity	Do not encourage increased respect for Emperor	Encourage increased respect for Emperor

Source: Kato (2014).

APPENDIX 3.B

Standard Errors, Expert Surveys, Japan, 2000–2005

Table 3B.1 *Standard errors for the means of parties' positions on new left issues as shown in Table 3.1*

	LDP	Komeito	DPJ	SDP	JCP	LIB
2000	2.300	0.428	2.729	1.711	2.285	4.075
2003	2.609	1.399	3.399	1.207	2.561	N/Avail
2005	3.150	1.556	3.066	1.441	2.655	N/Avail

Source: Calculated from Kato (2014). The Liberal Party (LIB) was only in existence until 2003, when it disbanded with the DPJ.

APPENDIX 3.C

DALP Survey Codings for Japan

Table 3C.1 *Positions of Japanese parties on new left issues, DALP dataset*

	Mean score	Standard error
LDP	8.21	1.27
Komeito	5.67	1.94
DPJ	4.33	1.12
SDP	2.42	1.43
JCP	2.95	1.90

Source: DALP dataset (2008–9). 1 = most liberal, 10 = most conservative. See explanation for Table 3.2 for exact question wording.

The results shown in the table above corroborate the results already shown from the expert surveys and the CMP data. The DALP survey places the LDP to the right, followed by the Komeito, the DPJ, the JCP, and the SDP. This ordering of parties is identical to the findings from Kato's (2014) expert surveys shown earlier in this chapter.

4 | *The History of the Lay Judge System Debate in Japan up to 1996*

Overview

This chapter outlines the history of the jury/lay judge issue in Japan prior to the debate over the introduction of a new system that began in the late 1990s. The chapter covers three periods: the prewar era, the US occupation era, and the postwar period up to 1996. During the prewar era, a jury system was introduced in Japan in 1928 and remained in effect until 1943, when it was suspended due to the intensifying war effort. During the Occupation era, the US occupiers considered reviving the jury system, but ultimately they shelved the question. After the occupation ended, the revival of the jury system did not emerge onto the policy agenda until the late 1990s, but Japanese legislators continued to ask about the possibility of reinstituting the system throughout the postwar period. Drawing on content analysis of Japanese parliamentary debates between 1947 and 1996, this chapter shows that while conservative politicians were more active in raising the issue of the jury during the immediate postwar period, after the 1950s the issue became more of a concern for politicians of the left.

The chapter will proceed as follows. The following section offers a brief overview of the prewar jury system in Japan. The third section describes the debates that occurred during the US Occupation of Japan as to whether or not to revive the prewar system or whether it should be re-introduced in new guise. The fourth section presents results from quantitative content analyses of parliamentary statements that referred to juries during the 1947–96 period. The fifth section summarizes and concludes.

The Japanese Prewar Jury System

Debates over introducing a jury system began fairly early in Japan's modern history. According to Mitani (2013), who offers the most comprehensive historical study of the prewar Japanese jury system to date, architects of the Meiji Constitution of 1889 did discuss the possibility of introducing a jury. The Meiji Constitution ultimately did not include a clause providing for the introduction of a jury system in Japan, but debates continued thereafter.

A draft bill for the introduction of a jury system was written in 1918 during the Takashi Hara Cabinet. Mitani (2013) notes that Hara's motivation for pushing for a jury in Japan was twofold. First, he had become inspired about the jury while on a six-month tour of Western countries that he had taken during 1908–9. Secondly, he saw the jury as a means of shielding the emperor from political conflict. Trials in Japan had hitherto been held in the name of the emperor. Hara feared that if the public became disgruntled with court rulings, it could turn against the emperor as well. By introducing a jury, the judicial system could at least partially shield the emperor from possible political repercussions.

After Hara was assassinated in 1921, the Korekiyo Takahashi Cabinet continued to push for the introduction of a jury system, and the bill was passed in 1923. After a five-year preparation period, the jury system came into existence in 1928.

The prewar jury consisted of twelve jurors. Jurors were chosen from literate males over the age of thirty who had lived in the same municipality for over two years and had paid three yen or more in national taxes. According to Toshitani (1984: 6), under these rules, fewer than two million individuals were eligible to serve as jurors, or the equivalent of only one in every eleven voters. Note that Japan had introduced universal male suffrage in 1925.

Under this system, crimes that carried heavier sentences, specifically death penalty, life sentence, or imprisonment, were subject to a jury trial. The professional judges would inquire of the jurors whether they agreed or disagreed that the facts present in the case would constitute a crime. The jurors decided by majority rule.

However, the defendant in such cases could refuse to be tried by a jury. In addition, for certain categories of crimes, specifically crimes that carried three or more years of sentence and that fell under the jurisdiction of local district courts, defendants could request a trial by jury instead of a trial by professional judges. Moreover, at any time during a jury trial, the defendant could change their minds and request to be tried by professional judges instead. If the defendant chose to be tried by a jury and was found guilty, at least part of the costs of the trial had to be borne by the defendant. These costs would include travel expenses and compensation for the jurors. This provision made the system very unpopular, leading to very limited use of the jury trial (Deguchi 2001).

Further undermining the power of the jury was a provision that allowed the professional judges to summon a new group of jurors if they did not agree with the jury's rulings. This meant that in effect, the jury's rulings were not binding on the professional judges, since, in theory, professional judges could keep summoning new jurors until the jurors ruled in a way that would be acceptable to the professional judges.

A final limitation of the prewar jury system was that there were very limited provisions for appealing a jury trial ruling. According to a postwar survey conducted by the Tokyo Bar Association of sixty-eight lawyers who had participated in prewar jury trials, most of the respondents believed that the limited grounds for appeal was the primary reason why the prewar jury system was unpopular (Tokyo Bar Association 1992: 60, 68).

The use of the jury system fell precipitously over time. From a high of 133 cases in 1929, the year after the system was introduced, the number of cases ruled by juries fell every year thereafter, down to only four cases in 1938 and two cases in 1942, and the system was suspended in 1943 (ibid: 366). Despite the limited nature of the prewar jury system, its effects were significant. A total of 611 defendants were tried under jury trial between 1928 and 1943, of which 94 were acquitted (ibid: 36). This 15.4% acquittal rate was much higher than the overall acquittal rate at the time, which was below 4% (Toshitani 1984).

Debates over Reviving the Jury during the Occupation Era

Following World War II and the arrival of the Supreme Commander for the Allied Powers (SCAP) to occupy Japan in August 1945, the Japanese judicial system underwent a dramatic transformation (Shiomi 1975). The courts, which had been under the jurisdiction of the Ministry of Justice during the prewar era, were made formally independent from the administrative branch (ibid). The courts were also given the powers of judicial review, which they had not had under the prewar legal system. In addition, the Supreme Court gained the power to make its own internal rules and regulations (Constitution of Japan 1946, Article 77), further enhancing the autonomy of the courts from the legislative and administrative branches.

During the Occupation, a debate also emerged as to whether or not the prewar jury system should be revived, but ultimately SCAP did not make a concerted push to make the Japanese (re-)adopt a jury system. According to Toshitani (1975), the adoption of a jury system was included in SCAP's early drafts for a new Japanese constitution, but it was deleted from later drafts. It is not clear why this deletion was made, but historians have speculated that perhaps the staff members drawing up the constitution did not have sufficient time to debate this issue and decided to postpone making a decision. After all, such a system could be introduced later by the passage of a law if it were deemed to be desirable (ibid: 111; Deguchi 2001).[1]

Some individuals within SCAP, most notably Anthony J. Maniscalco of the Public Safety Division, did attempt to push for a law that would institute a revised version of the prewar Japanese jury system (Deguchi 2001). He proposed this as part of the overall revision of the Code of Criminal Procedure between February and May 1946. Maniscalco's proposals were based on a close study of the prewar Japanese jury system and its weaknesses. For instance, Maniscalco's proposal included making the jury verdicts binding, as opposed to non-binding, as they had been under the prewar rules. Maniscalco's proposed jury system would also allow for verdicts to be appealed, which was only possible under very limited conditions in the prewar system. Also unlike the prewar system, defendants would not have a choice as to whether to be tried by a jury. The Ministry of Justice is said to have staunchly opposed Maniscalco's proposals, but believing that they represented the position of SCAP overall, the Ministry is said to have reluctantly accepted, at least for a while, that the introduction of some form of jury or lay judge system would be inevitable (Toshitani 1975). Thus, the Ministry of Justice launched several commissions consisting of lawyers and legal scholars to explore what kind of system would be acceptable. The debates covered a broad range of issues, including whether a pure jury or a mixed jury would be more desirable, and

---

[1] In an excellent article, McElwain and Winkler (2015) argue that one of the distinguishing characteristics of the Japanese constitution compared to other constitutions around the world is that it is short and vague, and thus it leaves much to be stipulated by law.

whether juries should be limited to criminal cases or whether they should also rule on civil cases. Throughout the debates, the Ministry of Justice expressed a preference for mixed juries over pure juries, although when some scholars expressed the concern that a mixed jury may not be compatible with the new constitution, the Ministry of Justice did not try to push hard for a mixed jury either.

Maniscalco was the most vocal proponent of reviving a jury system in postwar Japan in a new guise, yet in reality his view never became the mainstream position even within SCAP. The prevailing view that emerged among those engaged in judicial reform within SCAP was one of skepticism towards the viability of a jury system on Japanese soil. After 1946, Alfred C. Oppler and Thomas L. Blakemore, both in the Government Section (GS) of SCAP, led the effort to transform the Japanese judicial system. Oppler, a native German and an expert on German law and on civil law systems more generally, had been specifically summoned to serve in Tokyo because of his familiarity with continental-style civil law systems (Deguchi 2000). Blakemore was an expert on Japanese law. Both were more cautious than Maniscalco about introducing what they saw as an American institution in Japan. Oppler and Blakemore were also more willing than Maniscalco to allow the Japanese side to take greater initiative in reforming its judicial system according to its preferences. Oppler and Blakemore in fact openly criticized Maniscalco's proposal to introduce a revised jury system in Japan, noting that reforms should be incremental rather than radical, since radical reforms ran the risk of simply being rolled back once the occupation was over (ibid).

This does not mean that Oppler and Blakemore were critical of the institution of the jury per se, but simply that they did not believe that it was an appropriate time to introduce such a system in Japan. Looking back on his days during the occupation, Oppler later recounted: "The jury serves as a beneficial counterpoise to the doctrinaire American objectivism in criminal law and courts. Such counterpoise is certainly less needed in Japan" (Oppler 1976: 146). Indeed, while Oppler and Blakemore refrained from pressuring the Japanese into adopting a jury system, they did later insist on the insertion of a clause in the Court Act that read, "The provision of the court organization law does not exclude the establishment of jury system as provided elsewhere by law which will function in connection with the criminal trials" (Court Act 1947, Article 3[3]). The Japanese side appears to have been somewhat surprised by this proposal, which came abruptly in March 1947. They had been under the impression that Oppler and Blakemore were not interested in reviving a jury system and therefore suspected that Oppler had been pressured by authorities higher up to push for the inclusion of such a clause. Later scholars have also speculated that the initiative to open the door to the introduction of a jury system at a later date may have come from the Far East Commission or the State Department, but they have not found a paper trail (Toshitani 1975; Deguchi 2001). In any event, the law was passed in April 1947, with language that provided a legal basis for the future (re-)introduction of a jury system in Japan.[2]

The Ministry of Justice may not have liked this turn of events, but during the deliberations over the Court Law, Tokutaro Kimura, the Justice Minister, indicated that he believed that the jury system should be brought back in the future. For the time, however, he felt that fiscal constraints made it difficult to quickly revive the jury system. To begin with, many of the courthouses had burned down during the war and had to be rebuilt (Privy Council, cited in Toshitani 1975: 161).

It is important to note that although some scholars have later questioned whether a lay judge system would be constitutional under the postwar constitution (e.g. Nishino 2009),[3] the postwar Japanese government never publicly questioned whether such a system would be constitutional, and the justice minister who presided over the passage of the Court Act even seemed to believe it desirable to bring it back.

Content Analysis: Japanese Parties and the Jury, 1947–96

The jury system was thus not revived during the US occupation of Japan. Thereafter, the issue did not emerge onto the policy agenda

---

[2] As legislator Yasushi Yamakuma pointed out, technically this clause may have been unnecessary, since the prewar Japanese Jury Law had merely been suspended, not repealed (Toshitani 1975: 165–6). Nevertheless, the clause above would have the effect of providing additional proof that a jury system would be compatible with the new postwar constitution.

[3] Nishino's interpretation is controversial. Ashibe (1997), in his well-known constitutional law textbook, argues that an Anglo-American jury system would be constitutional only as long as the jurors' verdicts did not constrain the professional judges. On the other hand, Sato (1981), another popular textbook, argues that a pure jury system would be compatible with the existing constitution.

until the late 1990s. Nevertheless, various Japanese legislators did raise the issue in parliamentary debates throughout the postwar era. This section presents results of content analysis of parliamentary statements made by different Japanese legislators during the postwar era prior to the judicial reforms of the late 1990s. Which parties were more enthusiastic about re-introducing a lay judge system, and during which periods? And which types of jury/lay judge systems did the different parties endorse? The data show that while the ruling LDP only began seriously to consider the idea of re-introducing a lay judge system in the late 1990s, various opposition (i.e. leftist) parties had expressed positive feelings for such a system throughout the postwar era, and continued to do so with increased vigor since the 1980s. These findings help to shed light on their positions over the introduction of the lay judge system when the issue did emerge onto the agenda during the 1990s.

Examining Japanese Diet Deliberations

Why examine parliamentary deliberations as a window onto measuring Japanese political parties' policy positions? There exist three perspectives on the significance of Diet deliberations in Japanese politics. One view is that the Diet deliberations are essentially irrelevant. In his classic *MITI and the Economic Miracle*, Johnson (1982) argued that the Diet simply "rubber-stamps" bills that have been written by elite bureaucrats without subjecting them to close scrutiny. In recent years, however, this view has become less influential as scholars have increasingly noted the vibrant legislative activity that occurs within the LDP (e.g. Muramatsu 1981; Inoguchi and Iwai 1987; Ramseyer and Rosenbluth 1993).

In recent years, a lively debate has emerged as to whether the Japanese Diet is consensus-based or majoritarian (Fukumoto 2000, 2004; Masuyama 2000, 2003, 2004, 2006). If the Diet operates in a consensual manner, committee-level deliberations should have substantive importance in forging that consensus. If it is majoritarian, committee-level deliberations may be more *pro forma* than aimed at reaching any consensus among parties. This latter view of the Japanese Diet is superficially closer to the "rubber-stamp" view of the Japanese Diet advanced by Johnson, but it is actually very different. In Johnson's view, the Japanese Diet merely "rubber-stamps" legislation because politicians are uninterested and/or lack the competence to understand bills written by elite bureaucrats. In the majoritarian view of the Japanese Diet, by contrast, the Diet "rubber-stamps" because bills that are submitted to the Diet have already undergone extensive intra-party debate within the ruling LDP and thus there is no need to repeat the debate in parliament. But even proponents of the majoritarian view still stress that legislative debates serve a purpose. In this view, the Diet presents a crucial arena for legislators of all parties to engage in position-taking, even if committee-level deliberations do little to influence the actual substance of legislation (Masuyama 2004, 2006). Such position-taking may help their electoral prospects (Sannabe 2014) and, in turn, improve their prospects for promotion within the party as well (Fujimura 2013).

Thus, whether we accept the consensual or majoritarian view of the significance of Japanese Diet deliberations, both views concur that these deliberations offer an important window through which to assess the policy positions of different political parties.

Coding Scheme

The study set out to identify how often legislators of different parties referred to the word "jury" (*baishin*) during parliamentary debates in the postwar era. The coding was conducted as follows. A keyword search of all of the minutes of the parliamentary debates, whether in committee or plenary meetings was conducted using the search engine for Japanese Diet proceedings, which is available at the National Diet Library website (National Diet Library n.d.). The study coded how many times legislators of different parties referred to the word "jury" in their statements from 1947 to 1996. To cast as broad a net as possible, this study chose not to discriminate between parliamentary statements focusing mainly on the jury and those referring to the jury simply in passing.[4] The coding in this chapter covers roughly a fifty-year period from May 20, 1947, the first postwar parliamentary session, to December 31, 1996. The coding ends in 1996 because the LDP began to look into the possibility of introducing major judicial

---

[4] Government officials and various witnesses also made some references to the jury during parliamentary deliberations. But since this book is interested in references to the jury by legislators, such references were excluded.

reforms in 1997. The post-1997 period will be covered in the next two chapters.

Of course, a reference to the word "jury" does not necessarily mean that the statement or question itself relates to the introduction of a jury system to Japan. Nevertheless, usage of the word implies some interest in the system. Note that the Japanese word for "jury" is used almost exclusively in the legal context, unlike the English word "jury," which may refer to a range of topics (e.g. "The jury is still out"). Still, the coding had to be sensitive to the possibility of the word being used with other meanings. Thus, several exceptions were made to the coding rule. First, references to "grand jury (*daibaishin*)" were excluded, since the grand jury is a fundamentally different institution than the trial jury. The author did initially code the references to the "grand jury," but it turned out that in the overwhelming majority of cases, the reference was to Japanese companies that had run into legal problems in the United States and had been indicted by the grand jury or in connection to political scandals (e.g. findings by the American grand jury relating to the Lockheed scandal in Japan), so these seemed irrelevant to the question at hand. The results for references to "grand jury" are thus not reported here. Also, several references to "panel examinations" ("*baishinshiki shiken*") were made in the late 1940s in relation to introducing a standardized examination for the certification of public accountants. Since these also had little to do with the issue of interest to this book, these references were also excluded from the data.

Between 1947 and 1996, there were a total of 450 references to the word "jury" in 187 statements (both plenary and committee) in the House of Representatives (lower house), and 138 references in 72 statements in the House of Councillors (upper house). For the House of Representatives, this roughly means that there were on average 9 references and 3.74 statements per year that referred to the word "jury," and for the House of Councillors, 2.76 references and 1.44 statements per year. These are hardly negligible numbers, especially given that the jury system was not even in existence. The vast majority of statements were questions to the government.

Because legislators often made several references to the word "jury" in the same statement, the data presented below are on the number of statements that made at least one reference to the word "jury," rather than the number of references. One statement is made every time a legislator has the floor to speak. If a legislator asks a question to the government, an official from the government responds, and then the same legislator asks a follow-up question, this was counted as two statements.

Not surprisingly, the overwhelming majority of statements and questions relating to the jury were made in the Committee on Judiciary Affairs. However, the coding also includes statements and questions regarding the jury were made in other settings, such as the Plenary Session or the Budget Committee.

"*Baishin*" is not the only word referring to "jury" in Japanese; the word "*sanshin*" is typically used to refer to "mixed juries" of the civil law tradition. The author thus coded the number of times legislators of different parties used the word "*sanshin*" as well, although the references were much less frequent compared to references to "*baishin*." In the House of Representatives, there were just twenty-five references in fifteen statements between May 20, 1947, and December 31, 1996,[5] while in the House of Councillors, there were only twelve references in eight statements.[6] This is the equivalent of an average of 0.50 references a year in the House of Representatives and 0.24 references a year in the House of Councillors. Since the number of references to "sanshin" was exceedingly small, details of the coding results will not be analyzed extensively.

To simplify the presentation, the results shown below will only be for major parties that were in existence since the 1960s: the LDP, the Japan Socialist Party (JSP), the Clean Government Party (CGP until 1994; later Komeito), the Japan Communist Party (JCP), and the Democratic Socialist Party (DSP). These parties were generally large enough to have representatives present at the major committee meetings as well as the plenary sessions. Since different parties were in existence for different periods of time, however, the study standardized the number of references

---

[5] Ten of the twenty-five references were made by JSP legislators, and seven were made by DSP legislators. The remaining eight references were made either by Dietmembers of the LDP or by those who belonged to parties that later formed the LDP. As with the references to "*baishin*," the overwhelming majority of the references to the "*sanshin*" by LDP legislators were made during the 1940s and 1950s. In fact, after 1959, there was only one reference to the "*sanshin*" by an LDP Dietmember.

[6] Seven of the twelve references were by JSP Dietmembers, two by a CGP Dietmember, and one by a JCP Dietmember. No LDP Dietmember made a reference to the mixed jury in the House of Councillors.

to the word "jury" by every 1,000 meetings attended by each party.[7] Standardizing the data by the number of Diet meetings attended provides a rough baseline for comparison of parties' level of interest in the issue of the jury. It is true that parties receive different time allocations depending on their number of seats, so using total numbers of statements by party as a baseline could be more precise, but would require much more labor, for probably not very different results.

Note that conservative parties that made references to the jury between 1947 and 1955 and which later merged to form the LDP in 1955, specifically the Kaishinto, Kokumin Kyodoto (People's Cooperative Party), Kokumin Minshuto (People's Democratic Party), Minshu Jiyuto (Democratic Liberal Party), Democratic Party (*Minshuto*), and the Japan Liberal Party (*Nihon Minshuto*) are shown below as "LDP." This may have the effect of overstating the figures for the LDP for the 1947–55 period. Note also that there is no data on the DSP until the late 1950s, or the CGP until the early 1960s, when they first won seats in parliament. Moreover, the results for the DSP are only through 1994, since the DSP disbanded in 1994 to join the NFP (the NFP made no references to the jury between 1994 and 1996). The DPJ is also excluded since it did not come into existence until September 1996, towards the very end of our coding period. In fact, the new DPJ made no reference to the jury during the three months to the end of 1996, which is where this chapter ends. In subsequent chapters, however, it will be shown that DPJ legislators became very interested in the question after 1996.

Results

How often did Japanese legislators of different parties refer to the word "jury" during the postwar era to 1996? The results, standardized by the number of meetings attended by each party, are shown in Figure 4.1.

Figure 4.1 shows that the DSP most frequently made statements that referred to the "jury" during the period under study, followed closely by the JSP. Both parties made more than 3 statements out of

---

[7] During this fifty-year period, there were on average 829.9 meetings a year in the House of Representatives and 636.7 meetings a year in the House of Councillors.

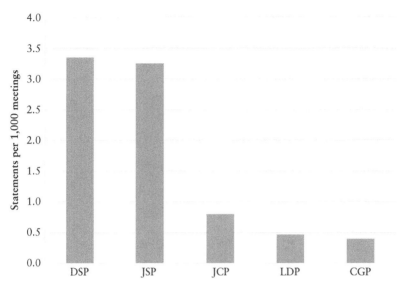

Figure 4.1 Number of statements referring to "jury," per 1,000 meetings attended, by party, Japanese House of Representatives, 1947–96
Source: National Diet Library (n.d.).

every 1,000 meetings attended that referred to the "jury." Roughly, this is the equivalent of roughly 2.5 statements a year, for each party. The JCP, the LDP, and the CGP made many fewer statements referring to the word, with fewer than one statement referring to the word "jury" out of every 1,000 meetings attended, although the JCP was more likely than the LDP or CGP to refer to it.

The overall picture presented here roughly corresponds to a left-right cleavage; the left-leaning DSP, the JSP, and even the JCP were more likely to make statements referring to the jury than the LDP or the CGP. When we recall that many members of the DSP eventually joined the DPJ in the late 1990s, the ordering shown in Figure 4.1 roughly corresponds to the picture described in the previous chapter, that the JSP and the DPJ adopted new left issues to a greater extent than the LDP or the CGP. Also, perhaps it is not surprising that while the JCP and the CGP have often pushed for more "leftist" policies than the LDP in terms of social and foreign policies, they have not made as many statements referring to the new left issue of the "jury" as the DSP or the JSP. Indeed, the previous chapter showed the Komeito, previously

Figure 4.2 Number of statements referring to "jury" in parliamentary
debates, Japanese House of Representatives, 1947–96
Source: National Diet Library (n.d.).

CGP, to be less new left-oriented compared to the DPJ, and the JCP to
be somewhat inconsistent in its new left orientation. Parenthetically,
the fact that the CGP and the JCP are more hierarchical, centralized
parties than the DSP and JSP may help to explain why they were slower
to take up issues of participation.

How have the figures shown in Figure 4.1 evolved over time?
Figure 4.2 breaks down the figures shown in Figure 4.1 into different
time periods.

Figure 4.2 shows that interest in the jury among Japanese legislators has waxed and waned over time. During the late 1940s and early
1950s, there existed a considerable level of interest in the jury system,
and many legislators in fact asked about the possibility of reviving the
prewar jury system. During the 1947–50 period, in particular, almost
2 out of every 1,000 meetings included a statement that referred
to the jury. During the 1960s and 1970s, however, interest in the jury
subsided, possibly with the fading of the memory of the prewar jury
system. A dramatic resurgence in interest in the jury system occurred
during the 1980s, however. A qualitative look at the data indicates
that this new interest was sparked in part by the Supreme Court

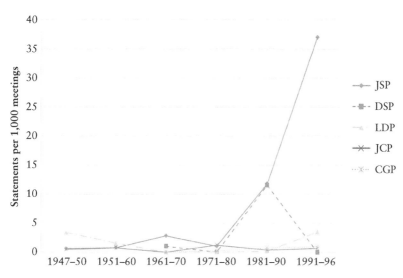

Figure 4.3 Number of statements referring to "jury," per 1,000 meetings attended, by party, Japanese House of Representatives, 1947–96, by decade
Source: National Diet Library (n.d.).

overturning a series of death penalties in re-trials. The Menda case (1983), the Zaidagawa case (1984), the Matsuyama case (1984), and the Shimada case (1989) attracted great media attention. These cases caused private attorneys and the media to point to the jury system as a possible bulwark against wrongful convictions. Legislators, especially among opposition parties, also became interested. This trend continued into the 1990s.

There also existed considerable variation in the levels of interest in the jury across different parties across different periods. This is shown in Figure 4.3, with the precise figures displayed in Table 4.1.

Figure 4.3 and Table 4.1 show that different parties exhibited quite different levels of interest in the jury system at different periods of time. During the early postwar era, conservative parties showed a relatively high level of interest in the jury system. For instance, in 1958, MP Chuichi Ohashi of the LDP, a former diplomat, argued: "Young judges today become judges straight out of college and have been exposed to red thought, and the newspapers say that that is affecting their rulings. To avoid such dangers, I believe that we must have civilians taking

Table 4.1 *Number of statements referring to "jury," per 1,000 meetings attended, by party, Japanese House of Representatives, 1947–96*

	DSP	JSP	JCP	LDP	CGP
1947–50	0.00	0.62	0.48	3.42	0.00
1951–60	0.00	0.78	0.73	1.52	0.00
1961–70	1.02	2.81	0.00	0.00	0.00
1971–80	0.00	1.03	1.21	0.00	0.22
1981–90	11.59	11.82	0.40	0.20	0.72
1991–96	0.00	37.04	0.66	3.49	0.95

Source: National Diet Library (n.d.).

part in court."[8] From this perspective, the jury system was seen as a potential bulwark against communist thought.

But over time, conservative legislators lost interest in reviving the jury system, and the jury increasingly became an issue of the left. The JSP in particular became an increasingly vocal advocate for the jury system. During the 1940s and 1950s, the percentage of statements referring to the "jury" by the LDP and its conservative predecessor parties outnumbered those by the JSP, but since the 1960s, the percentage of statements by the JSP far outnumbered that by the LDP. The difference became increasingly lopsided in the 1980s. The DSP and the JCP also made many more statements referring to the jury. For instance, in 1977, MP Daisuke Kawaguchi of the JSP accused the criminal justice community for its handling of a case in which a defendant who had been sentenced to fifteen years in prison for murder by the Supreme Court had his sentence reversed in a re-trial twenty years later. This case was in fact one of the precursors to the series of overturned death sentences that materialized in the early 1980s. Kawaguchi posed a question to the government in the Budget Committee:

However much this individual will be compensated, irreparable damage has been done to his life. It has been reported that the truth came to light after a newspaper journalist, who had been unconvinced by what he had heard

[8] Remarks by Chuichi Ohashi, Minutes of House of Representatives Committee on Judicial Affairs No. 17, 28th Session of the Diet, March 27, 1958.

in the trials, unearthed new facts on his own. Newspaper journalists are not legal experts . . . [But such] lay people often have good common sense. Japan used to have a system of jury trials . . . I believe it was suspended for various reasons, but does the government have any plans to revive the system in the future?[9]

Kawaguchi's view of the jury system as a possible safeguard against wrongful rulings was rooted not in the distrust of the political motives of judges, but in the distrust of justice officials as being unrepresentative of the broader community.

From a similar perspective, MP Takashi Miura (DSP) also posed a question to the government in 1984:

If we can't directly elect justices or have a jury system, there has to be strong evidence that amateurs cannot handle [legal affairs]. The Jury Law in Japan has been suspended since 1943 . . . The law says that the jury system will be revived after the war ends. Nevertheless, the system has not been revived. Why not?[10]

Japanese leftist parties during the early 1980s thus began to converge on an anti-professional rationale for introducing a jury system in Japan. When they did refer to the jury, it was typically to push for the (re-)introduction of the system. Note that this timing also coincides with the growing eagerness of Japan's leftist parties to take up new left causes. Both the JSP and the JCP enjoyed great electoral success during the early- to mid-1970s on an anti-pollution platform (Calder 1988), and both parties also submitted freedom of information bills to the parliament in the early 1980s.

In addition, though not obvious in Figure 4.3, Table 4.1 shows that the CGP also exhibited a steady increase in the number of statements referring to the "jury" throughout the postwar era. Starting from zero references during the 1960s, the frequency of statements referring to the jury by the CGP increased from 0.22 per 1,000 meetings attended in the 1970s, 0.72 in the 1980s, to 0.95 in the 1990s. Though less

---

[9] Remarks by Daisuke Kawaguchi, Minutes of House of Representatives, First Subcommittee of the Budget Committee, No. 2, 80th Session of the Diet, March 12, 1977.

[10] Remarks by Takashi Miura, Minutes of House of Representatives, Committee on Judiciary Affairs, No. 5, 101st Session of the Diet, March 9, 1984.

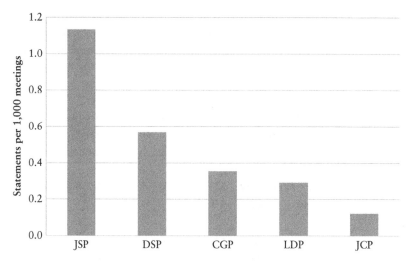

Figure 4.4 Number of statements referring to "jury" in parliamentary debates, per 1,000 meetings attended, by party, Japanese House of Councillors, 1947–96
Source: National Diet Library (n.d.).

dramatic than the surge of activity shown by the JSP, the JCP, or the DSP, the CGP nevertheless also exhibited a steady rise in the attention accorded to the jury throughout the period.

Table 4.1 also shows that even LDP legislators became more interested in the jury during the 1990s. However, much of the increase came in response to the growing frequency of statements referring to the jury by opposition party MPs starting in the 1980s. And despite the growing number of statements by LDP MPs, their interest in the topic reached nowhere near levels seen among JSP legislators during the 1990s or among JSP or DSP legislators during the 1980s.

The pattern that we have seen for the House of Representatives is largely similar for the House of Councillors, the upper house. Figure 4.4 shows the number of statements that referred to the word "jury" in the House of Councillors between 1947 and 1996, by party.

Figure 4.4 shows that as in the House of Representatives, the JSP and the DSP most frequently made statements referring to the word "jury" in the House of Councillors. The two parties were followed, in descending order, by the CGP, LDP, and the JCP. The CGP, which

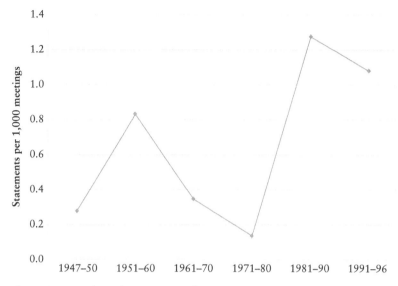

Figure 4.5 Number of statements referring to "jury" in parliamentary debates, per 1,000 meetings attended, House of Councillors, 1947–96
Source: National Diet Library (n.d.).

was in last place in the frequency of statements in the House of Representatives, is third in the House of Councillors, while the JCP, which was third in the House of Representatives, is fifth in the House of Councillors. For the CGP, however, the number of statements per 1,000 meetings attended was about the same for both Houses, at about just under 0.4 statements per 1,000 meetings attended. The JCP, on the other hand, made many fewer statements referring to the jury in the House of Councillors than in the House of Representatives. It had made almost 0.8 statements per 1,000 meetings attended in the House of Representatives, but it only made 0.1 statement per 1,000 meetings attended in the House of Councillors. It is not clear why this would be, although one possible reason may be that since the JCP typically had a fairly small number of seats in both Houses and thus very limited time to ask questions, as a tightly controlled hierarchical party, it may have chosen to ask different questions in the two Houses rather than repeat the same questions in both chambers.

Figure 4.5 shows the number of statements referring to the jury in the House of Councillors across different periods of the postwar era.

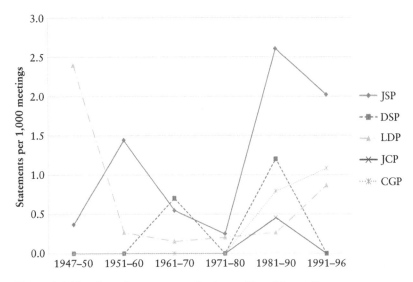

Figure 4.6 Number of statements referring to "jury" in parliamentary debates, per 1,000 meetings attended, by party, House of Councillors, 1947–96
Source: National Diet Library (n.d.).

Figure 4.5 shows that the frequency of statements referring to the word "jury" in the House of Councillors followed a largely similar trajectory as in the House of Representatives. The frequency of statements was relatively high in the early postwar period, but the references dropped precipitously in the 1960s and 1970s. As in the House of Representatives, the frequency of references surged again during the 1980s and remained high during the 1990s.

Figure 4.6 and Table 4.2 break down the figures shown in Figure 4.5 by the different parties.

Here again, the pattern shown in Figure 4.6 and Table 4.2 is largely similar to that shown earlier for the House of Representatives in Figure 4.3. As in the House of Representatives, the LDP and its conservative predecessors actually had the most number of statements per 1,000 House of Councillors meetings that referred to the jury during the immediate postwar period. But the JSP quickly overtook the LDP during the 1950s and continued to make statements referring to the jury most frequently until 1996. In addition, as in the House of

Table 4.2 *Number of statements referring to "jury," per 1,000 meetings attended, by party, 1947–96, Japanese House of Councillors*

	JSP	DSP	CGP	LDP	JCP
1947–50	0.37	0.00	0.00	2.40	0.00
1951–60	1.44	0.00	0.00	0.27	0.00
1961–70	0.55	0.70	0.00	0.16	0.00
1971–80	0.25	0.00	0.00	0.21	0.00
1981–90	2.61	1.20	0.79	0.27	0.46
1991–96	2.02	0.00	1.09	0.87	0.00

Source: National Diet Library (n.d.).

Representatives, the CGP began the postwar era with a low percentage of statements, but increasingly made more statements referring to the "jury."

Table 4.2 shows the precise numbers reported in Figure 4.6. The number of statements by the CGP rose from zero prior to 1981 to 0.79 per every 1,000 meetings attended during the 1980s to 1.09 statements during the 1991–6 period. This slow but steady increase in the number of references mirrors the trend of CGP statements seen in the House of Representatives. As in the House of Representatives, the JSP shows an abrupt rise in the number of statements during the 1980s, and the number of statements remained relatively high into the 1990s. As in the House of Representatives, the LDP shows a small increase in the number of statements referring to the jury during the 1990s, although even in the 1990s, there were still fewer statements by LDP legislators than by JSP or CGP legislators.

The data from both the House of Representatives and the House of Councillors thus show that while the conservative parties made more statements referring to the jury during the late 1940s, conservative interest in the jury dropped off soon thereafter. Instead, the jury became increasingly referenced by left-leaning opposition parties such as the JSP, the DSP, and to some extent the JCP, with the CGP also beginning to warm up to the issue especially starting in the 1990s.

Summary

This chapter traced the prewar and postwar evolution of the issue of the jury system in Japan. A jury system was introduced in Japan in 1928, but its institutional design severely discouraged defendants from using the system and use of the system declined every year until it was suspended in 1943. The jury system also was not revived during the US occupation of Japan, primarily because of reluctance on the part of Japanese policymakers and the unwillingness of senior SCAP officials to press the issue. Nevertheless, the issue remained in the minds of Japanese politicians, and they continued to pose questions regarding the jury throughout the postwar era. During the early postwar period, conservative legislators showed more interest in the issue than their leftist counterparts. Legislators lost interest in the jury during the 1960s and 1970s, as the memory of the prewar jury began to fade. But the issue saw a dramatic revival during the 1980s in the wake of a series of retrials that reversed death sentences. Note that this was also a time when Japan's leftist parties had increasingly embraced new left causes, such as environmental issues or freedom of information. After the 1960s, the jury became an issue of the left, with the JSP and the DSP, and, to a lesser extent, the JCP and even the CGP posing growing numbers of questions on the jury. Their questions revealed a growing interest in the jury as a corrective for an overly professionalized judiciary.

Thus, by the time the idea of introducing the jury finally emerged onto the Japanese policy agenda in the late 1990s, the more new left-oriented JSP and the DSP exhibited greater enthusiasm towards introducing a jury system, while the conservative LDP showed less, and the JCP and the CGP fell somewhere in between.

This pattern is consistent with the view presented in Chapter 2 that opposition parties in post-developmental states should be particularly eager to introduce a lay judge system than the conservative parties that form the cornerstone of the developmental state. Because conservatives in such states are committed to centralized technocratic policymaking and limiting transparency for the sake of development, opposition parties in developmental states often end up championing "post-materialist" issues such as greater transparency and citizen participation. The results presented in this chapter, that opposition parties in Japan were generally more willing than the LDP to push for a jury system, indeed lend support to this view.

It is also notable that the vast majority of the references to the lay judge system were to the "pure" jury (*baishin*), rather than the "mixed" jury (*sanshin*). This suggests that the leftist parties that favored the adoption of a lay judge system overwhelmingly favored a common-law style "pure" jury system on the American model, rather than the system that was ultimately adopted in the 2000s. That said, it is also possible that most legislators did not have a sophisticated enough understanding of the issue to be able to distinguish between "pure" and "mixed" jury systems, and they may also have been influenced by the memory of the prewar system.

5 | Bringing the Lay Judge System Back In, 1997–2004

Overview

Chapter 3 showed that until 1996, the Democratic Party of Japan (DPJ), the Social Democratic Party of Japan (SDP), and the Japan Communist Party (JCP) were more oriented towards the new left than the Liberal Democratic Party (LDP) or the Komeito. If the framework presented in this book is valid, the DPJ, the SDP, and the JCP should have favored instituting a jury/lay judge system that would undermine the powers of professional judges to a greater extent than the parties that have embraced new left issues to a lesser extent, namely the LDP or the Komeito. Since the Komeito, in turn, was found to be more new left-oriented than the LDP, it should have favored a greater transfer of powers from professional judges to lay judges than the LDP, although less so than the DPJ, the SDP, or the JCP. In addition, the final configuration of the resulting jury/lay judge system should be contingent upon the balance of power among the parties. To what extent are these predictions borne out by the empirical evidence?

The previous chapter showed that, starting in the 1960s, and especially from the 1980s, Japanese leftist parties increasingly championed the introduction of a jury/lay judge system. Although the conservative parties had more frequently referred to the jury system in the immediate postwar era, since the 1960s the overwhelming majority of references to the jury in the Japanese parliament have been made by the left, and especially by the more new left-oriented parties such as the JSP and the DSP. The new left-oriented parties' interest in the jury accelerated in the wake of the series of reversals of death penalty decisions during the early- to mid-1980s by the Supreme Court.

In the late 1990s, the question of introducing a lay judge system finally emerged onto the Japanese policy agenda. For the governing LDP, this was an unintended side effect of its broader effort to overhaul the judicial system. This chapter and the next highlight the key role that new left-oriented parties played in agenda-setting and in designing the new lay judge system. This chapter conducts qualitative historical process-tracing of the case of Japan to illustrate how the book's theoretical predictions are borne out empirically. It traces how partisan dynamics played a key role in keeping the lay judge issue on the policy agenda, as well as in shaping the contours of the new system. The next chapter will draw on quantitative content analysis of fifty years of Japanese parliamentary deliberations to further illuminate the different parties' levels of interest in the issues of introducing a jury/lay judge system, and the kind of system that should be introduced.

This chapter proceeds as follows. The following section traces the emergence of judicial reforms onto the policy agenda in the late 1990s. The third section describes the debates on lay participation within the blue-ribbon Justice System Reform Council (JSRC). The fourth section delineates how proposals by the Council were transformed into concrete legislation, and the role of various parties in this process. The fifth section turns to the counterfactual: what would the new system have looked like if the DPJ (founded in 1996 by legislators from the JSP, the DSP, and some from the LDP, and which soon became the major opposition party) had been as powerful when the final bill was submitted to the Diet in 2004 as it had been in 1999, when the bill to establish the JSRC was passed? The more new left-oriented DPJ favored a system that undermined the powers of professional judges to a much greater extent than the LDP or the Komeito, but its impact on policy had been curtailed by the time the final bill was submitted to the Diet. The sixth and final section summarizes and concludes.

Agenda-Setting under a Divided Parliament

Japan's big businesses had become increasingly frustrated with the slow-moving legal process in Japan, and during the early 1990s they began to demand major judicial reforms. They were particularly interested in seeing a dramatic increase in the number of lawyers and the introduction of various alternative dispute resolution measures. Introducing a system of lay participation was certainly not high on their agenda, if it was on it at all. In 1994, the Japan Association of Corporate Executives (JACE, *Keizai Doyukai*), one of Japan's major big business organizations, released a report titled "The Pathologies of

Contemporary Japan: Prescriptions [*Gendai Nihonno Byorito Shoho*]," in which it identified a number of problems it saw with existing Japanese institutions (Keizai Doyukai 1994). In particular, the report criticized the existing Japanese judicial system and argued that the government should establish what it called a "Judicial Reform Promotion Council" to draw up sweeping reforms of the system. Then in 1997, the JACE again released a report that pushed for an overhaul of the justice system, this time focusing more specifically on reforms of corporate law but again calling on the government to introduce reforms to expedite the legal process (Keizai Doyukai 1997). Notably, neither of the reports included a proposal to introduce a jury/lay judge system.

Another impetus for broad judicial reforms came from the Ministry of Justice (MOJ). The MOJ also supported an increase in the number of lawyers and the introduction of reforms that would make such an increase possible, at least in part because of the growing difficulties it was experiencing at the time in recruiting young prosecutors from the very small pool of individuals who had passed the bar exam (e.g. Miyamoto 2005). Thus for the MOJ, and for Japanese big business, introducing a system of public participation in criminal trials was not of great concern.

In response to these demands, in June 1997, the LDP established the Special Research Commission on the Justice System inside the LDP's Policy Affairs Research Council to discuss possibilities for judicial reform. The Commission was headed by Taku Yamazaki, an influential member of the LDP. In November 1997, the Commission released the "Basic Framework for Judicial Reform," which called for sweeping judicial reforms. This "Basic Framework" included a long list of possible reforms, including the establishment of US-style law schools and various measures to speed up court trials (Ueno 1998). Although big business had not pushed for US-style law schools *per se*, law schools would be compatible with an increase in the number of lawyers, which they did want (Keizai Doyukai 1994, 1997). The "Basic Framework" did not include proposals for a system of public participation in criminal trials, although we should note that it was not intended to be a final proposal. The commission subsequently split up into two sub-commissions, each of which met weekly between February and May of 1998 and continued to discuss proposals for reform (Mizuno 1999). According to Saito (1999), the Japan Federation of Bar Associations (JFBA), which took part in the commission discussions, strongly pushed for the introduction of a jury system around this time. Upon conclusion of discussions in the two sub-commissions, the LDP released a new report, "A Solid Framework for the Justice System for the 21st Century," which was released in June 1998. This report called for the establishment of a blue-ribbon government commission to devise a plan for overhauling Japan's judicial system, including the introduction of US-style law schools and various measures for expediting the legal process (Jiyu Minshuto 1998). In addition, owing at least in part to the JFBA's lobbying efforts, the "introduction of a system of public participation in the justice system" was also listed as one of the proposed reforms (ibid).

Just after the release of the "Solid Framework" in June 1998, the LDP suffered a major defeat in the Upper House elections in July. This electoral reverse brought down Ryutaro Hashimoto's government and caused a delay in setting up the blue-ribbon commission for judicial reform. The bill to authorize the establishment of the commission was approved by the Cabinet of Prime Minister Keizo Obuchi in February 1999 and submitted to the Diet shortly thereafter.

Despite the specific recommendations of the LDP's "Solid Framework" report, including the proposal to establish a "system of public participation in the justice system," the initial bill that the Obuchi Cabinet submitted to parliament for the Law Concerning the Establishment of Justice System Reform Council did not provide a list of concrete reforms for it to consider. Instead it gave *carte blanche* to the new Council to set its own agenda. This vagueness in the bill received fierce objections from opposition party members of the Committee on Judicial Affairs in both Houses of the Diet. For instance, during the parliamentary debates over the bill, Soya Fukuoka of the DPJ complained in his question to Takao Jinnai, the Justice Minister (LDP):

Article 2 of this bill stipulates that this Council should "Clarify the role that the judicial branch should play in our country in the twenty-first century . . ." This is the same as simply saying that the Council should undertake judicial reform and is very vague about specifics . . . The mission of the Council is both very abstract and very unlimited. It is written in such a way that it can take up anything and everything . . . Rather than giving *carte blanche* to the Council in this manner, would we not want to specify some of the more urgent issues that it should take up . . . giving it a more specific mandate? Is it not the responsibility of this Committee [on Judicial Affairs] to come to some agreement regarding the mission of this Council . . .?[1]

Nobuto Hosaka of the SDP concurred in his parliamentary remarks: "The SDP supports judicial reform, but we have some serious doubts about this bill as it has been submitted . . . Asking the parliament to give *carte blanche* to the cabinet is like asking it to relinquish its own responsibility, and I strongly doubt that this is the way for us to go."[2]

The government responded that the rationale for not offering a list of specific issues that the Council would take up was that such a list would conflict with the principle of separation of powers between the administrative and judicial branches of government. The newly established Council, it argued, should be free to discuss whatever reforms it deemed necessary.[3] But opposition party MPs were not satisfied with this reasoning, and they rallied around the idea of adding a provision to mandate the JSRC to take up the issue of introducing a jury system in Japan. Many opposition party members of the Committee on Judicial Affairs, such as Hidenori Sasaki (DPJ), Yoshio Urushihara (CGP, now renamed Komeito), as well as Hideo Kijima (JCP), actively voiced support for introducing a jury/lay justice system. Sasaki, for instance, noted during committee debates:

[C]ompared to other countries, I feel that Japanese citizens have very limited opportunities for participating in the judicial system. It may not necessarily be appropriate to directly import the American or British jury systems or the German mixed jury system into Japan, but this is a great opportunity to think about what measures might be introduced to bring the courts closer to the people.[4]

Urushihara concurred: "If the judicial branch is to be well understood by the people and to be supported, it should not be remote from

---

[1] Remarks by Soya Fukuoka, Minutes of House of Representatives Committee on Judicial Affairs No. 6, 145th Session of the Diet, March 31, 1999.

[2] Remarks by Nobuto Hosaka, Minutes of House of Representatives Committee on Judicial Affairs No. 7, 145th Session of the Diet, April 13, 1999.

[3] Remarks by Seiichi Fusamura, Ministry of Justice, Minutes of House of Representatives Committee on Judicial Affairs No. 6, 145th Session of the Diet, March 31, 1999.

[4] Remarks by Hidenori Sasaki, Minutes of House of Representatives Committee on Judicial Affairs No. 5, 145th Session of the Diet, March 30, 1999.

the people. . . To this end, I believe that encouraging greater popular participation in the judicial system would be very important."[5] Kijima also expressed support: "I believe that democracy necessitates popular participation in the justice system, and [a jury would] contribute to reducing the power of bureaucrats in the justice system. . ."[6] The opposition parties' support for a jury/lay judge system will be discussed more systematically in the next chapter.

As will also be shown in the next chapter, LDP MPs were much less eager to take up the issue of participation, and most of their questions to the government focused on issues that were of greater interest to the business community, such as increasing the number of lawyers or the expansion of mediation schemes.[7]

The government, on the other hand, offered neither much opposition to the idea of introducing a lay judge system, nor much enthusiasm for it. For instance, Jinnai, the Justice Minister (LDP), noted in his parliamentary remarks: "We recognize that introducing a jury system or other system of participation in criminal trials would be quite important for promoting greater public input in the justice system. . . Since such a system would alter the basic contours of our justice system, I believe that the issue should be debated carefully from many different perspectives."[8] Jinnai's cautious statement clearly contrasts with the strongly favorable statements on the part of opposition party legislators.

Dissatisfied with the bill's failure to specify what issues the new council should take up, opposition parties prepared to submit an amendment to the bill to mandate the JSRC to take up a number of specific issues, including the issue of how public participation in the justice system might be expanded. The LDP conceded, and in the House of Representatives, the LDP and six opposition parties, i.e. all parties except the now tiny SDP, jointly submitted an amendment proposal that explicitly mandated the JSRC to take up specific issues, including citizen involvement in the judicial process.

---

[5] Remarks by Yoshio Urushihara, Ministry of Justice, Minutes of House of Representatives Committee on Judicial Affairs No. 6, 145th Session of the Diet, March 31, 1999.

[6] Remarks by Hideo Kijima, ibid.

[7] See, for instance, remarks by Okiharu Yasuoka, ibid.

[8] Remarks by Takao Jinnai, Minutes of House of Representatives Committee on Judicial Affairs No. 6, 145th Session of the Diet, March 31, 1999.

The LDP's concession to accept this amendment can be explained by the particular balance of power among parties in parliament around the time that the bill to establish the JSRC was submitted in early 1999. Opposition parties did not hold a majority in the House of Representatives (the lower house), but in July 1998, they won control of the House of Councillors (the upper house), creating a situation of "divided parliament." The LDP entered into coalition with the Liberal Party in November 1998 in order to alleviate the situation, but the two parties still only held a combined total of 114 of the 252 seats in the House of Councillors (Kanda 2014). The strongest opposition party in the House of Councillors at the time was the DPJ, with 47 seats, followed by the JCP (23 seats), the Komeito (22 seats), and the SDP (13 seats). Moreover, the LDP lacked the two-thirds majority in the House of Representatives that it needed in order to override a rejection of the bill in the House of Councillors (Ito 2011). Rather than amend the bill in the House of Councillors and then have to pass the amended version again in the House of Representatives, the LDP chose to speed up the process by agreeing to amend the bill in the House of Representatives. The amended bill was passed by the House of Representatives on April 22, 1999, and by the House of Councillors on June 2, 1999.[9]

In addition, both houses of the Diet adopted a supplementary resolution to the bill that urged the JSRC to take up a number of "important issues," including popular participation in the justice system and increasing the number and quality of legal professionals in Japan. As Masuyama (2006) notes, Japanese parliamentary resolutions are not binding, but the combination of the amendment – which is binding – and the resolution would send a strong message to the new JSRC. Thus, in effect, the parliament had mandated the JSRC to take up the issue of popular participation in criminal trials, i.e. to discuss the possible adoption of a jury/lay judge system (Yanase 2007).

The fact that leftist opposition parties held a majority in the House of Councillors was thus crucially important in setting the agenda for the newly established JSRC. As we have seen in Chapter 3, these opposition parties – the DPJ, the SDP (previously JSP), the Komeito (previously CGP), and the JCP – were more new left-oriented than

---

[9] Thies and Yanai (2014) show that under "divided parliament," *ceteris paribus*, the Japanese government submits fewer bills to the parliament and that the percentage of amended bills and rejected bills increases.

the LDP, and thus more eager to push for an expansion of popular participation. Indeed, all four parties were eager to see the introduction of an US-style jury. Of course, they could not get everything they wanted from the LDP. The amendment's phrase "popular participation in criminal trials" was vague enough that the JSRC would still have leeway in how to design this new system of participation. In fact, the amendment had merely mandated the JSRC to discuss the issue, not necessarily to propose to adopt a jury/lay judge system.[10] It is also certainly possible that the JSRC would have taken up the question even without the urging of the Diet. Nevertheless, the Diet had now given the JSRC a clear mandate to explore the issue.

Discussions over the Lay Judge System in the JSRC

Composition of the JSRC

The JSRC consisted of thirteen blue-ribbon members chosen by the Prime Minister's Office and the MOJ (Tsuchiya 2005: 113). As Tani (2002) notes, six out of thirteen members were legal scholars or current or former lawyers, striking a "balance between legal insiders and outsiders." The thirteen members consisted of one former judge, one former prosecutor, and one former private attorney; five academics, three of whom were legal scholars; two members from the business world; one labor representative; one member from a consumer organization; and one novelist. No active officials of the courts, prosecution, or the bar association were included. As Teijiro Furukawa, the Deputy Chief Cabinet Secretary noted, this was because in the overall judicial reform being contemplated, "Judges, prosecutors, and lawyers are carp on a cutting board. Carp should not be allowed to hold knives" (Yamazaki 2001: 1).

Koji Sato, a constitutional scholar and professor at Kyoto University, was appointed to chair the JSRC. Sato had been a member of the Administrative Reform Council (1996-98), and during his service he had won the trust of both Furukawa and Okiharu Yasuoka, one of

---

[10] Other issues that the JSRC had been mandated to take up, such as the hiring of larger numbers of experienced private attorneys as judges, were in fact discussed in the JSRC but did not materialize.

the main proponents of judicial reform within the LDP (Furukawa 2004: 7–8; Yasuoka 2008: 90).

Sato had also offered expert testimony at the House of Councillors Committee on Judicial Affairs when the bill for the Law concerning Establishment of Justice System Reform Council was under deliberation. There, he had enthusiastically endorsed the introduction of a jury system in Japan.

> I would very much like to see . . . this Council seriously discuss the possibility of introducing a jury system . . . The biggest reason for this is that . . . the Japanese citizenry seems to think that courts are very remote from them, and that justice is something that brings itself about . . . More specifically, in a jury, citizens must be present in the courtroom to bring about justice themselves and to determine people's fate. Having such an opportunity should help to make people realize that there is more human drama involved in trials and in the judicial system than they see now. This, in turn, should help to make them realize that the justice system belongs to them . . . [11]

Sato thus saw the jury system as an avenue for civic education. In his highly regarded textbook *Kenpo [Constitutional Law]*, which is one of the most widely read textbooks on Japanese constitutional law among Japan's law students, Sato had also argued that introducing a "pure" jury system would be compatible with the existing constitution (Sato 1981). However, his views on the jury were not the reason he was selected to lead the panel. Moreover, as will be seen later, in his role as chair, Sato carefully kept his own personal views in check and did not attempt to impose his views about the jury on the rest of the JSRC. Conceivably, the government might not have selected him for the position if it had believed that he would try to impose his views.

Perhaps a better reflection of the government's views on the lay judge system was the appointment of Masahito Inoue, a criminal law scholar at the University of Tokyo, to serve on the JSRC. Like Sato, Inoue had served on several other important government commissions prior to the JSRC, such as the National Bar Examination Commission and the Advisory Committee on the Rules of the Supreme Court. It is important to note that the government was well aware of the positions of these key scholars prior to appointing them on the JSRC.

---

[11] Remarks by Koji Sato, House of Councillors Judicial Affairs Committee No. 11, 145th Session of Diet, May 18, 1999.

The JSRC met sixty-six times over two years between July 1999 and June 2001. To ensure transparency, the transcripts and minutes of the meetings were made available online and were also published in *Gekkan Shiho Kaikaku (Judicial Reform Monthly)*. Beginning with the eleventh session, the press was allowed to watch the televised meetings live via a monitor placed in a separate room.

It should also be noted that in the midst of the JSRC's debates, the LDP released its own new set of proposals for judicial reform in May 2000, titled "A Firm Step Forward for the Judicial System in the 21st Century: Towards a Judicial System that is Trusted by both Citizens and the World." The main focus of this document was on civil and corporate legal matters, and the LDP laid out specific proposals for expediting the legal process, introducing new schemes for alternative dispute resolution, and related reforms. On the jury system in particular, the document argued that an US-style jury system would not be appropriate for Japan. "A system [like the jury] in which legal professionals do not participate in the determination of facts is fundamentally at odds with the existing legal system of our country. There is thus no basis for such a system to function smoothly in this context" (Jiyu Minshuto 2000). On the other hand, the LDP was not averse to introducing a continental-style lay judge system. ". . . [O]ne of the ways to reflect the diverse views of citizens in the legal process, and/or to respond appropriately to legal disputes in highly specialized issue areas, may be the introduction of a 'mixed' jury system, and we believe that the introduction of such a system should be considered" (ibid). Thus, members of the JSRC were well aware of the ruling party's position when debates over the jury/lay judge system began in the JSRC in the fall of 2000.

Debates over the Lay Judge System

The JSRC debated a broad range of major reforms, including the introduction of an US-style law school system, reform of the intellectual property system, expansion of alternative dispute resolution schemes, and public participation in the justice system. The issue of public participation was taken up starting in the thirtieth session of the JSRC, in September 2000. Again, these discussions began just after the LDP had released its own set of proposals in May.

On September 12, 2000, in the thirtieth session of the JSRC, representatives from the Supreme Court, the Public Prosecutor's Office, and the

JFBA were invited to present their views on the possible introduction of a jury/lay participation system. Perhaps emboldened by the LDP's position on the issue, Takao Nakayama of the General Secretariat of the Supreme Court and who spoke formally on behalf of the Supreme Court, expressed vehement opposition against an Anglo-American jury system.

"The jury system rests on a fundamentally different judicial framework than our own, and it is implausible that such a system would work effectively by importing it into our existing justice system,"[12] Nakayama argued. The reason, he claimed, was that "The jury only gives a verdict – guilty or not guilty. There is no disclosure of the reasons leading to that verdict or of the debates that took place among the jurors. A jury system, then, does not help to unveil the truth."[13] Nakayama did express support for a variant of a continental-style lay justice system, but only a system in which the lay justices would have no vote.[14] Even if they have no vote, Nakayama offered, "Lay justices could participate in discussion with professional judges and express their views, in turn, making it possible to reflect public opinion in criminal rulings."[15] As will be shown in Chapter 7, the Japanese Supreme Court's initial preference for a non-binding lay judge system was strikingly similar to the preference of the Taiwanese Judicial Yuan during Taiwan's debate on this issue.

Nakayama's view met with fierce objections from several members of the JSRC, particularly Kohei Nakabo, who was a former president of the JFBA. Nakabo objected that the Supreme Court was much too reluctant to reform.[16] The JFBA had favored an Anglo-American style jury system since the 1980s (Kage 2015) and Nakabo echoed this view in the discussions in the JSRC as well.

The debate continued for several sessions, but a major rift emerged between those who favored an US-style jury system, including Nakabo,

---

[12] Minutes of the 30th Session of the Justice System Reform Council, September 12, 2000, http://www.kantei.go.jp/jp/sihouseido/dai30/30gijiroku.html, accessed April 5, 2014.

[13] Ibid. Note that Nakayama's assertion that jury systems do not require juries *not* to provide a reason for the verdict or sentence is not necessarily true. The Spanish jury system in fact requires juries to offer a reason for their verdict (Thaman 1997).

[14] Minutes of the 30th Session of the Justice System Reform Council, September 12, 2000, http://www.kantei.go.jp/jp/sihouseido/dai30/30gijiroku.html, accessed April 5, 2014.

[15] Ibid.

[16] Ibid.

Tsuyoshi Takagi, the labor representative, and Hatsuko Yoshioka, who represented consumers; and those who preferred a more continental-style lay judge system that would preserve the powers of professional judges to a much greater extent, including Morio Takeshita and Masahito Inoue, both of whom were legal scholars. Sato, who chaired the JSRC, carefully refrained from imposing his own views.

JSRC participants and observers concur that a turning point in the debates came at the forty-third session of the JSRC, which met in January 2001 (Iimuro 2000; Sato and Aoyama 2001; Tsuchiya 2005: 126–128). In this session, three prominent scholars – Koichiro Fujikura, an expert in Anglo-American Law, Koya Matsuo, a specialist in criminal procedures law, and Taichiro Mitani, a political historian – offered their expert opinions. All three had read the minutes of the previous JSRC meetings and were aware of the split within the JSRC on the issue.[17] All three took the position that the difference between the US-style jury system and a continental-style lay justice system could be bridged.[18] The suggestions by Matsuo, who was a leading expert in criminal procedure law, were especially specific. He argued, first, that the defendants should not have a choice as to whether to be tried by lay judges; second, that because the Japanese public had become accustomed to seeing criminal rulings accompanied by extensive explanations of the rationale for that ruling, the US-style jury verdict, which is not accompanied by an explanation of its decision, would not work well in the Japanese context; third, that a system in which the lay judges sit alongside professional judges, in contrast to the US-style jury system, may be more conducive to both sides "sharing their own insights," and, in turn, to a more in-depth discussion; and fourth, also from the perspective of "sharing insights," lay judges should be involved in ruling not only on verdict but also sentencing.[19] Matsuo also coined the term "*saiban-in*," which eventually became the name of the Japanese lay judge system (e.g. Tani 2002; Tsuchiya 2005: 127).

Matsuo's proposals helped to bridge the rift inside the JSRC. They were also likely to be more palatable to the LDP than a "pure" jury system, since professional judges would be involved in all stages of the

[17] Minutes of the 43rd Session of the Justice System Reform Council, January 9, 2001 http://www.kantei.go.jp/jp/sihouseido/dai43/43gijiroku.html, accessed April 6, 2014.

[18] Ibid.

[19] Ibid.

criminal trial process, rather than leaving the verdict solely to jurors. Note here that like Sato, Takeshita, and Inoue, Matsuo had also served on numerous government commissions and had just been appointed to chair the Legislative Council of the Ministry of Justice. Thus, like Sato, Takeshita, and Inoue, Matsuo was not only a leading scholar but also a figure highly trusted by the government. Sato also later recounted, "After this [forty-third] session . . . I could see that the introduction of a lay judge system had become a real possibility . . ." (Sato and Aoyama 2001: 17). Many of the proposals that Matsuo made at this meeting, such as not giving defendants the choice of opting in or out of a lay judge trial, that lay judges would serve on both guilty and not guilty plea cases, and that lay and professional judges would deliberate together to reach *both* verdict and sentence, were adopted in the JSRC's final report. These formed the basis for the bill that was passed by the Diet in May 2004 as well.

The JRSC ended its mission in June 2001 when it submitted its final report to the cabinet. The report included a number of major proposals, such as the expansion of various schemes for alternative dispute resolution and reform of the intellectual property system, but undoubtedly the two major pillars of the report were the introductions of an US-style law school system and a lay judge system. The report sketched out the main contours of the new lay judge system, in line with Matsuo's vision, but other important aspects of the new system still needed to be hammered out. In particular, a major issue left unresolved was the number of lay and professional judges.

Coalition Dynamics and the Design of the *Saiban-in* System

By the time the JSRC had submitted its final report, an important shift had occurred in the partisan politics of the Diet. In October 1999, the Komeito broke with other opposition parties to form a governing coalition with the LDP and the Liberal Party. This gave control of the Upper House back to the government. The Liberal Party left the coalition in early 2000, but the LDP-Komeito coalition still retained control of both Houses of the Diet. Since, as we have seen in Chapter 3, the Komeito was more new left-oriented than the LDP or the Liberal Party, it also introduced a broader spectrum of political views into the government. This was to have important repercussions for the design of the lay judge system.

After the JRSC submitted its final report, the Office for the Promotion of Justice System Reform was established within the Cabinet Office.[20] The Office was given a period of three years to oversee the enactment of proposals advanced by the JRSC. Eleven investigative committees were established within the Office to devise concrete legislative proposals based on the JSRC's final report. Each committee covered a key reform issue that had been proposed by the JSRC: one was to focus on the new lay judge system, another on introduction of US-style law schools, a third on the reform of the intellectual property system, and so on.

The investigative committee for the lay judge system was comprised of eleven members, including five legal scholars, five active or former lawyers (including one who also counted as a legal scholar), one police bureaucrat, and a journalist. Inoue, who, as member of the JSRC, had been quite hostile to the notion of an US-style jury, was appointed to chair this committee.

A rift quickly emerged within the committee over the relative number of lay and professional judges who should sit on trials. It was believed by actors on both sides of the issue that a larger number of lay judges relative to professional judges would give greater influence to the lay judges. The MOJ and the Supreme Court therefore favored a smaller number of lay judges; the JFBA, a larger number.

As Tani (2004) argues, the difference in views over the desired number of lay vs. professional judges also reflected a more fundamental disagreement over the objective of introducing a lay judge system in the first place. Those who wanted a larger number of professional judges and fewer lay judges tended to stress the civic education function of the system; they hoped that participating in court trials would help to educate the public regarding the workings of the judicial system and to instill public-mindedness in the citizenry. This view also assumed that the existing judicial system was already functioning quite well, as reflected in the 90%-plus public approval ratings for the judicial system, and therefore that the judicial system itself did not require fundamental reform. By contrast, those who hoped to see a larger number of lay judges tended to see more flaws in the existing system. Professional judges were out of touch from the real world and were not keeping step with broader social changes. Proponents of this

---

[20] This section relies on Tani (2004); Yamaguchi (2004); Yanase (2009, Chapter 1); Wang and Fukurai (2011); and Ogura (2013).

view pointed to the series of mistrials, as well as the 99.9% conviction rate in Japan, as symptomatic of deeper underlying problems in
the judicial system. From this perspective, instilling a healthy dose of
public opinion would lead to rulings that would be more in line with
public expectations and, in turn, help to enhance the legitimacy of the
judicial system. The discussion entered a stalemate.

With the experts unable to agree, the debate went to the politicians.
There was considerable discussion within the LDP over the number of
lay judges vis-à-vis the number of professional judges. Many believed
that the new lay judge trials should have three professional judges,
which had been the norm for Japanese criminal trials throughout the
postwar period. As noted earlier, this position was also favored by
the MOJ and the Supreme Court. But some within the LDP, and the
Komeito, which had become the LDP's coalition partner some months
before, pushed to reduce the number of professional judges to two.
Those who favored two professional judges often tended also to favor
a larger number of lay judges. As noted earlier, the JFBA supported
this position. In fact, in the investigative committee, the JFBA supported a proposal for one or two professional judges and between nine
and eleven lay judges.

Observers concur that the mainstream LDP members' push for a
smaller number of lay judges was driven by a conservative desire to
preserve the power of professional judges and to keep the reform as
incremental as possible (e.g. Tani 2004; Ogura 2013). By the same
logic, the opposition parties, as well as the Komeito, appear to have
believed that a larger number of lay judges would mark a more fundamental break from the existing professional judge system. Indeed, the
Komeito explicitly argued that a larger number of lay judges would
be desirable in order to reduce the status difference between professional and lay judges and to foster a climate that would allow the
latter to speak up more freely (Tani 2004). The Komeito's proposal for
the lay judge system, released in December 2003, titled, "Designing
the *Saiban-in* System," argued: "The *saiban-in* system should not be
viewed as an extension of the existing system. Thus, in designing the
system, it should be viewed as an entirely new system, of the people,
by the people, and for the people" (Komeito 2003, cited in Tsuji 2015:
372). "The number of lay judges should be relatively large, so that the
diversity of societal views can be reflected and that it is clear that the
citizens are in charge" (ibid: 376).

From the perspective of existing studies on small-group deliberation, the assumptions made by all parties in these debates can be questioned. Social-psychological research on small-group deliberation typically finds that, *ceteris paribus*, smaller groups are more conducive to active deliberation and reduce the power of factions compared to larger groups (e.g. Devine et al. 2001; Delli Carpini et al. 2004). A smaller number of lay judges, then, might actually *enhance* the power of lay judges vis-à-vis professional judges; and consequently, a system with a smaller number of lay judges would actually represent a greater break from the existing professional judge system than one with a larger number of lay judges. It appears, though, that the politicians were not aware of these insights and, as a result, the conservative LDP paradoxically advocated fewer lay judges, while new left-oriented parties, including the Komeito, pushed for a greater number of lay judges.

In April 2003, the LDP established the Subcommittee on the Lay Judge System within its Research Commission on the Justice System in order to draw up a proposal for the new lay judge system. Headed by MP Jinen Nagase, the Subcommittee met for discussions on a weekly basis, inviting various speakers, including lawyers, legal professors, and the police. In August, the Subcommittee released a draft preliminary proposal that advocated for lay judge trials consisting of three professional judges and between three and six lay judges.

At this point, however, several LDP legislators began to push for two professional judges. The JFBA, which favored two lay judges, had launched a vigorous lobbying campaign with the LDP Dietmembers. The Supreme Court, in turn, lobbied hard to keep the three-judge system. In the completed preliminary proposal released on September 26, the Subcommittee report actually included proposals for both the two-judge system and the three-judge system, revealing considerable disagreement within the LDP.

However, several of the main LDP proponents of the two-judge system, including Seiichi Ota and Hideo Usui, lost their seats in the November 9, 2003, General Elections, dealing a blow to the JFBA and those who favored two professional judges. On December 9, the LDP Subcommittee released its final report, which recommended a three-judge system. The report also proposed that the number of lay judges should be around four, although it conceded that the number could range between two and six.

The Komeito, on the other hand, came out in favor of two judges and seven lay judges. "It is important that the system invites citizen participation, and that citizens can feel a sense of accomplishment upon completion of their task" (Komeito 2003, cited in Tsuji 2015: 375). This position was much closer to the JFBA's, and in fact many of the leaders of the Komeito, including Chief Representative Takenori Kanzaki, and Secretary General Tetsuzo Fuyushiba, were private attorneys themselves. Thus, in some ways, at the partisan level, the disagreement between the MOJ-Supreme Court on the one hand and the JFBA on the other was reflected in the rift between the LDP and the Komeito.

After considerable discussion, the two parties reached agreement towards the end of January 2004. The new lay trials would involve three professional judges and six lay judges. Thus, while the three-judge system was preserved, in line with the preferences of LDP conservatives, the number of lay judges was closer to the number preferred by the more new left-oriented Komeito. The LDP also agreed to a Komeito proposal that when the defendant pleaded guilty, and when the prosecutors and defense attorney agreed, the court could also hold a trial with one professional judge and four lay judges. The Komeito also won other important concessions from the LDP, such as lowering the minimum age for lay jurors from twenty-five to twenty, expanding the scope of cases that would fall under lay judge trial, and reducing the penalty on lay judges for disclosing confidential information obtained during trial (e.g. Tani 2004).[21] With these last major issues resolved, along with some other minor issues, the *Saiban-in* Law passed the House of Representatives on April 23, 2004, and the House of Councillors on May 21, 2004. The law mandated a five-year preparation period prior to the introduction of the new lay judge system, and the system was officially launched in May 2009.

In sum, after the JSRC's proposals, the final design of the *saiban-in* system was largely shaped by negotiations between the two governing coalition partners, the LDP and the Komeito. Since these two coalition partners held a majority in both Houses of the Diet, other parties had very little input in the last stage of designing the *saiban-in* system.

[21] The LDP had not put an upper limit on the severity of possible punishment, but the Komeito argued that violators should not be subject to more than a fine. As a compromise, the two parties agreed that violators could be subject to either a fine or a jail sentence (Tani 2004).

It should be noted here that the more strongly new left-oriented Japanese parties such as the DPJ, the SDP, and the JCP expressed a clear preference for a system that would impose even greater constraints on the power of professional judges than the one that was ultimately agreed upon between the LDP and the Komeito. However, due to the lack of influence of the opposition parties around the time that the *saiban-in* bill was submitted to the Diet, the impact of these parties on the final design of the *saiban-in* system was much more limited than the influence of the Komeito.

Counterfactual Reasoning: Proposals by the DPJ, SDP, and JCP

As noted earlier, by the time that the judicial reforms emerged onto the Japanese policy agenda in the late 1990s, the DPJ had replaced the JSP, now Social Democratic Party of Japan (SDP) as the largest opposition party, while incorporating many ex-DSP and JSP members into its ranks. As seen in Chapter 3, the DPJ also embraced new left causes to a greater extent than the LDP or the Komeito. Perhaps not surprisingly, then, the DPJ at the beginning of the debates over judicial reform advocated the introduction of a "pure" jury rather than a mixed jury. Soon after the JSRC began its discussions, Satsuki Eda, the DPJ shadow Justice Minister and himself a former judge, released the DPJ's proposals for judicial reforms. Included in the list of proposals was the introduction of a "pure" jury system.[22] The proposal argued that "By participating in juries, trials will become a part of citizens' daily lives. This will bring a breath of fresh air into the judicial system" (Eda 2000). "If a pure jury is adopted, courts will try to explain legal procedures in a more accessible manner, bringing the courts closer to the people" (ibid). The DPJ also advocated for a much broader range of cases to be subject to a "pure" jury trial and pushed for the inclusion of not only criminal but also administrative cases.[23] When the JSRC released its final report, the DPJ shadow cabinet expressed dissatisfaction that the JSRC had not proposed administrative cases to be subject to *saiban-in* trials (Eda 2002).

---

[22] The DPJ's proposals are available on https://www.eda-jp.com/dpj/shihou.html, accessed February 19, 2015.

[23] The DPJ also proposed a "mixed" jury system for civil cases (ibid).

In December 2003, the DPJ also compiled its own version of the *Saiban-in* bill (Minshuto 2003). Since, by this point, the JSRC's final report had proposed a mixed, rather than pure, jury system, the DPJ's bill stipulated a mixed jury system, but with just one professional judge and ten lay judges. Note that this was a more radical proposition than the Komeito's, which pushed for two professional and seven lay judges. The DPJ's thinking was that reducing the number of professional judges would much diminish their influence and have the overall effect of enhancing the influence of lay judges. In order to encourage the participation of women as lay judges, the bill also stipulated for the provision of childcare and elderly care facilities within the courthouse. As with the Komeito, the DPJ also proposed that all citizens who were eligible to vote should be eligible to serve as jurors.

However, the loss of the Upper House greatly reduced the influence of the DPJ over the substance of legislation. The DPJ did succeed in amending the final bill so that the penalties for lay judges who disclosed information obtained during service would be further reduced; this issue had been of concern to the Komeito as well. The DPJ also won a supplementary resolution that would urge the government to introduce videotaping and/or recording of interrogations. But these were minor concessions, and the overall framework of the lay judge system remained largely unchanged after the LDP-Komeito agreement of January 2004. If the DPJ and other new left-oriented parties had had more seats in the parliament, they would likely have been able to transfer more powers to the lay judges.

The SDP and the JCP had even less leverage over the design of the new system than the DPJ. At the time that the *Saiban-in* bill was submitted to the Diet, neither the SDP nor the JCP had enough seats in the House of Representatives to assign any of its members to the Judicial Affairs Committee (Tani 2004; Yanase 2008). The JCP did have one member on the House of Councillors Judicial Affairs Committee, but the SDP had none (ibid).

Nevertheless, when the interim report of the JSRC was released in November 2000, Mizuho Fukushima, the head of the Judicial Affairs Division of the SDP and herself a private attorney, released a statement suggesting that the JSRC should consider the introduction of a "pure" jury system (Fukushima 2001).

The JCP also initially advocated the introduction of a pure jury system. Later, once the introduction of the *saiban-in* emerged onto the agenda, the JCP pushed for a system consisting of one professional judge and nine lay judges.[24] As with the DPJ's proposal, this proposal was for a more radical departure from the existing system than the Komeito's proposal. Satoshi Inoue, the sole JCP member of the Committee Judicial Affairs Committee of the House of Councillors, remarked in his parliamentary question to the government: "We have asked many times about the question of how many judges should serve with how many lay judges. We believe that this is a crucially important issue for ensuring that the *saiban-in* be able to speak freely in the presence of [legal] professionals."[25]

Summary

Process-tracing of the introduction of the Japanese *saiban-in* system reveals that partisan dynamics crucially shaped both the introduction and the configuration of the new lay judge system in Japan. The more new-left oriented parties – the DPJ, SDP, and JCP – expressed a preference for pure jury systems over mixed jury systems, and for *saiban-in* systems consisting of a larger number of lay judges vis-à-vis professional judges. The LDP supported a mixed jury system, and it consistently favored a smaller number of lay judges than the other parties. The Komeito's position was somewhere in between that of the LDP, on the one hand, and the DPJ, SDP, and the JCP, on the other. This partisan distribution of views is precisely what we would expect from the findings shown in Chapter 4.

While the conservative LDP remained in power throughout the period of deliberation, new left-oriented parties played a key role in shaping the configuration of the Japanese system at key junctures. New left-oriented parties held a majority in the House of Councillors during the 1999 debates over the Bill Concerning the Establishment of Justice System Reform Council, and they played a major role in inserting an amendment that mandated the JSRC to take up the issue of popular participation in the justice system. This amendment paved the way for the issue of introducing a jury/lay judge system to be taken up by the JSRC.

---

[24] Remarks by Satoshi Inoue, House of Councillors Judicial Affairs Committee No. 15, 159th Session of Diet, May 11, 2004.

[25] Ibid.

Moreover, even after the opposition lost control of the Upper House due to the Komeito's entry into a governing coalition with the LDP, the presence of the Komeito in the coalition ensured that new left views remained influential. The Komeito played a key role in expanding the number of lay judges, based on the (mistaken) belief that this would help to dilute the power of professional judges. On the other hand, if the DPJ, SDP, and JCP had been more influential within the overall party system at the time that the *Saiban-in* bill was being debated, the resulting system would probably have undermined the powers of professional judges to a much greater extent than the one that actually transpired.

This historical process-tracing of the introduction of the Japanese lay judge system also offers intriguing insights into the relationship between politicians and experts. The chapter shows that even in a highly technical issue-area such as judicial politics, politicians, rather than legal scholars or practitioners, controlled the direction of reform. In selecting the members for the JSRC, the LDP chose figures they knew well and had previously worked with. By performing this key gatekeeping function, the politicians were able to ensure that the resulting outcome would not be far from their preferences, even if politicians did not understand all of the technical issues.

The Japanese lay judge system that resulted from this long process does not constrain the power of professional judges as much as the Spanish system does. For instance, the lay judges deliberate together with the professional judges. The scope of cases to be tried by lay trial is also narrower in Japan compared to Spain. This relatively weaker reform can be attributed to the influence of the conservative LDP. In Spain, by contrast, the jury system was introduced by the new left-oriented Socialist Party. Nevertheless, the Japanese reform imposed greater constraints upon professional judges compared to the cases of Korea and Taiwan, primarily due to the greater influence of new left-oriented parties within the Japanese party system at the time that the issue was under debate. Japan's new left-oriented parties played a major role in pushing the introduction of the lay judge system onto the agenda. They also played an important role in expanding the scope of cases that would fall under lay judge trial, as well as the pool of potential jurors.

One more point is in order. A recent study by Matsumoto and Matsuo (2010) showed that legislators who had previously served as judges, prosecutors, or private attorneys were substantially more likely to speak in the Committee on Judicial Affairs than those with other career backgrounds. Indeed, a large number of legislators who posed questions to the government in the deliberations over the JSRC bill were also lawyers. For instance, legislators who have been mentioned over the last few chapters as having spoken in the committee debates, such as Soya Fukuoka (DPJ), Hidenori Sasaki (DPJ), and Hideo Kijima (JCP), were all private attorneys. But note that the legislators' positions were consistent with what one would expect on the basis of the new left-orientations of their parties. Party affiliation and ideology shaped these politicians' preferences to a greater extent than their individual career backgrounds.

In fact, a case in point is Satsuki Eda (DPJ). As noted earlier, Eda is a former judge who was serving as the DPJ's shadow Justice Minister when the issue of introducing a jury/lay judge system emerged onto the policy agenda. Eda had served as a professional judge for almost ten years before leaving the judiciary and running for office in 1977. Despite Eda's background as a professional judge, he eagerly pushed for the adoption of a pure jury system. Thus, rather than the lawyer-legislators' expertise driving their positions on the issue of introducing a lay judge system, party affiliation drove lawyer-legislators' positions on this question.

6 | *Setting the Agenda: New Left-Oriented Parties and Deliberations in the Japanese Parliament*

Overview

This chapter presents a more systematic examination of the respective parties' positions on public participation in criminal trials based on a content analysis of deliberations in the Japanese Diet over the establishment of the Justice System Reform Council (JSRC) in 1999. As noted in the previous chapter, the influence of new left-oriented opposition parties was crucial in passing the amendment that mandated the JSRC to take up the question of popular participation in criminal trials. The fact that the ruling Liberal Democratic Party (LDP)-Liberal Party coalition did not have a majority in the House of Councillors allowed new left-oriented opposition parties to push through the amendment in both Houses of the Diet. As shown in Chapter 5, this was a crucial turning point leading to the establishment of the *saiban-in* system.

There are at least four reasons to assess how the positions of different parties mapped out specifically during the deliberations over the Bill Concerning Establishment of the Justice System Reform Council (hereafter the JSRC Bill). First, it allows us to pinpoint the position of the Democratic Party of Japan (DPJ) on this issue. The mid- to late 1990s were a time of upheaval for Japan's political parties, as the electoral system changed from the single non-transferable vote system to a mixed-member proportional system. The Japan Socialist Party (JSP) and the Democratic Socialist Party (DSP), which had most actively raised the issue of the jury in parliamentary debates between 1947 and 1996, had all but disappeared from the Japanese party system by the time that the JSRC Bill was submitted to the Diet. The DSP disbanded in late 1994, and most members of the party initially joined the New Frontier Party and then the DPJ, which was formed in late 1996. The JSP did not disband, but most of its members left the party to join the new DPJ in 1996. The JSP, now renamed the Social Democratic Party (SDP), was left with only fifteen legislators in the

122

House of Representatives and five in the House of Councillors by the time that the Bill was submitted to the Diet.

Therefore, it is crucial to examine the position vis-à-vis the question of introducing a jury/lay judge system of the newly founded DPJ, which largely consisted of former members of the leftist JSP and the DSP, but also a considerable number of former members of the LDP. The previous chapter showed that the DPJ not only pushed for the introduction of a lay judge system, but that it favored an American-style "pure" jury system that would impose stronger, rather than weaker, constraints upon professional judges. This point needs to be explored in more systematic fashion, with quantitative content analysis similar to that which was presented in Chapter 4 on the period up to 1996.

The second reason to take the content analysis forward beyond 1996 is that until 1996, the issue of introducing a jury/lay judge system was largely a hypothetical question, since the ruling LDP exhibited little or no interest in the question. It was the 1999 JSRC Bill that offered legislators the first opportunity since the occupation era to specifically debate the introduction of a jury/lay judge system. Did the positions of different parties' legislators change once the introduction of a jury/lay judge system became a real possibility, rather than a hypothetical issue that they would only debate in the abstract? Or did their positions remain largely unchanged, only now perhaps much more insistently expressed?

Thirdly, as will be shown later, after judicial reforms emerged onto the policy agenda in 1997, legislators also gained a much better understanding of the jury/lay judge issue. They began to distinguish between different systems, such as the "pure" jury and the "mixed" jury, rather than simply referring to all systems as "jury" systems, as they mostly had between 1947 and 1996. Thus, we can use content analysis of the post-1996 period to investigate different parties' interest in different *types* of jury/lay judge systems, rather than simply evaluating their general level of interest in the topic, as was done in Chapter 4.

Fourth, the deliberations over the JSRC Bill also present a useful window through which to assess the preferences of different parties over introducing a jury/lay judge system, because parties had a broad range of options as to which specific judicial reform issue to take up in the parliamentary debates. As noted in the previous chapter, a major impetus for judicial reforms had come from big business. Thus, in theory, parties could choose to take up questions that were of greater concern to big business, such as offering a greater variety of schemes for alternative dispute resolution or intellectual property cases, or they could choose to address more new left-oriented concerns, such as the introduction of a jury/lay judge system. Because parties had a choice in selecting which issues to take up, the extent to which they actually addressed the question of introducing a jury/lay judge system reveals much about different parties' policy preferences and priorities.

Thus, a systematic assessment of whether, and to what extent, the earlier political divide among Japan's major parties over the issue of introducing a jury/lay judge system changed after the issue actually emerged onto the agenda serves as an important complement to the qualitative process-tracing analysis that was presented in Chapter 5. This is the task of the present chapter.

The next section outlines the basic procedures for a bill to become law in Japan. The third section presents results of content analysis of the deliberations over the JSRC Bill in the Committee on Judicial Affairs of the House of Representatives. The fourth section shows the results for the Committee on Judicial Affairs of the House of Councillors. The fifth section combines the results from the House of Representatives and the House of Councillors. The sixth section summarizes and concludes.

How a Bill Becomes a Law in Japan

Japan has a parliamentary system, and typically 70–80% of bills submitted to the Diet are submitted by the Cabinet (Koga et al. 2010).[1] The Japanese Diet is also bicameral, and bills may be submitted first either in the House of Representatives or the House of Councillors.[2] Upon submission of a bill, it is referred to a committee of the House.[3] For bills submitted by the Cabinet, a member of the Cabinet typically first explains the objective of the bill to the committee, after which the

[1] Individual legislators may also submit bills to the Diet as well, as long as the bill has the support of at least twenty legislators, in the case of the House of Representatives, of ten or more legislators, in the case of the House of Councillors. House of Representatives (n.d.), www.shugiin.go.jp/internet/itdb_english.nsf/html/statics/guide/legislat.htm, accessed February 11, 2015.

[2] The exception is for budget proposals, which must first be submitted to the House of Representatives.

[3] See Matsumoto and Matsuo (2010) for an excellent study of the determinants of how much Japanese legislators speak in committee meetings.

government is subjected to questioning by the committee members. In general, parties are allocated question time in the committee depending on the share of seats that they hold in each House (House of Councillors n.d.). Typically, however, LDP Dietmembers spend much less time questioning the government, and they often relinquish their own questioning time to opposition parties (Matsumoto and Matsuo 2010).[4] After committee-level questioning, a vote is taken in the committee, and once the bill passes the committee, it then moves to the plenary session for a full vote. This process is then repeated in the other House. Once the bill passes both Houses, it becomes a law. If the House of Representatives passes a bill but the House of Councillors votes it down, the former can override the latter veto with a two-thirds majority.

In the deliberations on the JSRC Bill, Justice Minister Takao Jinnai (LDP) laid out the purpose of the bill in the House of Representatives on March 23, 1999, and the Committee on Judicial Affairs spent the next four sessions deliberating the bill. An amended version of the bill passed the Committee on April 21, 1999, and was then passed by the plenary session of the House the following day. Thereafter, it was sent to the House of Councillors. The Committee on Judicial Affairs in the House of Councillors debated the bill over four sessions between May 18 and May 27, 1999. The bill underwent no further amendments in the House of Councillors and passed the Committee on May 27 and the plenary session on June 2, with all parties in favor except the SDP.

Since in-depth debates over the bill took place in the Committee on Judicial Affairs rather than in the plenary session, this study presents results of analysis of the committee-level debates only.

Deliberations in the House of Representatives

First, the present study conducted content analysis of all four meetings of the House of Representatives Committee on Judicial Affairs that took up the JSRC Bill: the meetings of March 30, March 31, April 13, and April 21, 1999. In order to measure different parties' levels of interest in the question of introducing a jury/lay judge system, the

---

[4] Yasuhiro Hanashi, an LDP Dietmember, wrote in 2004 that "For every one hour of question time allotted to LDP MPs, the DPJ gets four hours" (Hanashi 2004). This may be an exaggeration, but the opposition parties as a whole are typically allotted more question time than the ruling LDP.

study counted the number of times that legislators referred to three key words: "pure" jury (*baishin*), "mixed" jury (*sanshin*), and the more generic term participate/participation (*sanka*).

The content analyses in Chapter 4 examined the number of statements in which at least one reference was made to the word "jury," rather than the actual number of references to the jury. This was because the aim in Chapter 4 was to conduct a broad survey of parties' tendencies to refer more or less frequently to the term, at a time when the issue was far from being at the top of the national policy agenda. In contrast, this chapter seeks to examine, in more detailed fashion, how often legislators of different parties made references to the jury, and also the finer distinctions that the legislators drew, e.g. between "pure" jury, "mixed" jury, and participation. Thus, the analysis below reports on the number of references, rather than number of statements.

Table 6.1 shows the number of times that members of the Committee on Judicial Affairs mentioned the above three words across four days of debates.

As shown in Table 6.1, seventy-seven of eighty-four references to "pure" jury, "mixed" jury, or "participation" were made by opposition parties, while the governing LDP–Liberal Party (LIB) coalition only made a combined total of seven. The Komeito most frequently referred to one or another of the three terms of "pure jury," "mixed jury," and "participation." It was closely followed, in descending order, by the JCP and the DPJ. The Komeito made almost 30% of all references, and the JCP and the DPJ made more than a quarter each. The LDP made the fewest number of references to the three terms, followed by the Liberal Party. Indeed, the differences among parties are quite stark; the Komeito, which most frequently referred to the three terms, made more than eight times as many references as the LDP, which made the fewest references.

References to "pure" jury, "mixed" jury, and "participation" were fairly evenly split. Overall, legislators made more slightly more references to "participation" than to "pure" or "mixed" jury; but references to either of the two jury systems outnumbered the references to "participation" overall. There is some variation across different parties as to which term was more favored; for instance, the Komeito most frequently used the term "pure" jury, and its combined references to "pure" or "mixed" jury outnumbered its references to "participation" by more than two to one. In contrast, the JCP preferred the term

Table 6.1 *Number of references to "pure" jury, "mixed" jury, participation, by party, Committee on Judicial Affairs, House of Representatives*

	"Pure" jury	"Mixed" jury	Participation	Total	% of total
Komeito	10	8	7	25	29.76
JCP	5	5	12	22	26.19
DPJ	7	5	9	21	25.00
SDP	5	1	3	9	10.71
LIB	3	0	1	4	4.76
LDP	2	1	0	3	3.57
Total	32	20	32	84	100.00

Note: Figures refer to number of times that legislators of each party referred to each of the three terms during deliberations in the Committee on Judiciary Affairs, House of Representatives, on March 30, March 31, April 13, and April 21, 1999.
Source: National Diet Library (n.d.).

"participation," and the number of references to this term exceeded the number of references to either form of jury. The SDP referred to the "pure" jury five times as often as the "mixed" jury, reflecting its strong preference for the former over the latter system. The DPJ's rhetoric was more balanced.

Note that whereas Chapter 4 found that the overwhelming majority of references in the pre-1996 period were to the "pure" jury (*baishin*), in the 1999 debates the references to "mixed" jury (*sanshin*) increased dramatically. In the parliamentary deliberations between 1947 and 1996 shown in Chapter 3, the number of references to the "mixed" jury only comprised 5.6% of the number of references to the "pure" jury in the House of Representatives. In 1999, the number of references to the "mixed" jury reached more than 60% of the number of references to the "pure" jury. The rapid increase in the number of references to the "mixed" jury suggests that legislators had done their homework after the issue finally emerged onto the policy agenda and had gained a more sophisticated understanding of the issue by the time that the government submitted the JSRC Bill to the parliament.

Table 6.2 *Number of references to "pure" jury, "mixed" jury, participation, by party, per 10,000 characters, Committee on Judicial Affairs, House of Representatives*

	Total number of references (A)	Number of characters (B)	Number of references per 10,000 characters (10,000*A/B)
JCP	22	24,657	8.92
Komeito	25	29,594	8.45
SDP	9	19,427	4.63
DPJ	21	58,678	3.58
LIB	4	16,273	2.46
LDP	3	17,048	1.76
Total	84	165,677	5.07

Source: National Diet Library (n.d.).

As noted earlier, different parties are allotted different amounts of time for questioning in the parliament depending on their shares of seats, but the LDP usually spends little time on questions. Thus, Table 6.2 above standardizes the figures shown in Table 6.1 by dividing them by the total number of Japanese characters uttered by legislators of each party. Unlike in the English language, word count is not typically used in Japanese to measure text length; the number of characters is the more commonly used measure.

Table 6.2 shows that when the figures shown in Table 6.1 are standardized by the number of characters uttered by legislators of each party, the overall picture does not change dramatically. The top two, the middle two, and the bottom two parties are the same as in Table 6.1. There were some changes within these three pairings. When standardized on a per-character basis, the JCP, rather than the Komeito, actually made the most frequent references to the three terms, with roughly nine references per 10,000 characters. And the SDP, which had trailed behind the DPJ in terms of raw number of references, actually outnumbered the DPJ on a per-10,000 character basis. But even when standardized by character count, the LDP still made the fewest references, and again the Liberal Party made the next fewest.

As noted earlier, judicial reforms in Japan during the late 1990s and early 2000s did not revolve solely around the question of introducing a jury/lay judge system. There were other prominent issues as well, such as the introduction of American-style law schools or the expansion of various schemes for alternative dispute resolution. Thus, parties could choose to pay attention to issues other than the question of participation, and that is what the conservative parties clearly did. The opposition parties consistently exhibited greater interest in the question of introducing a jury/lay judge system than the LDP-Liberal ruling coalition.

An alternative way to assess different parties' levels of interest in issues of participation may be to count the number of *questions* relating to participation. For instance, if all of the references to the jury/lay judge system were made in one question, this might not reveal a high level of party interest in the system, despite the large number of references on one occasion. Conversely, if several questions made points relating to the jury/lay judge system, this would signal a greater level of interest in the issue of participation on the part of that party. Moreover, politicians might ask questions relating to the jury/lay judge system without actually using the term; for instance, if a question that is posed to one expert is again posed to another, politicians might not repeat the question but simply ask them to answer the same question.[5] It is thus useful to count the number of questions posed that were related explicitly to the issue of introducing a jury/lay judge system.

Towards this end, the study counted the number of questions that were specifically related to the introduction of the jury system posed by legislators of each party, and divided that number by the total number of questions asked by each party. Note that if the question started out referring to the issue of the jury but ended up asking about something else, it was not counted. The results are shown in Table 6.3.

Table 6.3 shows that consistent with trends shown in this chapter thus far, the LDP-Liberal conservative coalition asked a combined total of just three of sixteen questions, while the leftist opposition (including Komeito) asked a combined total of thirteen. The JCP and the Komeito still exhibit the highest levels of interest in the jury/lay judge system, while the LDP is near the bottom. Nevertheless, there

---

[5] See, for instance, remarks by Atsuo Nakamura, House of Councillors Committee on Judicial Affairs No. 11, 14th Session of Diet, May 18, 1999.

Table 6.3 *Questions relating to introduction of a jury/lay judge system,*
as a percentage of all questions posed, by party, Committee
on Judicial Affairs, House of Representatives

	# of questions	Total # of questions	% of questions
JCP	5	38	13.16
Komeito	4	60	6.67
LIB	2	37	5.41
DPJ	3	87	3.45
LDP	1	29	3.45
SDP	1	74	1.35
Total	16	325	4.92

Source: National Diet Library (n.d.).

are some important differences between the results shown in Table 6.3
and those shown in Table 6.2. For instance, the SDP, which had been
third among six parties in number of references, now is sixth out of six
parties in terms of the number of questions posed relating to the jury/
lay judge system. In fact, all of the SDP's references relating to participation were posed in the same question. The Liberal Party, which had
been second-to-last in terms of number of references, was third in the
percentage of questions to the jury/lay judge system, just behind the
Komeito. But of course these are all small numbers.

Deliberations in the House of Councillors

For the House of Councillors, the study again counted the number
of times that legislators referred to the words "pure" jury (*baishin*),
"mixed" jury (*sanshin*), and participate/participation (*sanka*) during
the four meetings of the Committee on Judicial Affairs on May 18,
20, 25, and 27, 1999. Recall that the opposition was in control of
the House of Councillors at this time, so the views of these MPs were
very important for the ultimate legislation. Table 6.4 presents the
results.

As shown in Table 6.4, in the Upper House the four opposition parties were responsible for the lion's share of the references. The DPJ

Table 6.4 *Number of references to "pure" jury, "mixed" jury, participation, by party, Committee on Judicial Affairs, House of Councillors*

	"Pure" jury	"Mixed" jury	Participation	Total	% of total
DPJ	9	7	12	28	45.90
JCP	8	5	2	15	24.59
Independents	7	0	2	9	14.75
SDP	2	2	4	8	13.11
Komeito	1	0	0	1	1.64
LIB	0	0	0	0	0.00
LDP	N/A	N/A	N/A	N/A	N/A
Total	27	14	20	61	100.00

Source: National Diet Library (n.d.).

made the most references to the terms "pure jury," "mixed jury," or "participation"; indeed, more than 45% of all references came from the DPJ. The JCP was a distant second, with fifteen, or close to a quarter of all references, followed by the SDP, the Komeito, and the Liberal Party, in descending order. The LDP did not have any references because it did not pose any questions in the Upper House deliberations. In addition, unlike in the House of Representatives, there was an independent MP without party affiliation, Atsuo Nakamura, who was permitted to speak in the committee hearings, and he made a considerable number of references, especially to the "pure" jury. Nakamura was a former actor who had also been involved in the founding of Amnesty International Japan (Maeda 2014). He went on to found what some consider to be the first national-level green party in Japan, the Green Congress, in 2002, which dissolved in 2004 after failing to win any seats in the House of Councillors elections in 2004 (Higuchi et al. 2009). In short, he is a prototypical new left politician.

Here again, there is considerable variation across parties in the frequency with which different terms were used. The DPJ and SDP were relatively balanced among the three terms. In contrast, the JCP made many more references to the "pure" jury than either the "mixed" jury or "participation." The independent Nakamura also exhibited a

Table 6.5 *Number of references to "pure" jury, "mixed" jury,*
participation, by party, per 10,000 characters, Committee on
Judicial Affairs, House of Councillors

	Total number of references (A)	Number of characters (B)	Per 10,000 characters (10,000*A/B)
Independents	9	5,991	15.0
JCP	15	14,425	10.4
DPJ	28	32,887	8.5
SDP	8	10,755	7.4
Komeito	1	17,985	0.6
LIB	0	5,066	0.0
LDP	N/A	N/A	N/A
Total	61	87,109	7.0

Source: National Diet Library (n.d.).

marked preference for "pure" jury. The LDP and the LIB remained
silent on the issue.

Table 6.5 above standardizes the figures shown in Table 6.4 and
divides the figures by the total number of characters spoken by legislators of each party across the four committee meetings.

Table 6.5 shows that when the figures shown in Table 6.4 are standardized by the number of characters, Nakamura, the independent,
actually made the most references to juries or participation. Although
he did not use the terms as frequently as the DPJ or the JCP in absolute
terms, he was far ahead of party politicians in terms of the percentage
of text relating to participation. Among the parties, the JCP made the
largest number of references per 10,000 characters, as was the case
in the House of Representatives. This time the JCP was followed by
the DPJ and SDP, with Komeito far behind. The Komeito, which had
been second in the standardized number of references in the House of
Representatives, is only fourth among political parties in the House of
Councillors.

While the LDP remained completely silent in the House of
Councillors deliberations, we may still gain a sense of the contrast

Table 6.6 *Questions relating to introduction of a jury/lay judge system, as a percentage of all questions posed, by party, Committee on Judicial Affairs, House of Councillors*

	Number of questions (A)	Total number of questions (B)	% of questions (100*A/B)
Independents	6	27	22.22
JCP	4	43	9.30
DPJ	4	74	5.41
SDP	2	50	4.00
LIB	0	16	0
Komeito	0	36	0
LDP	N/A	N/A	N/A
Total	16	246	6.50

Source: National Diet Library (n.d.).

between parties that are more and less new left-oriented by comparing the JCP, DPJ, SDP, and the Komeito, on the one hand, and the Liberal Party, on the other, because as shown in Chapter 3, according to the expert survey conducted by Junko Kato, the Liberal Party stood just barely to the left of the LDP on new left issues and to the right of the other major parties. Strikingly, the Liberal Party made no references to any of the key terms, despite voicing more than 5,000 characters. In contrast, the JCP, DPJ, SDP, and the Komeito altogether made fifty-two out of sixty-one references to juries or participation, and Nakamura added nine more. Thus, it is clear that the new left cleavage matters for explaining the Upper House MPs' interest in this issue.

In addition to the number of references, the study again counted the number of questions explicitly relating to the introduction of a jury/lay judge system. The results are shown in Table 6.6 above.

Table 6.6 shows that as in Table 6.5, the majority of questions about this issue were posed by new left-oriented opposition parties. Nakamura posed the most questions relating to the introduction of a jury/lay judge system, followed, in descending order, by the JCP, the DPJ, and the SDP. The Liberal Party and the Komeito did not pose any questions relating to participation. There are some important differences between the results shown in Table 6.5 and those shown in Table 6.6.

Table 6.7 *Combined number of references to "pure" jury, "mixed" jury, and participation, by party, Committees on Judicial Affairs, House of Representatives and Councillors*

	"Pure" jury	"Mixed" jury	Participation	Total	% of all references
DPJ	16	12	21	49	33.8
JCP	13	10	14	37	25.5
Komeito	11	8	7	26	17.9
SDP	7	3	7	17	11.7
Independent	7	0	2	9	6.2
LIB	3	0	1	4	2.8
LDP	2	1	0	3	2.1
Total	59	34	52	145	100.0

Source: National Diet Library (n.d.).

For instance, the DPJ was far ahead of other parties in the number of references to participation, but in terms of the percentage of all questions that it asked, it was not as insistent on this issue as the JCP.

Deliberations in Both Houses

Parties with fewer numbers of seats may choose to strategically allocate their question time so that they do not ask the same questions in the House of Representatives and the House of Councillors. It is thus useful to combine the results from the House of Representatives and the Councillors to gain a sense of how different parties allocated their question time in parliament overall.

Table 6.7 above shows the number of times that MPs in either House referred to the words "pure" jury (*baishin*), "mixed" jury (*sanshin*), and participate/participation (*sanka*).

Table 6.7 shows that opposition parties took this issue most seriously. The DPJ made by far the most frequent references to "pure" jury, "mixed" jury, or participation, accounting for over a third of all references to the three terms in both Houses of parliament. The JCP was second, accounting for just over a quarter of all references, followed by the Komeito and the SDP. The LDP only accounted for

Table 6.8 *Combined number of references to "pure" jury, "mixed" jury, and participation, by party, per 10,000 characters, Committees on Judicial Affairs, House of Representatives and Councillors*

	Total number of references (A)	Number of characters (B)	Per 10,000 characters (10,000*A/B)
Independent	9	5,991	15.02
JCP	37	39,082	9.47
SDP	17	30,182	5.63
Komeito	26	47,579	5.46
DPJ	49	91,565	5.35
LIB	4	21,339	1.87
LDP	3	17,048	1.76
Total	145	252,786	5.74

Source: National Diet Library (n.d.).

2.1% of all references. Independents (MPs without party affiliation) only accounted for 6.2% since no independent asked a question in the House of Representatives. Strikingly, the conservative Liberal Party only accounted for 2.8% of all references to the three terms, despite the fact that its MPs asked many questions on various topics in both Houses of the Diet.

Table 6.8 above standardizes the figures shown in Table 6.7 by the number of characters.

Table 6.8 shows that once again, when standardized by the number of characters, the opposition parties were most interested in this issue, although the independents still made the most number of references to the "pure" jury, "mixed" jury, or participation, on the strength of Nakamura's personal interest in the issue. Aside from Nakamura, the JCP made the most frequent references in relation to its allotted airtime, followed, in descending order, by the SDP, the Komeito, and the DPJ. The LDP and the Liberal Party made by far the fewest references to the three terms, even when standardized by the number of characters.

Table 6.9 combines the results from the House of Representatives and Councillors on the number of questions relating to the introduction of a jury/lay judge system.

Table 6.9 *Combined number of questions relating to introduction of a jury/lay judge system, as a percentage of all questions posed, by party, Committees on Judicial Affairs, House of Representatives and Councillors*

	# of questions (A)	Total # of questions (B)	% of questions (100*A/B)
Independent	6	27	22.22
JCP	9	81	11.11
DPJ	7	161	4.35
Komeito	4	96	4.17
LIB	2	53	3.77
LDP	1	29	3.45
SDP	3	124	2.42
Total	32	571	5.60

Source: National Diet Library (n.d.).

Table 6.9 shows that in terms of the number of questions posed by each party, Nakamura, the independent, asked the most questions relating to the introduction of the jury/lay judge system; indeed, more than a fifth of the questions asked by Nakamura related to the issue. Here again, the JCP was second, followed by the DPJ, the Komeito, the Liberal Party, the LDP, and the SDP. The small number of questions by the SDP here is one of the few anomalies in otherwise overwhelmingly clear evidence that show the interest of new left-oriented opposition parties on this issue, especially in comparison to the lack of interest shown by the governing coalition.

Summary

This chapter presented results of content analyses of parliamentary deliberations over the JSRC Bill. As noted in the previous chapter, this was a crucial bill that mandated the JSRC to discuss the issue of lay participation in the justice system.

The results are largely consistent with the framework presented in this book. Regardless of whether the House of Representatives and the House of Councillors are examined separately or together, new left-oriented parties overall made more references and asked more questions relating to the issue of the jury/lay judge system than the conservative parties. The more new left-oriented DPJ and JCP consistently exhibited greater interest in the issue of introducing a jury/lay judge system in Japan compared to the conservative coalition parties of the LDP and the Liberal Party, with the Komeito falling somewhere in between. Chapter 4 showed the SDP to be the most new left-oriented party in the Japanese party system, and it made quite a few references to this issue in the committees, but it did not ask more questions relating to the jury compared to other parties, nor did it consistently push for a "pure" jury more strongly than a "mixed" jury. Of course, the SDP was a much diminished force by that time. The two parties that consistently showed a modest preference for a "pure" jury over a "mixed" jury were the DPJ and Komeito.

The results presented in this chapter also are largely consistent with the results shown in Chapter 4 on the number of references to the jury by different parties up to 1996. In Chapter 4 as well, Japan's leftist parties became champions of the issue of introducing a jury/lay judge system after the 1960s. This is reflected in the findings in the present chapter as well. In turn, the results shown in this chapter lend credence to the qualitative analysis shown in Chapter 5. The opposition parties' strong interest in the issue did not change after the introduction of a jury/lay judge system became a real possibility and legislators gained a better understanding of the issue. In addition, the findings presented in this chapter also reveal that after the SDP split in late 1996 to form the DPJ, the DPJ continued to pay close attention to the issue. It was joined in this by Komeito, which as noted in Chapter 4, had become increasingly become interested in this issue during the 1990s. While the parties could have chosen to allocate their limited question time to a range of different issues, the new left-oriented parties, including the DPJ and Komeito, chose to devote a substantial amount of time to discussing the jury/lay judge system.

The findings from the analyses thus show that it was indeed crucial for the outcome of judicial reforms in Japan that new left-oriented opposition parties held a majority of the House of Councillors precisely at the time that the JSRC Bill was submitted to the Diet. On the basis of these findings, one may reasonably surmise that had the new left-oriented opposition parties not held a majority, the amendment mandating the JSRC to take up the issue of participation would not have materialized.

7 | Proposals for Lay Participation in the Republic of China (Taiwan)

Overview

In the Republic of China (Taiwan), there was a concerted effort to introduce a lay judge system during the early- to mid-2010s. The Judicial Yuan (the judicial branch) had been exploring the possibility of adopting a lay judge system since the late 1980s. After two abortive attempts, in 2012 the Judicial Yuan finally submitted a bill to the Legislative Yuan proposing the adoption of what it has called a "lay observer system." Nevertheless, the bill stalled in the legislature and still had not been passed as of late 2016. Pilot experiments of the lay judge system have been launched by the Judicial Yuan in several cities across Taiwan, but a formal adoption of the system has not yet materialized.

Despite the unsettled status of this issue in Taiwan, the particular configurations of jury/lay judge systems that have been favored, respectively, by the two major parties in Taiwan offer a useful test of the framework advanced in this study. The preferences of different parties over the extent to which power is transferred from professional judges to juries/lay judges allow us to evaluate the book's main hypotheses empirically beyond the case of Japan. Moreover, the Taiwanese case helps to illuminate the conditions under which attempts to introduce a new system may fall short.

Taiwan is characterized by a two-party system, and Chapter 3 showed the Democratic Progressive Party (DPP) to be more new left-oriented than the Kuomintang (KMT). Since the DPP is new left-oriented, if and when the issue of lay participation emerges onto the policy agenda, the DPP is hypothesized to be more enthusiastic about introducing a system that imposes greater constraints upon professional judges, whereas the KMT should be more reluctant to transfer substantial powers to the citizens. As in Japan, the long history of one-party KMT rule in Taiwan should both reinforce the reluctance of the

KMT to change the existing system and strengthen the willingness of the DPP to change the system. Even when the KMT proposes reforms, it may be expected that those reforms would be more cosmetic than those proposed by the DPP.

The findings from the Taiwan case study confirm the validity of the book's theoretical framework. The present chapter shows that as in Japan, the new left cleavage crucially shaped the reforms proposed by Taiwan's two major parties. The Judicial Yuan under the KMT party government of President Ma Ying-jeou pushed for the introduction of a system in which the jurors' rulings would not be binding on the professional judges. Legislators of the new left-oriented DPP, on the other hand, were more eager to push for citizen participation in criminal trials than the KMT, and these DPP legislators criticized the Judicial Yuan's proposed lay judge system as not going far enough to constrain the judicial professionals. The DPP, however, was shut out of power between 2008 and early 2016 and was unable to make real policy impact during the Ma Administration.

Meanwhile, Ma found it difficult to rally legislators of his own party, the KMT, to support even his modest proposal, because of their lack of interest in the issue, as well as the institutional weakness of the president and his low popularity ratings. Thus, the bill to introduce the lay observer system made little progress toward adoption. The election of a new president, Tsai Ing-wen of the DPP, in early 2016 potentially opened the door to a more robust reform, but at the time of writing, the new administration is just taking office, so the analysis will stop with President Ma's tenure.

The chapter proceeds as follows. The next section offers a brief overview of the basic configuration of Taiwanese political institutions. The third section provides a pre-history of the debate over the jury/lay judge system in Taiwan. The fourth section traces the evolution of the recent debate over the introduction of the jury/lay judge system in Taiwan during the Ma Administration. The final section summarizes and concludes.

The material presented in this chapter draws on primary and secondary documents as well as on interviews conducted by the author with senior Judicial Yuan officials, legislators, scholars, legislative assistants, and NGOs in Taiwan during June and July 2015.

Semi-Presidentialism in Taiwan

The Taiwanese political system is a semi-presidential system. Samuels and Shugart (2010) have drawn a distinction between two variants of semi-presidentialism: the premier-presidential and the president-parliamentary systems. In premier-presidential systems, "the prime minister and cabinet are formally accountable *exclusively* to the assembly majority – and thus *not* to the president" (ibid: 30). In contrast, under president-parliamentary systems, "the prime minister and cabinet are *dually* accountable to the president and the assembly majority" (ibid).

At the formal institutional level, Taiwan's semi-presidential system exhibits elements of a premier-presidential system. The president may appoint the premier without consent of the Legislative Yuan, but there are no legal provisions as to whether the president may dismiss the premier. This makes the Taiwanese semi-presidential system a *de jure* premier-presidential system (Matsumoto 2013, 2014b).

However, as Matsumoto (2013) notes, in practice, the Taiwanese semi-presidential system has been run as a *de facto* presidential-parliamentary system. Taiwanese premiers have typically understood their positions to be subordinate to the president, and the president has been able to force premiers into resignation (Matsumoto 2013, 2014b). Shugart (2005) also classifies Taiwan as a president-parliamentary system in which the president has authority to dismiss the premier. In contrast, in premier-presidential systems such as France, the president has no authority to dismiss the premier short of calling fresh elections.

Even so, the power of Taiwan's president to induce cooperation from the legislature is relatively limited. Indeed, Kasuya (2013b) shows that the president's legislative power in Taiwan is weaker than in other semi-presidential systems in Asia, such as South Korea or the Philippines. To begin with, in contrast to the semi-presidential systems of France or Austria, the Taiwanese president has no power to dismiss the legislature and call new elections, unless the legislature passes a vote of no-confidence against the premier (ibid). Unlike in South Korea or the Philippines, the Taiwanese president also does not have a veto over legislative acts (ibid). The president's influence over legislators has been further eroded since the electoral reforms of 2005, which moved Taiwan's electoral system from a single non-transferable vote system to a mixed member proportional system similar to Japan's. Sheng (2009) and Tsai (2012) find that since 2005, Taiwanese legislators have become even more preoccupied with district-level concerns and less with national issues than they had been prior to electoral system change. Legislators have also become far more responsive to constituency-level concerns than party concerns (ibid).

In Taiwan, as in many countries, the president also typically serves as head of the party and may leverage her/his powers as party leader to win cooperation from individual legislators. Indeed, for most of his term as president, Ma also served as the chairman of the KMT.[1] However, Matsumoto (2014b) argues that changes in the KMT's candidate selection system in recent years have further eroded the influence of the party leadership over rank-and-file legislators. Until 2000, the KMT's candidate selection had been top-down (Fell 2013), but in 2000, it moved to a mixed primary system, and since 2004, candidate selection has been decided by a combination of a closed primary (30%) and public opinion polls (70%). The DPP has employed a similar mixed primary system since the 1990s as well (ibid; Sheng 2009). This candidate selection process has given legislators further autonomy from party leadership as well as incentives to prioritize constituency-level concerns over broader national policy.

Finally, scholars of Taiwanese politics also note that the popularity ratings of presidents may influence the incentives of legislators to cooperate with the president (Matsumoto 2013, 2014a). If the president is popular, legislators who belong to the same party may hope to benefit from coattail effects by cooperating with the president's policy agenda. However, if the president is unpopular, legislators may hope to distance themselves from the president as much as they can in order to protect their seats in the upcoming election. Ma fell short especially on this count. Ma was elected president in 2008 with 58.5% of the votes, the highest percentage ever by an incoming Taiwanese president. But after the first few months, his popularity slipped quickly, and those who disapproved of Ma's performance consistently far outnumbered those who approved of his performance (Taiwan Indicators Survey Research n.d.). Disapproval rates already exceeded 50% in Ma's first term (2008–11), and they came to exceed 70% in his second term (2012–15) (ibid).

---

[1] Unlike his predecessors, Ma refused to serve as president of his party during his first year in office as president.

The effect of these various arrangements has been to hamper the president's power to achieve desired legislation. Matsumoto (2014b) shows that between October 2009 and January 2012, only 51.2% of all bills submitted by the Executive Yuan (executive branch) passed the legislature, despite unified government in which the KMT held over 70% of the legislative seats *and* President Ma concurrently served as party president. Thus, by the time that administration officials began to push for a lay judge system in Taiwan around 2011, the overall political climate was hardly hospitable to such a major reform. The incentives on the part of individual legislators to cooperate with the unpopular president's policy agenda were particularly weak when it came to the proposed lay observer system, because supporting that reform would not serve particularistic interests of most legislators and thus not help their re-election prospects. Since the Judicial Yuan has the power to develop and propose legislation itself, despite the lack of interest on the part of KMT legislators, the lay observer system proposal did make it onto the legislative agenda in 2012, but it simply sat there until the Ma Administration left power in 2016. The chapter now turns to a detailed look at the Taiwanese judicial system and the evolution of the idea of introducing a jury/lay judge system.

The Taiwanese Judicial System

The Taiwanese judicial system inherited the system that the KMT had put in place in mainland China before recovering Taiwan from Japan in 1945. This system had been influenced primarily by continental legal systems, such as those of Germany, Austria, and Japan (Fukuyama 2002). Under this system, judicial powers were largely placed in the executive branch (Chiou 1998).

Beginning around the time of Taiwan's democratization, however, a series of judicial reforms were implemented to enhance the independence of the Judicial Yuan. For instance, reform of the budgeting system for the judicial branch in 1997 shifted the power to propose the Judicial Yuan's budget from the Administrative Yuan to the Judicial Yuan (ibid; Chiu and Peng 2001). In addition, a 1997 constitutional amendment stipulated that the president and the vice-president of the Judicial Yuan had to be appointed from among the justices of the constitutional court (Chiou 1998). Until this time, there were no provisions in the constitution as to who would be eligible to serve as president and vice-president of the Judicial Yuan, and Taiwanese leaders had often taken the liberty to appoint political appointees with little legal training. This practice came under fierce attack in the wake of democratization.

The move toward greater autonomy of the Judicial Yuan around the time of democratization was accompanied by extensive reforms in the area of criminal procedures as well (Wang 2006). In 1997, the Legislative Yuan revised the Code of Criminal Procedures, establishing the defendant's right to remain silent, which had been vague under the preexisting provisions. However, this revision did not provide for any penalties if law enforcement officials neglected to inform the arrested of their right to remain silent. In addition, new provisions stipulated that the police could not interrogate during "night" hours. In 1998, another revision required law enforcement officials to videotape all interrogations (Suzuki 2004; Wang 2006). Also, until 1997, the Taiwanese police had not been required to inform the accused of their right to counsel. In 1997, an amendment to the Code of Criminal Procedures stipulated that the police had to inform, prior to interrogation and all stages of the criminal procedure, of the accused's right to counsel (Wang 2011: 16).

The reform process continued into the 2000s. Although the judicial reforms began under KMT's Lee Teng-hui administration (1988–2000), they accelerated under the DPP's Chen Shui-bian administration (2000–8). The DPP's greater willingness to reform the justice system is not surprising, given that the post-war Taiwanese criminal justice system had been established under the KMT's developmentalist, authoritarian regime that the DPP opposed (Chen and Hsu 2014). In 2003, a provision was added to the Code of Criminal Procedures that would exclude all confessions from evidence if the accused had not been informed of their rights to remain silent and to a lawyer, unless the confession had been voluntary; and the burden of proof for demonstrating that the confession had been voluntary was placed on the prosecution (ibid). Further, in 2006, another revision to the Code of Criminal Procedures mandated the prosecution to appoint a lawyer for any accused individual who is unable to make complete statements due to "unsound mind" (ibid: 17). According to Wang (2011), this marked the first time that the government was required to appoint a lawyer during the pre-trial stage.

In 2002, in another revision of the Code, criminal trials in Taiwan took a step from a non-adversarial toward a more adversarial system

(Suzuki 2004; Wang 2006, 2011). Prior to 2002, the prosecutor would simply read the opening statement word for word, and the defense attorney had little role to play in the trial. After revision of the Code of Criminal Procedures, however, the burden of proof fell on the prosecution, not on the judge. The judge, in turn, came to play a much more neutral, passive role.

In spite of these victories, the Chen Shui-bian administration was unable to undertake a full overhaul of the judicial system due to the continuing dominance of the KMT in the Legislative Yuan, and the question of introducing a lay judge system was left to the Judicial Yuan.

Debates over Introducing a Jury/Lay Judge System in Taiwan: A Pre-History

Many legal scholars as well as private lawyers had long expressed support for the idea of introducing a jury/lay judge system in Taiwan, but prior to the late 1980s, the Judicial Yuan had been staunchly resistant. It had come up with a series of reasons why a jury/lay judge system would not be suited for Taiwan, for instance, that the Taiwanese people were far too "nice" and that they would allow their emotions to influence their decisions; that many cases would be too complicated for the lay jurors to understand; that the introduction of a jury/lay judge system would be too costly; and that even countries where jury/lay judge systems had a long history, such as the UK, were embarking on reforms to scale back the system (e.g. *United Daily News*, March 13, 1967).

The Judicial Yuan began to study various forms of jury/lay judge systems in 1988. This was also just around the time that the Japanese Supreme Court had also launched its study tour of jury/lay judge systems around the world (Kage 2015). The role of international diffusion cannot be discounted here. The Judicial Yuan dispatched officials to various countries around the world, including France, Switzerland, and Austria (*United Daily News*, November 17, 1988). During the same year, the Judicial Yuan established a commission to explore the introduction of a lay judge system (Chen 2012). Note that these efforts came prior to Taiwan's democratic transition.

After almost six years of deliberation, the Judicial Yuan put together a draft bill in 1994 that was modeled closely on the German mixed jury system. The proposal was for a weak lay judge system. The bill stipulated that lay trials would be held for crimes with heavier sentences, upon request by the defendant, and that the lay judge trials would consist of three professional judges and two lay judges (ibid). Lay judges would not be randomly selected from the public, but would serve upon recommendation of heads of local governments and would serve a fixed term of three years (ibid). The idea that the lay judges were to serve a fixed term, rather than serving on a case-by-case basis, made the proposed system closer to the German lay judge system than the Anglo-American jury system. Although proposing a modest reform, the bill ran into fierce opposition from judges and prosecutors and did not come to fruition. Nevertheless, this attempt by the Judicial Yuan to introduce a mixed jury system represented a major shift in its position.

As noted earlier, the Taiwanese government launched a full-fledged effort to reform Taiwan's justice system during the late 1990s. As part of this effort, the Judicial Yuan launched the National Judicial Reform Conference in July 1999 and invited 125 scholars, lawyers, and other intellectuals to participate over three days (Chang 2009). Among the propositions adopted in this conference was the notion of an "expert jury" system in which professionally qualified experts in specific fields would participate in rulings in juvenile, labor, medical, or intellectual property disputes (*United Daily News*, July 8, 1999). As this list indicates, experts were expected to participate in both civil and criminal cases. But the idea of an "expert jury" certainly represented a far smaller break from the existing system than a citizen jury/lay judge system.

Many of the proposals adopted in the National Judicial Reform Conference were implemented during the mid-2000s. For instance, in 2003, amendments to the Code of Criminal Procedure brought in a public defender system and a legal aid foundation (Huang et al. 2010). The Judicial Yuan devised a bill to introduce an expert jury system in 2006, but this bill also ran into opposition from many legal professionals, and the bill was never submitted to the Legislative Yuan.

The "Lay Observer" System

Thus, by the mid-2000s, the Judicial Yuan had unsuccessfully made two proposals for introducing a weak jury/lay judge system in Taiwan: the mixed jury system during the early 1990s and then the expert jury system during the mid-2000s (Chen 2012). But two major incidents led the Taiwanese government to undertake a third attempt at introducing a lay judge system. First, a Supreme Court ruling in August 2010 reversed a guilty judgment against a defendant charged with sexual offense against a four year-old girl (Huang and Lin 2013: 546). This reversal led to large-scale public demonstrations against the "dinosaur judges" who were viewed as being out of touch with the real world.

The public's ire at the judiciary was heightened even further by a major bribery scandal in 2010. Her Jyh-huei, a KMT legislator who had received a nineteen-year sentence in the lower courts, bribed judges in order to have his sentence lessened in the higher courts, and the High Court judges indeed acquitted him ("Corruption in Taiwan: Confirming the Worst Suspicions," *The Economist*, July 22, 2010). Twelve judges, prosecutors, lawyers, and others were indicted in this scandal (Sui 2010). Both the president and the vice-president of the Judicial Yuan resigned. The ROC President Ma pledged sweeping reforms to restore public confidence in the judicial system.

To overhaul the justice system, President Ma appointed outsiders as president and vice-president of the Judicial Yuan. The new president, Rai Hau-min, was the first private attorney to be appointed President of the Judicial Yuan. The new vice-president, Su Yeong-chin, was professor of law at National Chengchi University, also a close friend of Ma, and a long-time advocate of introducing a system of public participation in criminal trials. Rai and Su came into office with the slogan, "4C": "clean, crystal, considerate, and competitive," and pledged sweeping reforms including lay participation in trial proceedings (*United Daily News*, October 10, 2010). Ma, himself a lawyer, strongly endorsed the introduction of a lay judge system as part of the efforts to clean up the justice system, arguing that the best legal system is comprised of a combination of professional and public opinion (*United Daily News*, June 5, 2011).

In addition to the two incidents in Taiwan, both Japan and South Korea had launched jury/lay judge systems of their own by this time, which may also have influenced the willingness of the Judicial Yuan to make another attempt at introducing a new system in Taiwan.

In January 2011, the Judicial Yuan established a committee, chaired by Su, to draw up a proposal for a new jury/lay judge system. The eighteen members of the Taiwanese committee were comprised mostly of legal experts, including four legal scholars, five judges, one prosecutor, and two attorneys (Judicial Yuan 2012). Among the four legal scholars on Taiwan's committee, two had earned doctorates in the United States, one in Germany, and one in Japan. The membership of Taiwan's committee stands in contrast to the Japanese Justice System Reform Council, which had not included active officials of the courts, prosecutors, or the bar, and which had included consumers as well as producers of legal services. That the committee in Taiwan consisted of fewer outsiders to the legal profession than its earlier counterpart in Japan was an indication that the resulting proposal would make a less radical departure from the existing system. Also, unlike in Japan, the committee had not been set up by the Legislative Yuan,[2] which may have impacted the fate of the resulting proposal.

The committee met ten times between January and July 2011 and submitted its final report in July. During the course of the discussions, the group closely examined the jury/lay judge systems of Germany, Japan, and Korea. Scholars were invited from Germany, Japan, and Korea to deliver lectures on the systems in their respective countries.

In August 2011, a second committee was established to transform the blueprint devised by the first committee into concrete legislative proposals.[3] Eight of the members from the first committee remained to serve on the second committee, while the other members were replaced. This new committee again consisted overwhelmingly of members of the legal profession and included three legal scholars, five judges, three prosecutors, and four attorneys. This committee met six times between August and November 2011. Notably, this committee also conducted a series of mass surveys that tried to gauge public opinion on the question of participating in criminal trials. Building on this final report, the Judicial Yuan submitted a bill proposing the "lay observer system" in June 2012.

Under the proposed system, crimes that carried heavier sentences would be subject to a lay judge trial, regardless of whether the defendant pleaded guilty or not guilty. Juvenile crimes, however, would not be subject to a lay judge trial. Five lay judges would serve alongside three professional judges and would deliberate on both facts and sentences (Chen 2012). Lay judges would deliberate together with professional judges, but professional judges would refrain from offering their views

---

[2] I thank Professor Lin Yu-shun for pointing this out.
[3] Judicial Yuan (2012).

on facts and the application of laws until after the lay judges had deliberated on the facts and application of laws. At any time in the process, however, professional judges would be allowed to provide necessary explanation on admissibility of evidence, interpretation of laws, and so forth (Judicial Yuan 2014: 88–9). Lay judges would rule on guilty/not guilty, and, if the verdict was guilty, on sentence as well. Lay and professional judges would rule by majority vote, with the votes of both counting equally (ibid: 90). Crucially, however, the views of the lay judges would merely be advisory and would not be binding on the professional judges, hence the name "lay observer system." If professional judges decided to rule differently than the lay judges, the former were simply required to provide reasons as to why.

The Judicial Yuan stated that one of the reasons for proposing a non-binding system is that public opinion surveys showed that the Taiwanese public preferred it (*United Daily News*, March 18, 2014; October 2, 2014). But careful examination of the Judicial Yuan's surveys indicates that its questions were designed to elicit that response.

For instance, a question in the third wave of the surveys conducted by the Judicial Yuan reads, "Do you support a system where whether the defendant is guilty or not is only determined by citizens even if professional judges disapprove of the people's decision?" (Judicial Yuan n.d.). This question is ostensibly intended to ask respondents to indicate their level of support for an Anglo-American style "pure" jury system. But it is clearly a leading question. With the question phrased in this way, a plurality of the respondents indicated that they did not support a "pure" jury system. Even so, the responses were relatively even; 14.1% replied that they supported such a system very much, 27.1% somewhat supported, 32.0% somewhat opposed, and 13.4% opposed very much. Thus, even with such a leading question, the public only narrowly opposed the "pure" jury by 45.4% versus 41.2%. The Judicial Yuan, however, chose to interpret this result as a reason to reject the idea. It is not surprising that the judicial branch of a government, especially one that is ruled by a more conservative "developmentalist" party, would propose a lay participation system that would not bind the professional judges.

Indeed, another reason the Judicial Yuan offered for proposing a non-binding system was their concern that a binding system would be unconstitutional (Chen 2012). There exists considerable disagreement in Taiwan over whether or not a binding system would in fact be constitutional, with members of the DPP typically arguing that it would be, while those of the KMT and the Judicial Yuan claim that it would not. By way of comparison, recall that Takao Nakayama of the Supreme Court of Japan initially argued that a non-binding system would be most compatible with the Japanese constitution,[4] and it is not unusual for judges to argue that a binding system would violate the constitution in order to protect their own powers. So whether a binding system would be in fact be unconstitutional in Taiwan is open to question. But even if such a system were unconstitutional, the Taiwanese constitution has been amended relatively frequently, with seven revisions since 1991 (Rigger 2011), and thus if the political will were present, politicians could enact constitutional revision that would more clearly open the way for the introduction of a binding system. This book thus takes the position that the Taiwanese constitution does not pose an insurmountable obstacle to the introduction of a binding jury/lay judge system.

But to say that the Judicial Yuan favored a limited transfer of powers to the citizens is not to say that it was an opponent of reform *per se*. It was willing to make a major effort on behalf of its proposal. Beginning in 2012, the Judicial Yuan launched a series of mock lay observer trials in different district courts in Taiwan. The first of these was held at the Shilin District Court in February 2012 and, as of early 2016, forty-six sessions had been held in nine other district courts across Taiwan (Judicial Yuan n.d.). High-ranking officials of the Judicial Yuan, including President Rai and Vice-President Su, attended many of the mock trials. Their presence reflected the importance that they attached to this issue.

Partisan Responses to the Lay Observer System

Since submission, the Judicial Yuan's bill has made no progress in the Legislative Yuan, despite the KMT's majority in the Legislative Yuan (64 of 113 seats until mid-2016). A major reason is lack of interest among the KMT legislators. During my visits to Taipei, I asked several interview subjects whether there were KMT legislators who were active in pushing for any variant of a jury/lay judge system – and the

---

[4] Minutes of the 30th Session of the Justice System Reform Council, September 12, 2000, www.kantei.go.jp/jp/sihouseido/dai30/30gijiroku.html, accessed July 4, 2017.

question consistently drew blank stares. It is the case that two KMT
legislators have organized efforts to submit three separate bills to the
Legislative Yuan proposing the introduction of different variants of a
lay judge system.[5] One of these bills proposes a "mixed" jury system,
while the remaining two bills are more closely modeled upon the "lay
observer system" proposed by the Judicial Yuan. Both systems impose
much weaker constraints upon professional judges than those favored
by DPP legislators. But these bills have also made no headway in the
Legislative Yuan, due to lack of support from other legislators in either
party. In fact, my interviewees expressed doubt that even the legislators who proposed the bills had much interest in the issue. In Taiwan,
influential NGOs such as the Citizen Congress Watch rank legislators numerically according to their legislative productivity, creating an
incentive for legislators to submit bills even if they have little intention
of following them through.

The lack of interest among KMT legislators in even a limited reform
has several bases. First, the fact that the existing Taiwanese judicial
system was largely built during KMT rule would be expected to make
KMT legislators basically satisfied with the existing system, despite the
KMT president's desire for (limited) reform. Second, as noted earlier,
Taiwanese legislators have become increasingly constituency-oriented
since electoral reforms (Sheng 2009; Tsai 2012). Thus on this national
issue with little opportunity for pork-barreling, the lack of interest of
most Taiwanese legislators, whether they belong to the KMT or DPP,
may be expected.[6] But actually, in contrast to the KMT, several DPP
legislators are highly committed to the issue. For instance, between
June and July 2014, DPP legislative assistants joined the Taiwan
Jury Association and reform-minded private attorneys on a five-city
study tour to gain a better understanding of the American jury system
(Taiwan Jury Association 2014). Thus, the KMT legislators' lack of
interest in the lay participation issue clearly reflected their political

[5] Six other bills proposing some variant of a "pure" or "mixed" jury system
have been proposed. Details of the bills are available at www.judicial.gov.tw/
Guan-Shen/proposal.asp, accessed July 7, 2015.
[6] As Sheng (2009) points out, this is more true of legislators who have been
elected via single-member districts than via proportional representation. Under
the current electoral system, 73 of 113 seats are elected through single-member
districts, thirty-four from proportional representation, and six seats are set
aside for aboriginal representatives.

ideology as much as their focus on local constituency issues, while at least some DPP legislators' new left orientation was strong enough that it made them highly interested in this issue, despite the institutional incentives to focus on local constituency service.[7]

Adding to the KMT legislators' reluctance to support the "lay observer system" proposed by the Judicial Yuan were the low popularity ratings of Ma and the KMT (Taiwan Indicators Survey Research n.d.). As noted earlier, if there is little hope for legislators of a given party to ride on the coattails of the president, then there is little incentive for them to cooperate with the president. Indeed, they may hope to distance themselves from the president by sabotaging bills that are favored by the president, such as the lay observer system bill, to show their independence.

As noted above, DPP legislators have been more sympathetic than KMT legislators to the idea of introducing a jury/lay judge system. But they are strongly opposed to the Judicial Yuan's proposal. In contrast to KMT legislators, who have largely ignored the bill and the issue of judicial reform more generally, DPP legislators have repeatedly attacked the Judicial Yuan's bill, and the KMT, on grounds that it does not go far enough. In particular, the non-binding nature of lay judges' rulings in the proposals was subjected to fierce criticism from DPP legislators as well as influential NGOs such as the Judicial Reform Foundation, both of which favored an American-type pure jury system. For instance, at the Judicial and Legal System Committee meeting of the Legislative Yuan on December 31, 2014, legislator Ker Chien-ming of the DPP attacked the lay observer system as being not at all related to "participation in trials" as claimed by the Judicial Yuan.[8] Legislator Yu Mei-nu, also of the DPP, criticized the proposed system for not giving decision-making rights to citizens and said that there is a disconnect between the alleged purpose of the reform and the proposals that were actually being put forth.[9] Clearly, the greater new left orientation of the DPP matters for its position on the lay judge issue.

---

[7] Perhaps not surprisingly, these DPP legislators are typically either elected by PR or are those who have relatively safe SMD seats.

[8] Statement by Ker Chien-ming, Sixth Session of the Eighth Legislative Yuan, 23rd Plenary Meeting of the Judicial and Legal System Committee. Available at Legislative Yuan (n.d.).

[9] Statement by Yu Mei-nu, Fifteenth Plenary Meeting of the Judicial and Legal System Committee, Third Meeting Session of the Eighth Legislative Yuan, April 29, 2013. Available at Legislative Yuan (n.d.).

Frustrated that the Judicial Yuan only allows lay jurors to make advisory, rather than binding, rulings, these DPP legislators have submitted their own bills to the Legislative Yuan that propose an American-type jury system. NGOs such as the Judicial Reform Foundation have also attacked the "lay observer system" as only trying to make the most superficial changes to the existing system (*Taipei Times*, March 17, 2017) and have also lobbied DPP legislators to defeat the Judicial Yuan's proposal and to propose a more US-style "pure" jury system. Indeed, the DPP as a whole has formally endorsed the introduction of an American-style jury system (Democratic Progressive Party n.d.). Notably, Tsai Ing-wen, the new DPP president (2016–), included, on the top of her list of proposed judicial reforms in her 2016 presidential campaign, a proposal to establish "citizens' courts," a system in which citizens would have "some degree of decision-making power over the verdict" (Tsai 2015).[10] In this statement, Tsai criticized the Judicial Yuan's "lay observer system" because, in her words, "citizens have no power to actually participate in judgments. Thus the goal of democratization of the judiciary is not attained" (ibid). As of writing, Tsai had unveiled a plan to hold a national conference for judicial reform. The main objective of the conference would be to create a "judiciary for the people" and to "break down walls" that were preventing citizens from participating in the justice system (Chung and Chung 2016). As of writing, this national conference has not yet been held, and it remains to be seen whether the new president will be able to put her words into action.

Conclusions

The partisan cleavage between the KMT and the DPP over the new left issue, which in Taiwan also overlaps with the cleavages over national identity and economic issues, crucially shaped the debate over the configuration of a possible jury/lay judge system. President Ma and the Judicial Yuan under the conservative KMT favored a "lay observer" system that would largely preserve the power of professional judges. By contrast, the opposition DPP favored more sweeping reforms, especially a US-style jury system that would give more extensive decision-making powers to the citizens. While the KMT enjoyed a

---

[10] I thank Nick Horton for pointing this statement out to me.

comfortable majority in the Legislative Yuan between 2008 and 2016, the institutional weakness of the Taiwanese presidency, compounded by the low popularity of President Ma, and the generally conservative orientation of the KMT, made most legislators of that party reluctant to promote the introduction of a lay judge system. As a result, the Judicial Yuan's bill stalled in the Legislative Yuan.

Meanwhile, several influential legislators of the opposition DPP have submitted their own bills proposing a US-style "pure" jury system to the Legislative Yuan. But since the DPP was shut out of power in both the executive and legislative branches of government between 2008 and early 2016, their proposals made no headway in the legislature. In its campaign for the 2016 presidential and legislative elections, the DPP signaled that the introduction of a jury system was a high priority. It won the elections in a landslide. But it remains to be seen if the new unified government under the DPP will push hard for a major transfer of power away from professional judges.

8 Introducing Jury Systems in South Korea and Spain

Overview

This chapter further tests the validity of the hypotheses presented in the book by drawing on the cases of South Korea and Spain. As noted previously, these cases offer useful variation in the extent to which new jury/lay judge systems have imposed constraints upon the power of professional judges. At one end, Spain's jury system has transferred the most extensive powers from the professional judges to the jury among the four cases under study. Spain's system lists a set of crimes for which a jury must be empaneled. The jury's verdict is binding on professional judges, and the jurors deliberate in isolation from professional judges. At the other end, South Korea's jury system has imposed the weakest constraints upon professional judges among the three cases of completed reforms. Professional judges have the authority to decide which cases should be ruled by a jury trial and which solely by professional judges, and even after a jury is empaneled, its rulings can be overruled by the professionals.

Chapter 2 hypothesized that the more new left-oriented the party, the more it should favor jury/lay judge systems that greatly undermine the powers of professional judges. Chapter 2 also hypothesized that the stronger these new left-oriented parties are within the overall political system, the more likely that they will succeed in imposing their preferences on the reform when the issue rises to the political agenda. Chapter 3 drew on expert surveys and party manifestoes to develop specific expectations for the four country cases under study. On the basis of data shown in Chapter 3, the book hypothesized that new left-oriented parties should have had the greatest impact over the introduction and design of the jury/lay judge system in Spain, where leftist parties were consistently new left-oriented and enjoyed the most influence within the political system. Chapter 3 also showed that new left issues failed to consistently divide the conservative from the leftist parties in South Korea, at least during the period under study; the leftist Millennium Democratic Party (MDP)-United Democratic Party (UDP) adopted more new left positions than the conservative Grand National Party (GNP) in some elections, but not in others. This reflected the fact that the Korean party system at the time was undergoing a partisan realignment. Thus, even though a leftist party held the presidency in South Korea at the time that a jury/lay judge system was being debated, the data does not indicate that it would necessarily favor a reform that imposed strong constraints on the power of professional judges. Moreover, the leftist President Roh Moo-hyun lacked a majority in the legislature for most of his term. Thus, even if Roh personally hoped for a system that imposed strong constraints upon the power of professional judges and had some success in forcing legislators from his party to fall into line, such a proposal was unlikely to be accepted by the conservative legislative majority.

This chapter shows that the cases of Spain and South Korea bear out the theoretical expectations of the book. Spain transferred the most extensive powers away from professional judges to jurors among the four countries under study. South Korea, on the other hand, introduced more limited reform during leftist party rule. Roh not only suffered from weak support from his own party but also faced an opposition-controlled legislature for most of his term. Thus, the resulting jury system was a product of much compromise with those forces who wished to preserve the power of professional judges.

The remainder of the chapter proceeds as follows. The following section examines how the Spanish Socialist Party engineered the introduction of the jury system in Spain. The third section traces the path to the introduction of the jury in South Korea. The fourth section summarizes and concludes.

Spain

Party Politics in Spain

Spain transitioned to democracy in 1978 with the promulgation of a democratic constitution after almost forty years of dictatorial rule under General Francisco Franco. Franco had banned political parties during his rule. In the wake of democratization, over 200 parties sprang up to run for the 1977 general elections, the first general election after democratization (Encarnación 2008: 52). The centrist Unión de Centro Democrático (UCD) won a near-majority of seats in the 1977 and 1979 elections, leading to the installment of the Adolfo Suárez cabinet. Suárez had been personally hand-picked by King Juan Carlos I to transition the country to democracy, and he initially enjoyed enormous popularity (ibid: 54–5; Gunther and Montero 2009).

The UCD carried out a number of key reforms to consolidate Spain's fledgling democracy, such as the enhancing of civilian control over the military and reaching agreement with Catalonia, the Basque Country, and Galicia over their autonomy charters (Encarnación 2008: 56). However, its popularity was short-lived. In the 1982 elections, the UCD's seats declined from 168 to twelve, as its vote share plummeted from 35% in the 1979 general elections to 6% in 1982. After the 1982 election, the UCD disappeared from electoral competition. Since then, the People's Party (Partido Popular, PP) and the Socialist Party (Partido Socialista Obrero Español, PSOE) have rotated in power, although regionalist parties have also been key power brokers (Hopkin 1999).

The PSOE took power in 1982. Reforms within the PSOE beginning in the late 1970s had contributed to its growing popularity (Encarnación 2008). PSOE leader Felipe González steered through some key reforms for the PSOE, most notably dropping Marxist rhetoric from its platform. In 1982, the PSOE became the first party after democratization to win a majority of seats in the Spanish parliament, winning 202 out of 350 seats. Under González, the PSOE undertook major economic reforms, expanded social spending, and it also led Spain's entry into NATO and the EEC. The decision to join NATO was particularly controversial within the Spanish left and represented the PSOE's turn from "red" to "pink."

The PSOE remained in power until 1996, albeit as a minority government between 1993 and 1996. It was during this period that the jury system was introduced in Spain.

Introducing the Jury in Spain

Spain had experimented with jury/lay judge systems during several junctures during its modern history.[1] According to Thaman (1997),

---

[1] Not many sources offer information on the Spanish criminal justice system in the English language. See Bergalli (1995) for a useful overview.

a jury system was first introduced in Spain in 1820. Jury trials were suspended in 1844 but were restored again briefly during 1855. They were re-adopted for a short period between 1864 and 1867 for cases involving the press and again between 1872 and 1874, and once more between 1888 and 1923 (they were suspended in Catalonia and Gerona in 1907). The jury was revived again in Spain in 1931 but was gradually suspended in areas conquered by Franco during the Spanish Civil War, and an end was put to all jury trials in Spain with Franco's victory in 1939 (ibid; Jimeno-Bulnes 2004).

With the end of the Franco regime, a liberal constitution was put in place in 1978. Article 125 of the 1978 Spanish constitution stipulates for the establishment of a jury system.[2] But legal provisions for the founding of a jury system were not passed by the legislature until 1995. In the meantime, a debate raged over whether Article 125 in fact mandated the introduction of a jury system at all, with proponents of the jury system arguing that it did, and opponents arguing that it did not. Parenthetically, many Latin American constitutions also include provisions for jury trials, including the Argentine and Mexican constitutions, but most of those countries have not introduced jury systems (e.g. Hendler 2008/9; Fukurai et al. 2009). Among those proponents who did support the adoption of some form of lay participation, there was also considerable support for a mixed, rather than pure, jury system, due to Spain's continental legal tradition (Thaman 1997, 1999; Jimeno-Bulnes 2007).

Despite the controversy about whether the constitution *required* a jury system, the constitution certainly opened the door to legislation instituting a jury system. Gustavo López-Muñoz y Larraz, the President of the Pro-Jury Association, proposed a draft jury bill in 1982 (Jimeno-Bulnes 2004). The first formal legislative attempt to introduce a jury in Spain after democratization came in 1983 from Basque regionalist party legislators. The Basques pushed for a "pure" jury consisting of nine jurors, but the bill was not debated in parliament. In 1986, the far-left Izquierda Unida (IU) Party included the introduction of a jury system as its top agenda item under the heading of "judicial reforms."[3] Once again, this minor party was unable to create much momentum for reform.

---

[2] According to Jimeno-Bulnes (2004), the PSOE was instrumental in inserting this language, using the word "jury."

[3] "La ausencia de Sartorius evita a Ledesma responder en el Congreso sobre el retraso de la ley del Jurado," *El Pais*, March 2, 1988.

In March 1994, Juan Alberto Belloch, Justice Minister of the Socialist Felipe González Cabinet, submitted a Draft Jury Law to the Spanish parliament. The push for a strong jury proposal at that time was largely due to Belloch, a respected jurist whom González had brought in as Justice Minister in May 1993 in order to boost the popularity of his cabinet in the wake of a series of corruption scandals (Davison 1993). Belloch had in fact wanted to introduce a jury in Spain since 1974.[4] The ruling Socialists had initially favored a mixed jury system, but Belloch himself pushed hard for a "pure" jury system, and as Justice Minister, he was in a strong position to promote his views (Jimeno-Bulnes 2004). The Basques (PNV) and the far-left IU also demanded a pure jury system that would give the jurors alone the power to decide the verdict, which was consistent with their longstanding positions on this issue. Although the PSOE was not in coalition with either the PNV or the IU, the PSOE had lost its absolute majority in the both houses of parliament in the 1993 elections and needed cooperation from these parties in order to ensure passage of the bill. The vote in the Lower House passed by 182 to 124 in February 1995, with the conservative PP abstaining.[5] The Senate passed the same bill in May 1995, with the same parties' support.

The legislative debates over the bill offer a glimpse into the terms of the debate over introducing the jury system in Spain. In his address to the Chamber of Deputies on the legislation, Belloch stated that although prior judicial reforms had increased the "efficacy of the justice system in the service of the people," by contrast the primary goal of the new jury system was to bring about the "participation of the citizens in the penal justice system."[6] He noted that the citizenry was overwhelmingly in support of this reform, even though the juridical professionals were showing "a certain level of reticence."[7] He acknowledged that he understood why, as the legislation was greatly expanding the power of the citizenry and thus posed a challenge to the judicial professionals' sense of responsibility and capacity for change.

[4] *El Pais*, May 12, 1995.
[5] "El Pleno del Congreso da vía liber al jurado con la única abstención del Partido Popular," *El Pais*, February 24, 1995.
[6] Congreso de los Diputados, Pleno y Dip. Perm., núm. 128, de 23/02/1995 (texto íntegro), www.congreso.es/public_oficiales/L5/CONG/DS/PL/PL_128 .PDF, accessed April 7, 2016.
[7] Ibid.

But he stated that he saw many reasons for optimism that the new system of societal participation in the dispensation of justice would put down deep and strong roots, and he added, "We cannot permit the failure of the institution of the jury, which represents a call to direct participation of the citizens in the administration of justice."[8]

Diego López Garrido of the leftist IU expressed support for the strong linkage that Belloch drew between the jury and democracy. López Garrido was also critical of the PSOE, however, for delaying the introduction of the jury up until the mid-1990s. He stated that the long delay had undermined the 1985 Organic Law of the Judiciary, which had stated that legislation for the creation of a jury system would be introduced within one year. He reminded the House that the IU and other "progressive forces" had been consistent in their support of the introduction of a jury system.

Julio Padilla Carballada of the conservative opposition PP, on the other hand, gave a temporizing speech in which he claimed the PP was in principle supportive of the idea of introducing a jury system, but that the specific legislation offered by the PSOE was "very bad."[9] He complained that the PSOE had not taken seriously the eighty-four amendments offered by the PP. He joked that the PSOE was good at making compromises to stay in power, but it was less effective at making compromises to improve legislation.[10]

PSOE legislator Francisco Javier Valls García gave a strong reply to the criticisms made by Padilla Carballada. He said that the PSOE had taken in many suggestions from different parties.[11] There had been no effort to ramrod the legislation through parliament. The PP's very large number of suggested changes were rejected, he argued, because what the PP really wanted was to prevent the law from moving forward.[12]

Justice Minister Belloch was emotional upon the passage of the jury legislation by the Chamber of Deputies, saying that it was the most satisfying day that he had experienced since becoming minister. Indeed, he noted a "joyful democratic paradox" that the reform was approved on the date of February 23, which was the fourteenth

[8] Ibid.
[9] Ibid.
[10] Ibid.
[11] Ibid.
[12] Ibid.

anniversary of several military officers' failed coup d'état against Spain's new democracy.[13]

The PP's Attempts at Rolling Back the Jury

When the PP defeated the PSOE to return to power in 1996, it promptly attempted to roll back many of the judicial reforms introduced under the PSOE government. Specifically, it sought to narrow the scope of jury trials, to limit the jury to determining the facts rather than determining verdict, and also to increase oversight over jury decisions.[14] These measures, it argued, were necessary to correct the "rampant doctrinarianism" of the previous Socialist government.[15] In particular, the PP saw a window of opportunity to roll back the jury system after a controversial court case in the Basque country, in which a terrorist who had killed two Basque policemen was acquitted by the jury, sparking an uproar among the media and the public.[16]

But the PP had to tread carefully, because it was a minority government dependent on support from regionalist parties. In particular, the Convergència i Unió (CiU, the Catalan Party), objected to limiting the power of the jury. As seen in Chapter 3, the CiU stood to the right of the PSOE on new left issues, but its regionalist focus would lead us to expect it to push for a jury/lay judge system that transfers extensive powers from professional judges to jurors/lay judges, and this was precisely what happened. The CiU noted in reference to the jury's controversial decision in the aforementioned case in the Basque country, "If a sergeant mistakenly fires a gun, you do not take away all of the ammunition from the armed forces."[17] The CiU cited a report from the Attorney General that assessed the record of the implementation of the jury law. The report by the Attorney General, published in October 1997, actually gave a favorable view of the jury system. It only recommended some minor reforms, for instance, that kidnapping and genocide be included in the list of crimes subject to jury trials, and that bureaucratic corruption should be excluded from jury trials.[18]

---

[13] *El Pais*, February 24, 1995.
[14] "La Reforma del Jurado," *El Pais*, October 19, 1997.
[15] *El Pais*, April 23, 1997.
[16] *El Pais*, October 19, 1997.
[17] Ibid.
[18] Ibid.

Due to the CiU's importance in parliamentary terms, the CiU's resistance meant that the PP's proposals for watering down the jury system were shelved indefinitely.

Nevertheless, the PP continued to look for opportunities to roll back the jury system. In 2000, for instance, the PP included in its electoral platform a policy of replacing the existing "pure" jury system with a "mixed" jury.[19] The PP won an absolute majority that year, but it did not mount a major challenge to the existing system. The PP did manage to pass some minor reforms of the jury law in 2002, but the changes were mostly technical in nature.

The PSOE returned to power in late 2004, and during this period, the jury was left untouched. Also during this period, the PP appeared to become increasingly resigned to accepting the system and did not raise objections to it during its victorious 2011 electoral campaign. However, returning to power with a large parliamentary majority, it proved highly responsive when, in 2012, about twelve environmental groups filed a petition that asked to exempt wildfires from jury trials.[20] Lack of evidence on who started the fires was leading to a large number of acquittals. A resolution by the European Parliament in 2009 that member states should make stricter rules against forest fires had encouraged the petition, and the PP did not mind restricting the jury where it could. A reform of penal code on March 27, 2015 removed forest fires from jury trial (articles 352–4).[21]

Part of the reason for the PP's grudging acceptance of the jury system over time appears to be that prosecutors and judges have found ways to undermine its full implementation. A report of the *Consejo General del Poder Judicial* (General Council of the Judiciary) in 2015 documented a steady decline in the number of jury trials in national courts from the high point of 785 in 1998 down to only 364 in 2014 (Consejo General del Poder Judicial 2015). This decline is even more dramatic if we consider the number of court cases in relation to the overall Spanish population, which grew over the time period. In 1998, there were 1.97 jury trials for every 100,000 inhabitants; by 2014, this figure was down to 0.78. The falloff was less severe in the provincial courts. In 1998, there were 404 jury trials in provincial courts; this

[19] *El Pais*, January 20, 2000.
[20] *El Pais*, April 4, 2012.
[21] *El Derecho*, April 6, 2015.

number went up to 448 in 2002, before declining to 308 in 2008, then bouncing back to 346 in 2014 (ibid).

According to Jimeno-Bulnes (2011), the fall in the number of jury trials has been caused at least in part by the courts reinterpreting the Spanish Jury Law to increasingly restrict the scope of cases that are subject to jury trial, as well as the increasing turn to a practice of reaching "confirmidad," or what in the United States would be analogous to plea bargaining. Jimeno-Bulnes suggests that this latter practice in particular does not comply with the law as written. She concludes that the law should be amended if the practice is to be continued (ibid).

Summary

Spain adopted the most extensive reforms among the four countries studied in this book, opting for an Anglo-American jury system rather than the "mixed" jury that is much more common among civil law systems. The Spanish jury's verdict is binding, rather than advisory. As Jimeno-Bulnes (2004) notes, Spain presents one of the rare cases of a civil law system that has introduced a common law-style jury system.

The case highlights the crucial role of partisan dynamics in shaping the design of new jury systems. The jury issue has long divided the left and the right in Spain, going back to the early nineteenth century. Nevertheless, it is clear that the reform of 1995 was strongly influenced by new left ideas of civic participation and deliberation, as noted by its champion, the PSOE Justice Minister Belloch. The new Spanish jury system was adopted under the new left-oriented PSOE, which initially leaned toward a mixed jury system but ultimately opted for a pure jury system. This was partially due to Belloch's personal preferences, partially due to the fact that as a new left-oriented party, the PSOE was more amenable to the idea of expanding grassroots participation, and partially due to the fact that although the PSOE was in power at the time, it lacked a majority in the parliament and needed cooperation from the regionalist PNV and the far-left IU, both of which also favored a pure jury. Thus, from the perspective of this book, it is not surprising that Spain's new system made the most radical departure from the existing professional judge-dominated system.

The Spanish case also highlights the continued importance of partisan dynamics once a jury system has been introduced. After the center-right PP returned to power in 1996, it quickly attempted to roll back the jury. However, it was hindered in this effort by the regionalist CiU, on which the PP was dependent for support. Conceivably, if the PP had been in power alone, it may have seen greater success in rolling back the jury.

South Korea

Overview: The South Korean Party System

As noted in Chapter 3, the early- to mid-2000s was a period of partisan realignment in South Korea. After democratization in the late 1980s, the South Korean party system had primarily been split along a regional cleavage, with the Yongnam region voting for the GNP, the Honam region voting for the opposition, and the Seoul area serving as the "swing" region. During the early- to mid-2000s, however, the Korean party system saw a period of realignment in which the regional cleavage was ultimately supplanted by a left-right ideological cleavage (Asaba 2009; Hix and Jun 2009; Kim 2010; Hellman 2014; Onishi 2014). As noted in Chapter 3, the left-right ideological cleavage that was gradually emerging around the time, and remains largely in place to this day, revolves primarily around economic and foreign policy issues (Steinberg and Shin 2006; Onishi 2014). The conservatives usually favor the protection of *chaebol*, the Korean industrial conglomerates, a more pro-American foreign policy, and more hawkish measures toward North Korea. The left, in contrast, is more willing to promote an expansion of workers' rights and exhibits stronger anti-American attitudes and a greater willingness to introduce softer policies on North Korea (Onishi 2004, 2014). It is important not to exaggerate the intensity of this ideological cleavage; research by Lupu (2014), for instance, finds that the Korean party system is only moderately polarized relative to most developed countries. But this does not mean that partisan conflict is not intense, and even when policy differences are not stark, there is often an *appearance* of polarization.[22]

The question of introducing a jury/lay judge system emerged precisely during this period of partisan realignment, when legislators'

---

[22] In turn, Jeon and Machidori (2015) argue that strong party discipline in the Korean legislature is driven by party leaders' control over candidate nomination and campaign financing.

political platforms and loyalties were in flux. Chapter 3 showed that because the party system was undergoing realignment, new left issues did not consistently divide the left from the right in South Korea in contrast to Japan, Spain, or Taiwan.

President Roh Moo-hyun, who represented the left wing of the leftist MDP, came into power in 2003 with the slogan "Government of Participation." As shown by this slogan, his rhetoric was often new left-oriented. But Roh's party lacked a majority of the legislature for most of his tenure. The majority of Korean presidents since democratization have faced divided government, but as Kang and Asaba (2015) note, Roh was the first to face a divided government in which the opposition held a supermajority in the legislature. This weak power position was one factor that precipitated Roh's impeachment in 2004, although Roh was reinstated by the constitutional court and served out the rest of his term, which ended in 2008. The strength of the conservative opposition meant that many of Roh's bold policy proposals failed to materialize, such as the moving of the Korean capital from Seoul and the ratification of the US-Korean Free Trade Agreement (Onishi 2014). Under Roh, a jury system did come into being, but it represented a much more modest change than many of its advocates had hoped for.

Introducing the Jury System in South Korea: Pre-History

While Imperial Japan had a jury system between 1928 and 1943, it did not introduce the system in its Korean colony (Dobrovolskaia 2016). As in Japan, the US occupation debated whether to introduce a jury/lay judge system in Korea after the World War II but ultimately decided against it (Choi 2008; Lee 2009). For the next half-century, the introduction of a jury/lay judge system never emerged onto the policy agenda in South Korea, which spent much of that time as a military-sponsored dictatorship.

The reform of criminal procedures was an important pillar of the democratization process in South Korea starting in the late 1980s, as we have seen it was in the case of Taiwan. Before democratization, pro-democracy groups tended to focus on issues of judicial independence or criminal procedure; the introduction of a jury/lay judge system was not particularly high on their agendas (Cho 2008). This remained true in the early years after democratization, when progressive groups pushed for, and won, important reforms of criminal procedures. The 1995 revision of the Criminal Procedure Law, for instance, limited the power of authorities to arrest individuals unless they had obtained a prior warrant from a judge (Cho 2002). The 1995 revision also introduced a bail system for suspects who requested *habeas corpus* (ibid).

In 1995, center-left President Kim Young-sam established the "Globalization Committee," which was charged with the task of drawing up proposals to bring the Korean public sector up to international standards. One of the main pillars of the Committee's reform proposals was judicial reforms. While the discussions did touch upon the possible introduction of a jury system, it was still seen as a medium- to longer-term issue and did not become a subject of extensive debate (Kudo 2004b). The main issues debated in the Committee relating to the judiciary were the expansion of the bar and the possible introduction of an American-style law school system (Yoon 2001).[23]

In May 1999, President Kim Dae-jung, Kim Young-sam's successor who was further to his left, but also from the older generation that was less interested in new left concerns, set up an advisory committee, the "Committee for Propelling Judicial Reform," to overhaul the Korean judicial system. The Committee consisted of eighteen members, including lawyers, legal scholars, and intellectuals (Yoon 2001). Cho (2008) notes that the establishment of the Committee was motivated by a series of bribery scandals involving judges and lawyers that had emerged just before Kim Dae-jung's inauguration, thus undermining public trust in the judiciary. The Committee released a final report in 2000, and among its proposals was a call for a system of lay participation in trials, although the report still cautioned that this would be a goal for "the medium- to long-term future" (Committee for Propelling Judicial Reform 2000: 337, cited in Cho 2008: 272).[24] Thus, despite the power of international norms in the South Korean

---

[23] The Globalization Committee and the Supreme Court agreed on a dramatic expansion of the bar, but the Supreme Court resisted the introduction of a US-style law school.

[24] One reason why the reform was pushed back appears to be that the Korean Supreme Court did not feel prepared to begin debating the issue. Soon after the "Committee for Propelling Judicial Reform" released its report, the Supreme Court undertook an extensive study of lay judge systems around the world (Lee 2011a).

political mindset, the idea of introducing a jury system was still not high on the agenda.

Judicial Reform under Roh Moo-hyun

Momentum toward the introduction of a jury/lay judge system finally accelerated under Roh Moo-hyun, Kim's successor, who came into power in 2003. Elected under the slogan, "Government of Participation," Roh was himself a leftist human rights lawyer, and this career background clearly heightened his interest in judicial reforms. In October 2003, the President and the Supreme Court agreed to establish a blue-ribbon Judicial Reform Committee (hereafter JRC) under the Supreme Court to devise concrete measures for overhauling the judicial system. Following a year of deliberation, the JRC submitted its final report in December 2004 (Choi 2008). This section will first review the series of events that led up to the adoption of the Korean jury system, and the next will offer an explanation for the design of the new system. Unfortunately, the information on the Korean case is less extensive than the other three, so the argument in these sections will rely on more circumstantial evidence.

The JRC consisted of twenty-one members (Ginsburg 2012). It was headed by a lawyer who had also been one of the founding members of the *Minbyeon [Lawyers for a Democratic Society]*, a group of lawyers who represented pro-democracy protesters who had been arrested. Roh himself had been a member of *Minbyeon*. As in Taiwan, but in contrast to Japan, the majority of the blue-ribbon committee's twenty-one members consisted of lawyers and legal scholars. The exceptions were two members representing the mass media, one member representing business, one member from the Ministry of Education, one member from the Ministry of Defense, and one member representing women. Thus, fifteen out of twenty-one committee members were either lawyers or legal scholars.

The JRC met twenty-seven times and engaged in heated deliberation. The JRC debates occurred in two sub-committees, the first of which considered the reform of judicial appointments and legal education, and the second of which debated issues relating to public participation in the justice system, including the introduction of the jury/lay judge system, as well as reforms of military tribunals (Kudo 2004a). Mirroring the earlier experience of Japan's JSRC, in the Korean JRC the introduction of a jury/lay judge system and the founding of US-style law schools were the two main issues of debate. Indeed, Ginsburg (2012) notes that members of the JRC were well aware of the debates over justice system reform in neighboring Japan (also Han 2015). But in addition, given that "Government of Participation" was the Roh administration's main slogan, it was not surprising that the introduction of a jury/lay judge system would be high on the agenda.[25] As the discussions began, major reform-minded NGOs such as the People's Solidarity for Participatory Democracy (PSPD) sensed an opportunity and rushed to submit proposals to the JRC demanding the introduction of an Anglo-American style jury system (Ha 2010).

The JRC soon split between those who believed that a jury/lay judge system would be constitutional under existing Korean law and those who believed that it would not. Moreover, as in Japan's JSRC, those JRC members who believed that such a system would be constitutional were divided between those who pushed for a "pure" jury system and those who preferred a "mixed" jury (Min 2011; Shin 2012). On the issue of constitutionality, the JRC ultimately reached a compromise that side-stepped the question of constitutionality by proposing that the jury's decisions should merely be advisory rather than binding; at least, it was claimed, for the first five years of the system's operation (Shin 2014). After that, the system would be reviewed, and, if necessary, reformed as appropriate (Han 2015). Also to side-step the ostensible issue of constitutionality, defendants who wished to be tried by jury trial would be required to make a formal request, and a jury trial would only be held if professional judges approved the defendant's request.

Second, the committee also adopted a compromise that Korea should adopt a hybrid of the "pure" and "mixed" jury systems. Specifically, the jurors would initially discuss whether or not the defendant is guilty in isolation from professional judges. But if half of the jurors agreed, the jurors could invite the professional judges to give their opinion. If the jurors failed to reach a unanimous verdict, the professional judges and the jurors were to jointly discuss whether or not the defendant is guilty.

---

[25] Park (2010: 547) notes that other measures to expand public participation were also introduced during the Roh administration, such as the adoption of "citizen standing" measures for the average citizen to challenge government action, making various local issues subject to mandatory popular referendum, and the lowering of the voting age.

Third, the JRC recommended that the new system be introduced in 2007, with only felony cases being subject to jury trials for the first five years.

Following the submission of the JRC's final report, the Presidential Committee on Judicial Reform (PCJR) was set up to convert the JRC's recommendations into concrete legislative proposals. In May 2005, the PCJR submitted the Bill on Lay Participation in Criminal Trials, and the bill passed the National Assembly with only minor revisions on April 30, 2007. The delay was mainly caused by the legislature's long stalemate over an unrelated issue, the controversial revision of the Private School Law (Lee 2011a; Park 2014).[26]

As shown in Chapter 1, the final design of the Korean jury system delegated much less power to the jurors than the new systems in Spain or Japan. Jury trials would only be held upon request of the defendant and if the request was approved by professional judges. In addition, the jurors' rulings could be overruled by the professional judges. Indeed, although the JRC had recommended that the jury's verdict be advisory for the first five years between 2007 and 2012 and to potentially become binding thereafter, the final bill passed by the National Assembly made no provision for such a shift (Cho 2008: 279).

In 2012, the "Committee on Civil Participation in the Judiciary" (CCPJ) was established to discuss the "final form" of the Korean jury system. The CCPJ was attached to the Korean Supreme Court. In 2013, the CCPJ submitted a bill that would make the jury's rulings on verdict and sentencing more binding (Choi 2013b; Lee 2016).[27] In 2013, the Ministry of Justice also submitted a separate bill that sought to allow the prosecution to bring a motion to dismiss a petition for a jury trial. It also sought to exclude a number of crimes from jury trials, particularly violations of the Public Election Act. As of late 2016, neither bill has passed the legislature.

Explaining the Weakness of Reform

There are several reasons why the South Korean reform was so weak. The proximate cause, as Min (2011) notes, was that an important

---

[26] This was a controversial policy in which Roh sought to, and largely succeeded in, expanding government regulation of private universities. Roh saw this policy as one of the four main pillars of his policy agenda. For a good overview of this case, see Umakoshi (2010), Chapter 7.

[27] Choi (2013b) provides a detailed discussion of the CCPJ's proposal.

emphasis of the reform effort was to design a system that would pass in the legislature. To this end, Roh also needed to make sure that legal professionals were kept reasonably happy. Indeed, Ginsburg (2012) notes that the President's office and the Supreme Court were in close communication as the debates within the JRC unfolded.

Making sure that the proposal would satisfy everyone was no small order given the highly charged political climate at the time. As noted earlier, the JRC came into being in the fall of 2003, shortly after Roh came into office. At that time, the conservative opposition controlled a supermajority in the legislature (Asaba 2009; Onishi 2014). Roh was then impeached in early 2004, leading to a suspension of all presidential powers over two months, until the constitutional court rejected the motion to dismiss the president (Ginsburg 2010). Roh did maneuver to win a majority of the legislature in the 2004 legislative elections, but only by a slim margin, and he lost his majority just ten months later, when his Uri Party was defeated in by-elections. Indeed, Roh lacked control of the legislature for most of his tenure as president. During his five-year term between 2003 and 2008, Roh's party only held a majority in the legislature for ten months, between mid-2004 and early 2005 (Kang and Asaba 2015). This significantly hampered Roh's efforts to push through major reforms. Roh's weak position is reflected in the fact that only 51.1% of bills submitted to the National Assembly by the Administration between 2004 and 2008 were passed. This was a marked decline from the 1996–2000 and the 2000–2004 periods, when the corresponding figures were 81.7% and 72.4%, respectively (Okumura 2009).[28]

The JRC, which debated the reform between the fall of 2003 and late 2004, was well aware of Roh's weakness. Thus, while many members of the JRC were sympathetic to a system that would transfer greater powers to the jurors/lay judges, the architects of the new system also needed to ensure that the new system would be acceptable to professional jurists and members of the more conservative GNP.

The need for compromise was further accentuated by the fact that Roh did not even fully control his own party during much of his term in office. Crucially, the Korean party system was undergoing a major realignment at the time and partisan loyalties became increasingly

---

[28] Unlike in the American presidential system, the Korean presidential system allows for the Administration to submit bills to the legislature (Okumura 2009).

fluid as legislators frequently switched parties in search of best opportunities for re-election. This severely undermined Roh's leadership within his own party, while also reducing the salience of new left ideas for party legislators.

Other factors also contributed to Roh's weakness vis-à-vis his own party. Unlike most of his predecessors, Roh chose not to head his party during most of his term as president, which broadened the rift between him and his party (Ka and Nishino 2015). Even if Roh had headed his own party, the typical Korean president does not always have many levers at her/his disposal to control party members compared to other Asian countries (Asaba 2013; Kasuya 2013b). As Rich (2014) shows, between 2004 and 2008, Korean party members defected from the party line in about one-third of all legislative roll-call votes. As Asaba et al. (2010) point out, this low level of party discipline in part reflects the different electoral cycles for presidential and legislative elections in South Korea, in which presidential elections are held every five years, whereas legislative elections occur every four. The typical Korean president thus faces one legislative election at some point during her/his term. The president's control over campaign financing and the candidate nomination process serves as leverage to influence the behavior of legislators during the run-up to the elections, but not after. Roh came into power in 2003 and enjoyed considerable control over party members until the 2004 National Assembly elections, but after that his influence over fellow party members declined precipitously. Furthermore, if the sitting president is unpopular, as Roh was, legislators prefer to distance themselves from the president (Ka and Nishino 2015). This is especially the case since Korean presidents cannot run for re-election. After the legislative elections, the president tends to become a lame duck, and presidential hopefuls, rather than the president her/himself, typically wield greater influence within the party (Asaba 2013). Given his weak position even within his own party, if Roh had any hopes of pushing though a jury/lay judge system, he needed to ensure that the proposed system would be one that would be palatable to the rest of his party and the opposition GNP, as well as other important stakeholders such as the Supreme Court.

Thus, it is actually quite impressive that Roh was able to obtain passage of any kind of lay participation bill at all. The price, however, was to water it down considerably from what Roh and other progressive-minded actors would have liked to see. If Roh had enjoyed greater control of his party and the legislature, he and his more reform-minded associates would have been able to exercise greater leverage over the design of the new jury system and to push for a system that would impose stronger constraints upon professional judges. But Roh did not have that power. Therefore, if he had hopes of passing any new jury/lay judge system, he needed to compromise his views with the more conservative forces that sought to preserve the power of the judiciary to a much greater extent. The resulting system reflects this compromise.

Summary

Roh Moo-hyun assumed power under the slogan, "government of participation." But efforts to introduce a US-style "pure" jury system were hampered by his weak position both vis-à-vis his own party and the legislature as a whole. In turn, this allowed proponents of more conservative views to exercise greater influence over the design of the new system, limiting it to a largely cosmetic reform.

Since defendants must petition for a jury trial, and because judges have relatively broad discretion to determine whether the petitions should be accepted, there have been relatively few jury trials in South Korea.[29] Between 2008 and 2013, 2,742 defendants applied for a jury trial, of which 1,054, or 38.4%, ultimately ended in a jury sentence (Shin 2014).[30] Even so, the system has not been completely devoid of impact. Shin (2014: 101) finds that 5.7% of those tried by a jury were found not guilty, which is higher than the rate for those tried solely by professional judges.[31] Chapter 9 delves more deeply into the impact of the new Korean jury system.

Summary

The cases of Spain and South Korea highlight how parties with different degrees of new left orientation favor removing powers from

---

[29] Lee (2008: 73) points out that during the deliberations over introducing the jury trial in South Korea, most policymakers agreed that between one hundred and 200 jury cases a year would be quite sufficient.

[30] In 2010, the jury system was amended to expand the scope of cases eligible for a jury trial to all cases that require a panel of professional judges.

[31] In 2010, the Act of Citizen Participation in Criminal Trials was revised, expanding the scope of cases that are subject to jury trial (Shin 2014).

professional judges to different extents. As shown in Chapter 3, Spain's PSOE was a more consistently new left-oriented party compared to Korea's MDP-UDP. Thus, in Spain, the PSOE government ended up proposing a system that would give extensive powers to the jury. In Korea, in contrast, the party system at the time was undergoing a major realignment and the new left cleavage failed to consistently structure the party system. Thus, while Roh himself was a relatively new left-oriented leader, he could not necessarily count on the rest of his party to share his policy preferences. He also anticipated tough opposition from legal professionals and political conservatives.

The two cases also offer contrasts in the relative power of new left-oriented parties to convert their preferences into actual policy. In both countries, a leftist party controlled the executive branch with a minority in the legislature. But in Spain, the PSOE was the ruling party in parliament, with support from more leftist parties, a situation that led to the adoption of an extensive transfer of power from professional judges to jurors. In South Korea, by contrast, Roh lacked control of the legislature for most of his term, which was in the hands of the right. This situation severely constrained those in the administration who wished to push for a stronger jury. The result was a weak system that gave the professional judges the authority to decide which cases should be a tried by a jury, and to also ignore the jury's verdict if they disagreed.

9 | *The Impact of New Lay Judge Systems*

Overview

This chapter examines some of the concrete impacts of new jury/lay judge systems. It asks: to what extent has the introduction of new systems led to changes in verdict and sentencing patterns? To what extent have the courts become more likely to convict or to acquit, or to give out heavier or lighter sentences? To what extent has the new system led to changes in practice in the realm of criminal procedure? What has been the impact on citizens? And how do these patterns vary systematically across countries that have transferred powers away from professional judges to different degrees?

This chapter offers a detailed analysis of the case of Japan to assess the impact of its new system on verdict, sentencing, and procedure. The chapter also offers a first attempt at comparing the effects of the new systems in Japan, South Korea, and Spain, although the chapter draws on more limited data for the latter two cases.

The chapter focuses mainly on the case of Japan because of the rich data available on this case. The original analysis of Japanese data presented in this chapter is important in and of itself because there are very few studies in the English language on how rulings and procedural practices change in the wake of the introduction of new jury/ lay judge systems (notable exceptions include Ibusuki 2010; Han and Park 2012; Kim et al. 2013; Lee 2016). The Japanese case is also particularly useful to examine because it represents a case of *moderate* reform. For instance, in the Japanese system, the lay judges deliberate together with professional judges to reach both verdict and sentence. It is often argued that in such systems of mixed tribunals, professional judges are likely to exert a greater influence over the course of discussion, and ultimately the rulings, to a greater extent than when jurors deliberate in isolation (e.g. Kaplan et al. 2006). On the other hand, substantial changes in verdict or sentencing patterns or in procedural practice in Japan would suggest a genuine transfer of power from the professional to the lay judges. Assessing the Japanese case can therefore illuminate how much difference a moderate transfer of power to lay judges make in terms of real judicial outcomes.

This chapter shows that the introduction of the *saiban-in* system in Japan was followed by a modest rise in acquittals, a decline in the number and percentage of death sentences and life sentences, and an increase in the percentage of suspended sentences with probations. These changes are in line with the hopes of at least some of the new left-oriented politicians and lawyers who pushed most strongly for the reform. The chapter also shows that the new Japanese system has led to a decline in the percentage of cases charged, a rise in the percentage of detention requests denied, and a rise in the percentage of detainees released before their final rulings. While many of these changes were already underway before the *saiban-in* system came into effect, the system has accelerated those changes. In South Korea as well, there is preliminary evidence of more lenient verdicts in jury trials. The effects of the new system in Spain are less clear, due to data limitations.

The material presented in this chapter also speaks to the scholarly debate over the punitiveness of juries vis-à-vis professional judges. Starting with the classic study of judge-jury agreement, *The American Jury* (Kalven and Zeisel 1966), as well as follow-up studies (e.g. Heuer and Penrod 1994; Eisenberg et al. 2005), scholars have found that American jurors tend to be more likely to acquit than professional judges.[1] By contrast, a study of the German mixed jury finds that lay jurors there were more likely to want to convict compared to professional judges, but also more likely to favor lighter sentences than the professional judges (Casper and Zeisel 1972). There also exists a lively debate over whether civil juries in the United States are more likely to give punitive damages than professional judges, with Eisenberg et al. (2002) finding no systematic difference between civil juries and professional judges, Hersch and Viscusi (2004) finding that civil juries are more punitive than professional judges, and Eisenberg et al. (2006, 2010) reporting civil juries to be more punitive in some categories of cases but judges to be more punitive in others.[2]

---

[1] For an excellent review of this literature, see Robbennolt (2005).
[2] For an excellent review of this literature, see Vidmar and Wolfe (2009).

The analysis presented in this chapter contributes to these debates with new data from Japan. In many developed democracies, including Japan, observers have pointed to the rise of "penal populism" among the general public. Many scholars in Japan expected that the increasingly harsh attitudes of the public toward criminal defendants would lead the courts to hand down tougher sentences once the *saiban-in* system came into effect (e.g. Honjo 2003; Tanioka 2007). The data presented in this chapter show that for the most part, these expectations have not materialized. Instead, the effects of the new Japanese lay judge system have generally been favorable to defendants, just as many of its new left-oriented advocates had hoped.

The chapter proceeds as follows. The next section delineates the changes that have occurred in Japan following the introduction of its new lay judge system. The third section draws on South Korean data. The fourth section presents available figures on the impact of the Spanish jury system. The fifth section summarizes and concludes.

The Impact of the Lay Judge System in Japan

This section lays out the changes in the delivery of justice that have occurred since the introduction of the new lay judge system in Japan. The overall impact of the new system can be assessed along at least three dimensions. The first is the effects on verdict and sentences. To what extent have courts become more likely to convict or acquit since the introduction of the new system? To what extent have sentences become more or less severe? How do these patterns vary between crimes that became subject to lay judge trial and those that did not? Scholars agree that since the late 1990s, sentencing in Japan has become harsher, as in many other industrialized democracies (e.g. Johnson 2008; Miyazawa 2008; also Pratt 2007). To what extent has the introduction of the lay judge system impacted this trend, if at all? This section offers original analysis of Japanese verdict and sentencing data to shed new light on these questions.

The second dimension is the effects on criminal procedures. What changes have occurred, if any, in the cases that are brought to trial? The introduction of the new system may have made prosecutors more likely to charge certain types of crimes than others. In addition, in many industrialized countries, courts not only deliver sentences; they also issue warrants that authorize the police and prosecution to make

arrests and/or detentions. In particular, Japan is well-known for per-
mitting lengthy pre-trial detentions (Johnson 2002). To what extent
has this changed since the introduction of the new system? Although
those decisions do not involve the lay judges directly, the knowledge of
them could affect the lay judges' opinions at a later stage, and therefore far-sighted prosecutors and judges may change their behavior
pre-emptively.

Third, the effects of the new system on citizens who have served in
the system, specifically the lay judges themselves, will also be examined.
As noted in Chapter 2, the classic Tocquevillian justification for the
jury system is that it serves as a "school for democracy" where citizens
may learn to become more civic-minded. To what extent do we find
evidence for this effect in Japan?

Chapter 1 noted that at the most basic level, one difference between
the effects of the new systems in Japan and Korea has simply been
the number of citizens who have served as jurors/lay judges. In
Japan, in the first seven-and-a-half years after the introduction of
the Japanese *saiban-in* (lay judge) system, between April 2009 and
October 2016, 53,828 randomly selected citizens served as lay judges
and ruled on verdict and, in the case of a guilty verdict, sentence, of
9,350 accused individuals (Saiko Saibansho 2016). This is the equivalent of over 7,000 citizens serving on trials every year. In contrast, in
Korea between January 1, 2008, and December 31, 2010, the first three
years since the introduction of the new system, 2,399 jurors served
on 321 trials, or just under 800 jurors a year (calculated from Lee
2011b: 198). Thus, far fewer Koreans were being asked to serve per
year. This was the case even though the Korean system permits up to
nine jurors per trial, whereas Japanese law allows only six. Admittedly,
the jury trial has gradually become more common in Korea, and, since
2012, the number of jury trials in Korea has ranged between 250 and
350 cases a year (Lee 2016). This is roughly the equivalent of about
2,400 jurors a year, but still fewer than in Japan, even if we normalize
the numbers for Korea's smaller population. In sum, the new Japanese
system has certainly generated more citizen participation. But what
have been some of the effects on judicial decision-making of the new
systems in the two countries, beyond simply the number of citizens
being mobilized?

It should be noted at the outset that as of writing, data on the implementation of the Japanese *saiban-in* system is only available for the

first six years since the introduction of the new system (2009–14). This is not many data points, and thus the present study can at best assess the short-term impact of the new lay judge system. A more thorough assessment of the longer-term impact of the new system will thus remain an issue for future study.

Changes in Verdict and Sentencing

Overview

How has the introduction of the new *saiban-in* system influenced verdict and sentencing patterns in Japan? Scholars typically find that the variance in sentencing has grown since the introduction of the new system (Foote 2014; Takamori 2015). This is not surprising, as different groups of lay judges may rule slightly differently on similar cases, but it raises important questions of equity. But beyond the question of variance, Japanese observers have disagreed over the basic question of whether the new system has, on average, tended to produce more guilty verdicts and tougher sentences or fewer guilty verdicts and lighter sentences (e.g. Yonekura 2012; Takeda 2014; Yamamoto 2015). To probe this issue, the study draws on different data than previous studies and examines the effects of the *saiban-in* system in light of long-term trends in verdict and sentencing patterns in Japan since the late 1970s.

Assessing whether or not any changes in verdict and sentencing patterns that have occurred *since* the introduction of the new system in 2009 are in fact a *result* of the new lay judge system is far from straightforward. There were other social and legal developments occurring around the same time that the new system was being launched that may also have affected court rulings, some of which will be alluded to in this chapter. To address this issue, at least partly, the present chapter compares changes in verdict and sentencing patterns for those crimes that are now subject to a lay judge trial, primarily murder and burglary leading to injury or death, with changes in patterns for some of those crimes that are still not subject to a lay judge trial, such as robbery, fraud, injury through negligence, or extortion. These latter crimes were chosen primarily because they represent the largest number of cases that are brought to criminal trial in Japan. If we observe different degrees of changes in verdict and sentencing patterns for crimes that are subject to a *saiban-in* trial versus crimes that are not, we may conclude with some measure of confidence that the differences were caused by the introduction of the new system. Nevertheless, the conclusions drawn in this chapter are necessarily tentative and should be interpreted with caution.

Because the *saiban-in* system has only been introduced at the district court level, verdict and sentencing patterns before and after the launch of the system will be compared at the district court level. Of course, the new system may have an impact on rulings by higher courts as well. But before we can begin to assess the impact of the new system on the higher courts, we need a sense of the impact of the new system at the district court level. In this regard, it is notable that by the end of May 2015, the higher courts had upheld 92.9% of lay judge decisions that had been appealed since the start of the new system. This figure is considerably higher than the 82.4% rate for the corresponding types of crimes between 2006 and 2008, i.e. before the new *saiban-in* system was introduced (Takamori 2015; see also Koike 2016).[3]

The Data

The overwhelming majority of existing analyses of changes in sentencing patterns since the introduction of the Japanese lay judge system (e.g. Ibusuki 2010; Harada 2013; Kojima 2015; Takamori 2015; Yamamoto 2015) rely on data on the *saiban-in* system that the Supreme Court has disclosed annually (Saiko Saibansho Jimu Sokyoku various years[a]) or on the report that it released in 2012 to assess the first three years of the new system (Saiko Saibansho Jimu Sokyoku 2012[c]). The latter, in particular, the "Report on the Implementation of the *Saiban-in* Trials [*Saiban-in* Saiban Jisshi Jokyono Kensho Hokokusho]" (Saiko Saibansho Jimu Sokyoku 2012[c]; hereafter the *Saiban-in* Report), published in 2012, offers detailed analyses of changes that occurred after the new system came into effect. The advantage of the *Saiban-in*

---

[3] It should be noted, however, that the percentage of *saiban-in* rulings that were appealed and reversed in the High Courts rose markedly between 2013 and 2014, from 6.8% to 11.3% (calculated from Saiko Saibansho Jimu Sokyoku (various years[b])). This figure was still lower than the percentage of rulings reversed in the higher courts in the few years prior to the introduction of the *saiban-in* system but it was actually higher than the percentage of non-*saiban-in* rulings reversed in 2014. Thus it is possible that the higher courts are becoming less respectful of *saiban-in* verdicts. But it remains to be seen whether the sharp increase in reversed *saiban-in* rulings in 2014 represented an anomaly or a more fundamental shift in the higher courts' attitudes.

Report is that it offers fine-grained comparisons of sentencing patterns before and after the introduction of the system for each category of crime that is subject to lay judge trial, such as murder and injury leading to death.

While offering rich information on changes that have occurred since the lay judge system came into effect, the figures presented in the *Saiban-in* Report also suffer from some drawbacks. One major limitation is that it compares verdict and sentencing data since the introduction of the new system against data from 2006 to 2008. But that is only three years, and given that political debates about the launching of the *saiban-in* system began in the late 1990s and that the Act on Criminal Trials with Participation of Saiban-in (hereafter the Act) was passed in 2004, we need to consider the possibility that professional judges may have begun to change their sentencing patterns even *before* the introduction of the new system in 2009. That is, the new system may have begun to impact sentencing patterns prior to its formal implementation. Indeed, between 2004, when the *saiban-in* system was passed, and 2009, when the system came into effect, the Japanese courts held more than 630 mock *saiban-in* trials across the country in cooperation with the Ministry of Justice and the Japan Federation of Bar Associations (Moriya 2015: 14). Thus, between 2004 and 2009, the professionals were already gaining a better sense of how citizens were likely to rule and may have started to adjust their behavior in anticipation. Therefore, in order to better evaluate the effects of the new system, we need to examine verdict and sentencing patterns before 2004 as well. Also, other social or policy-level changes may have been underway that affected sentencing patterns between 2006 and 2008. Only with a longer time frame can we properly assess the magnitude of changes that occurred after the system came into effect in 2009, and the reasons for those changes.

The present study draws primarily on statistics on verdict and sentencing patterns that are published in the *Criminal Cases* portion of the *Annual Report of Judicial Statistics*, which is compiled annually by the General Secretariat of the Japanese Supreme Court (Saiko Saibansho Jimu Sokyoku various years [b]). In order to gain a longer-term view of verdict and sentencing patterns, the study draws on data between 1979 and 2014, a thirty-five-year period. The year 1979 is taken as the starting point because postwar sentencing patterns became largely institutionalized during the late 1970s and early 1980s. For instance, the well-known "Nagayama standard," which set the standards for the sentencing of death penalties in Japan, was ruled by the Japanese Supreme Court in 1983.

It should be noted at the outset that there are also drawbacks to using the *Annual Report of Judicial Statistics* as a data source. For instance, as noted earlier, the Supreme Court's *Saiban-in* Report presents comparisons of verdict and sentencing patterns before and after the new system was launched for each category of crime that is subject to *saiban-in* trial, such as murder, injury leading to death, and burglary leading to death or injury. Such detailed comparisons are not possible with the *Annual Report of Judicial Statistics*, at least not for all categories of crimes. This is because, beginning in 1999, the Supreme Court vastly simplified the statistics that it published in the *Annual Report*. The upshot was that statistics for different subcategories of "injuries," such as injury, injury leading to death, assault, and other related crimes that fall under the category of "injury," which had been listed separately in the *Annual Report* until 1998, were subsumed under the single umbrella category of "injury." Similar simplifications were made with respect to other crimes as well, such as arson or crimes relating to obscenity, rape, and bigamy. This simplification of data poses little problem for our purposes with crimes such as murder and burglary leading to death or injury, since almost all of the subcategories of these crimes are subject to lay judge trial. But for simpler crimes of injury, the only subcategory of cases that must be judged by lay judges is injury leading to death, which comprises less than 10% of all crimes that are listed in the *Annual Report* as "injury." Comparing verdict and sentencing patterns for "injury" before and after the new system was introduced would therefore not yield an accurate picture of its impact. Similar problems exist with the categories of arson and crimes relating to obscenity, rape, and bigamy, among other categories.[4] Nevertheless, the data is useful for several important classes of crimes.

Part of the data since 1999 that is missing from the *Annual Report*, notably for crimes of injury leading to death, is actually made available

[4] Under the category of "arson," arson of inhabited buildings is subject to *saiban-in* trial, while other sub-categories of arson, such as arson of uninhabited buildings, are not; similarly, under the category of "crimes relating to obscenity, rape, and bigamy," rape leading to death or injury is subject to *saiban-in* trial, while other categories, such as public indecency or bigamy, are not.

annually by the Supreme Court in the journal *Hoso Jiho* (Saiko Saibansho Jimu Sokyoku Keijikyoku various years). Therefore, the chapter also includes relevant data presented in the *Hoso Jiho*.[5]

Thus, in the following discussion, the analysis of the impact of lay judge trials will rely primarily on data on verdicts and sentences for crimes of murder, burglary leading to injury or death, and, wherever possible, injury leading to death. These are the main categories of crimes for which figures are available over a long time series and comparable for both the pre-*saiban-in* era and the post-*saiban-in* era. Although it would be ideal to be able to compare statistics for all categories of crimes that have become subject to lay judge trial, these three categories of crimes nonetheless constitute well over 50% of all cases brought to lay judge trial (Saiko Saibansho 2016). Therefore, while not perfect, they can be assumed to provide a reasonably good representation of overall trends.

Verdict

First, has the introduction of the lay judge system in Japan led to changes in the frequency of convictions/acquittals? Japan is well-known for having an exceedingly high rate of convictions, with typically 99.9% of cases ending in conviction since the early 1980s (e.g. Johnson 2002). To what extent has this changed, if at all, since the passage and then the introduction of the new lay judge system? Figure 9.1 shows the trends.

Figure 9.1 shows that the percentage of acquittals as a percentage of cases charged had been falling steadily since the late 1970s and reached a nadir in 2000, when it hit 0.05% (seventeen cases). Since then, the percentage of acquittals began a slow recovery, reaching 0.14% (sixty-seven cases) in 2004, the year that the lay judge bill was passed. Thereafter, the percentage of acquittals continued to rise, hitting 0.17% (seventy-two cases) in 2007, and since the introduction

---

[5] The *Hoso Jiho* also includes data for other crimes that have become subject to lay judge trial, such as arson of inhabited buildings and rape leading to injury or death, but the data could not be presented in this chapter. Scholars and practitioners who have analyzed the *Saiban-in* Report have typically found rape to be one of the few categories of crimes in which sentencing has become harsher in the wake of the introduction of the new system (Shiroshita 2013; Takamori 2015). It is hoped that this question will be analyzed systematically in the future, based on the longer time-series data available in the *Hoso Jiho*.

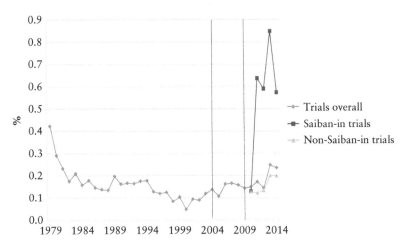

Figure 9.1 Percentage of acquittals among criminal cases charged, district court level, 1979–2014
Source: Saiko Saibansho Jimu Sokyoku (various years [b]).
Note that the vertical lines denote the year the saiban-in system was passed (2004) and the year that it came into effect (2009).

of the lay judge system, it has surged to even higher levels, reaching 0.25% (eighty cases) in 2013. While these figures are certainly minis- cule, they are also levels of acquittals not seen since the early 1980s.

Figure 9.1 also shows that the rise in the overall percentage of acquittals has been propelled by the much higher rate of acquittals in *saiban-in* trials compared to non-*saiban-in* trials. In 2010, the first full year of *saiban-in* trials, the percentage of acquittals was roughly the same in *saiban-in* trials as non-*saiban-in* trials, at 0.13%. But since then, the *saiban-in* trials have produced much higher rates of acquittals than non-*saiban-in* trials: 0.64% in 2011 (ten cases), 0.59% in 2012 (nine cases), 0.85% in 2013 (twelve cases), and 0.57% in 2014 (seven cases). Between 2011 and 2014, the acquittal rate for non-*saiban-in* trials also rose from 0.13% to 0.20%, but these are substantially lower figures than for *saiban-in* trials.

There is also some possibility that the rise in the percentage of acquittals in *saiban-in* trials has had the effect of pushing up the per- centage of acquittals among non-*saiban-in* trials. That is, the rise in acquittals in *saiban-in* trials began in 2011, but the rise in acquittals among non-*saiban-in* trials did not occur until 2013. This lag suggests the possibility that the professional judges in non-*saiban-in* trials have been influenced by the greater tendency to acquit that has emerged in the *saiban-in* trials, although a full assessment of this point requires more systematic investigation.

One alternative hypothesis for the rise in the overall rate of acquittals is the reform of the Prosecutorial Review Commission (PRC). Analogous to the grand jury in the United States, the PRC can, upon request from citizens, review prosecutors' decisions not to bring a charge. Recent reforms strengthened the PRC's authority. Under current rules, if the PRC rules twice that a case should have been charged, the case is automatically charged. This reform is another example of new left thinking producing greater democratization of the judicial system. Some observers have criticized the new PRC rules for producing a string of cases that ended in acquittals (e.g. Imaseki 2013). However, the PRC reforms are unlikely to be driving the results shown in Figure 9.1, for the simple reason that very few cases have been brought as a result of decisions by the PRC. Between 2011 and 2015, an average of 3.5 cases a year have been brought as a result of rulings by the PRC (Saiko Saibansho n.d.). This small number is not sufficient to make a significant difference in the overall acquittal rate.

To properly evaluate the impact of the introduction of the *saiban-in* system, it is also necessary to examine whether crimes that became subject to *saiban-in* trials also had higher rates of acquittals prior to the introduction of the *saiban-in* system. To assess this issue, we examine data on the percentage of acquittals before and after the introduction of the *saiban-in* system for two categories of crimes: murder and burglary leading to death or injury. The results are shown in Figure 9.2.

Figure 9.2 shows that the percentage of acquittals for murder cases had generally been relatively high in Japanese terms during the decades prior to the introduction of the *saiban-in* system. The acquittal rate for murder was typically around 0.5%, which was more than double the rate for all cases charged as shown in Figure 9.1. But the percentage of acquittals rose to even higher levels after the introduction of the new system in 2009. The rate of acquittals for murder in 2003 was 0.3% and 0.8% in 2006, the highest rate during the decade prior to the introduction of the system. But it surged to 3.1% in 2011. Again, these are still small numbers, but the rate of the increase is striking. The percentage of acquittals has fallen since 2011, and the most recent 2014 figure is very modest (0.35%). But this most recent data should not be interpreted as indicating that the lay judges are becoming less

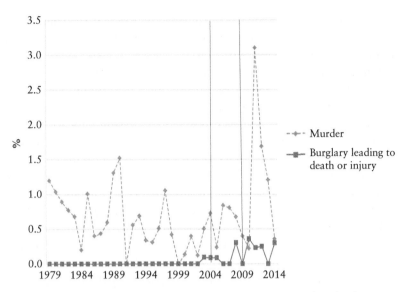

Figure 9.2 Percentage of acquittals among murder and burglary leading to death or injury cases charged, district court level, 1979–2014
Source: Saiko Saibansho Jimu Sokyoku (various years [b]).

eager to acquit. Rather, it is at least plausible that prosecutors learned from the jump in acquittals in the first few years after the launch of the *saiban*-in system, and therefore they began to steer clear of bringing cases that might end in acquittal (Takeda 2014). This hypothesis of how the *saiban-in* system has affected the types of charges brought by the prosecution will be further addressed later in the chapter.

There is also an increase in the percentage of acquittals for cases of burglary leading to death or injury. In contrast to murder, for much of the post-war period, it had been virtually impossible to obtain an acquittal for this class of crimes. Indeed, between 1979 and 2002, the percentage of acquittals stood at 0%. In 2003, 2004, and 2005, however, the percentage of acquittals for burglary leading to death or injury cases began to rise very slowly, reaching 0.1%, 0.09%, and 0.09%, respectively. The figure has continued to rise after 2009, with acquittal rates ranging between 0.2% and 0.4% of all burglary leading to death or injury cases in four of the six years between 2009 and 2014. While the percentage of acquittals in burglary leading to death or injury cases had never exceeded the rate for crimes overall prior to the introduction of the *saiban-in* system, after the system was launched in 2009, the percentage of acquittals in these cases exceeded the overall acquittal rate in four out of six years. In absolute terms, this is the equivalent of just one or two acquittals a year, so again, these are exceedingly small numbers.[6] But in percentage terms, they represent a stark change compared to 1979–2002 period.

Thus, both for murder and for burglary leading to death or injury, two of the crimes that carry the heaviest sentences, the percentage of acquittals reached its highest levels in the last thirty years in the wake of the introduction of the new system. Unfortunately, data limitations do not allow us to assess acquittal rates for injury leading to death.[7]

What about crimes that are not subject to lay judge trial? Figure 9.3 shows the trends for crimes that have had the most number of cases.

Figure 9.3 shows that for some cases of crimes not subject to lay judge trials, including injury through negligence and fraud, the percentage of acquittals has risen since the passage of the Act. This is consistent with trends seen earlier with murder and burglary leading to death or injury. But robbery, on the other hand, has not seen a marked rise in the rate of acquittals either since the passage of the Act in 2004 or the introduction of the *saiban-in* system in 2009. The pattern for extortion is also not entirely clear; there was an abrupt spike in acquittal rates in 2013, but in 2014 the rates appear to have returned to normal levels. Overall, however, the rise in the acquittal rate for some types of crimes not subject to lay judge trials suggests that the increase in the acquittal rate for crimes subject to lay judge trials may not solely be driven by the existence of the lay judge system. On the other hand, it may be that the greater tendency of lay judges to acquit is affecting the tendencies of professional judges even when

---

[6] The rise in acquittal rates for burglary leading to death or injury cases has largely been driven by the fact that the number of acquittals has not declined, while the number of defendants charged with this category of crimes has fallen precipitously in recent years. From a high of 1,119 cases in 2004, in 2014 the figure was 333 cases. This point will be discussed further later in this chapter.

[7] The *Hoso Jiho* data from 1999 does not include precise numbers of acquittals for different categories of crimes. While it does include the number of acquittals for categories of crimes that had two or more acquittals, when the number of acquittals was zero or one, they are simply grouped together with other categories of crime under "other." This presentation of the data unfortunately makes it impossible to calculate acquittal rates for each year.

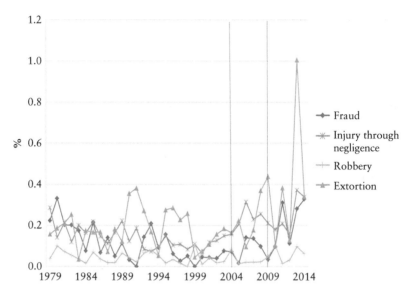

Figure 9.3 Percentage of acquittals, crimes not subject to lay judge trial, district court level, 1979–2014
Source: Saiko Saibansho Jimu Sokyoku (various years [b]).

they are deciding alone. Interestingly, for injury through negligence the rise in acquittals occurred during the 2012–14 period. This suggests the possibility that the professional judges are *following* the trend of rising acquittals among lay judge trials. This point deserves further examination in future studies.

Sentencing
The introduction of the *saiban-in* system has led to more acquittals. Has it also led to more lenient sentencing? This has been an issue of some contention among observers. The question is particularly important because Japan is one of the few developed democracies that still impose the death penalty, and under the *saiban-in* system, crimes that carry the possibility of a death sentence are all subject to a lay judge trial. Thus, the number and percentage of death sentences handed down for any type of crime provides a window onto the impact of the new lay judge system. How has the number of death sentences changed since the introduction of the *saiban-in* system in 2009? And how has it changed since the system was passed in 2004? Figure 9.4

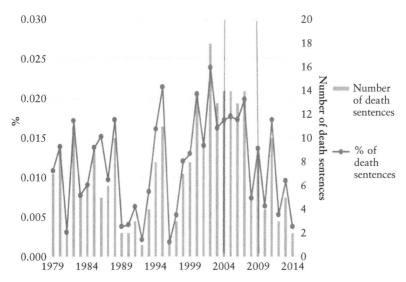

Figure 9.4 Number and percentage of death sentences among all cases charged, district court level, 1979–2014
Source: Saiko Saibansho Jimu Sokyoku (various years [b]).

shows the trends in both absolute number and the percentage of death sentences among all charges brought to district-level courts.

Figure 9.4 shows that, as Johnson (2008) noted, the number and percentage of death sentences in Japan had been rising sharply since the mid-1990s. Many observers had predicted that the introduction of the *saiban-in* system would precipitate a further rise in severe punishments (e.g. Hamai and Ellis 2008). Indeed, a survey finds that this was also the prevailing view among defense lawyers (Ota 2015). This expectation reflected the fact that public opinion polls show that support for the death penalty has consistently exceeded 80% and there has been no significant decline since the mid-2000s (Kimura 2015). However, there has been no increase in the number of death sentences. On the contrary, the first six years after the introduction of the new system brought a steady decline in the number of death sentences.[8]

[8] This point is not to deny that, as Miyazawa (2013) has noted, a higher *percentage* of cases in which the prosecution has asked for a death penalty has resulted in the delivery of a death sentence since the introduction of the lay judge system in 2009.

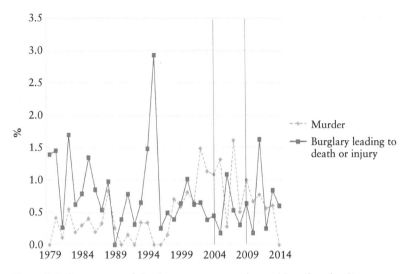

Figure 9.5 Percentage of death sentences, murder and burglary leading to death or injury, 1979–2014
Source: Saiko Saibansho Jimu Sokyoku (various years [b]).

In 2014, only two cases resulted in death sentences, the lowest figure since 1996. The trend of fewer death sentences had begun before the new system was launched in 2009, so the introduction of the new system may not have been the sole reason precipitating the decline in the number of death sentences. Nevertheless, the new system has not reversed this trend and instead appears to have accelerated it. Indeed, as noted in Chapter 1, some ex-lay judges have also formed a movement to oppose the death penalty.

Moving from absolute numbers to percentages, the story is largely the same. Since the low of 0.002% (or just one case) of death sentences in 1996, the percentage of death sentences among all cases charged rose into the 2000s, including after the passage of the Act in 2004. There was a steep decline in the number and percentage of death sentences in 2008, however, a year before the introduction of the *saiban-in* system, and the number and rate of death sentences has continued to fall since 2009. From 0.008% in 2008 (five cases), the figures have fallen to 0.004% (two cases) in 2014.

Figure 9.5 above breaks down the figures shown in Figure 9.4 into murder and burglary leading to death or injury cases, as a percentage of each of those crimes charged.

Figure 9.5 shows that murder cases saw a steady increase in death sentences between the late 1990s and the mid-2000s. For cases of burglary leading to death or injury, the percentage of death sentences actually declined from 1999. Between 2004 and 2009, the percentage of death sentences for both murder cases and burglary leading to death or injury cases was largely flat, although with some fluctuations. But since 2009, the percentage of death sentences among murder cases has dropped precipitously; indeed, in 2014, there was not a single case of murder that resulted in a death sentence, for the first time since 1996. For burglary leading to death or injury cases, the trends are somewhat more uneven, with a seemingly slight upward trend since 2009. However, it should be noted that with the exception of 2011, when there were seven death sentences, the numbers of death sentences for this category of crime have been exceedingly small (one in 2010, one in 2012, three in 2013, and two in 2014).[9]

The trends for life sentences are shown in Figure 9.6.

Figure 9.6 shows that as with death sentences, a surge in life sentences occurred between the late 1990s and 2000s, peaking in 2004, when 0.15% of cases (125 cases) resulted in life sentences. A correction of sorts occurred after 2004, with the percentage of life sentences falling to 0.08% (sixty-nine cases) in 2005, and 0.09% (sixty-three cases) in 2008. The decline has accelerated further since the introduction of the lay judge system in 2009, with life sentences falling to 0.04% of all charged cases in 2014, or only twenty-three cases in absolute terms. As with death sentences, the frequency and number of life sentences have declined nearly to the historical low point of the early 1990s.

The decline in the number and frequency of both death sentences and life sentences from 2009 suggests that contrary to the impression of some that the introduction of the lay judge system has led to more severe sentencing (e.g. Yonekura 2012; Takeda 2014), the new

---

[9] In an important study, Koike (2016) points to a February 2015 Supreme Court ruling that set relatively strict standards for *saiban-in* trials to hand out death sentences. He notes that while the higher courts in Japan have been relatively eager to allow *saiban-in* rulings to stand, even if they deviate considerably from sentencing trends by professional judges, the higher courts have begun to make an exception for death sentences and to limit the conditions under which death sentences by *saiban-in* trials would be upheld by the higher courts. It remains to be seen whether this ruling will have the effect of further discouraging district courts from delivering death sentences.

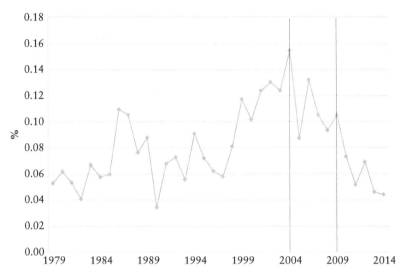

Figure 9.6 Percentage of life sentences among all cases charged, 1979–2014, district court level
Source: Saiko Saibansho Jimu Sokyoku (various years [b]).

system has coincided with a marked decline in the heaviest sentences. Of course, this does not mean that the introduction of the lay judge system has necessarily *caused* the decline in death sentences and life sentences. As noted earlier, the trend appears to have begun in the mid-2000s, before the new system was launched. However, it is possible that the decline in death sentences and life sentences after 2004 already reflected prosecutors' and judges' anticipation of the effects of the new system, since reform was passed in that year. It is also possible that the introduction of the system provided prosecutors and judges with a convenient excuse to cut back on what they perhaps had been beginning to see as excessively severe sentences. The bottom line is that the adoption of the new system appears to have played at least some part in reversing the trend of the late 1990s and early 2000s toward imposing more severe sentences.

If the percentage of death and life sentences has declined, has the frequency of long-term sentences risen? Since the heaviest sentences of death and life have declined, it is possible that more defendants are receiving fifteen- to thirty-year sentences instead. Indeed, a revision of

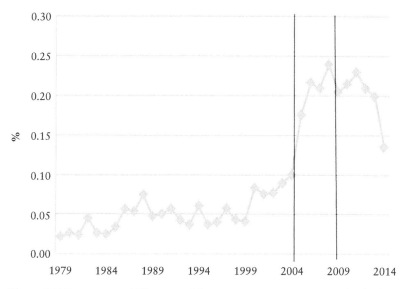

Figure 9.7 Percentage of fifteen- to thirty-year sentences among individuals found guilty who were sentenced to jail or prison terms, district court level, 1979–2014
Until 2004, the maximum sentence short of a life sentence was twenty years; since 2004, up to thirty years may be given.
Source: Saiko Saibansho Jimu Sokyoku (various years [b]).

the Criminal Code in late 2004 made it possible to sentence defendants to up to thirty years in jail or prison, as opposed to the previous maximum non-life sentence of twenty years. To what extent has the introduction of the lay judge system led to more frequent sentences in the fifteen- to thirty-year range? Figure 9.7 shows the overall trends, without separating lay judge cases from non-lay judge cases.

Figure 9.7 shows that the most dramatic surge in the percentage of jail or prison sentences between fifteen and thirty years occurred between 2004 and 2008, just before the introduction of the *saiban-in* system. In fact, the most rapid rise occurred between 2004 and 2005 when the percentage of the longest jail or prison terms as a proportion of individuals who were sentenced to jail or prison almost doubled from 0.1% to 0.18%. This sharp jump was likely driven by the passage of the revised Criminal Code in late 2004 that allowed for longer jail or prison terms. Thus the surge in long-term sentences

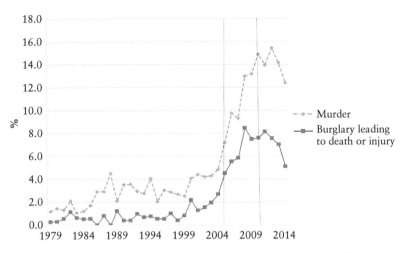

Figure 9.8 Percentage of defendants found guilty and sentenced to fifteen- to thirty-year sentences among those sentenced to jail or prison terms, crimes subject to lay judge trial, district court level, 1979–2014
Until 2004, the maximum sentence short of a life sentence was twenty years; since 2004, up to thirty years may be given.
Source: Saiko Saibansho Jimu Sokyoku (various years [b]).

between 2004 and 2008 should probably not be ascribed mostly to anticipation of the effects of the *saiban-in* system. Recall also that the frequency of life sentences declined precipitously between 2004 and 2005; conceivably, many of the defendants who might have received death or life terms under the old rules were now receiving fifteen- to thirty-year terms after 2004. The percentage of fifteen- to thirty-year sentences initially remained relatively stable after the introduction of the *saiban-in* system in 2009, but it fell abruptly in 2014 to 0.14%. It remains to be seen whether this decline represents a longer-term trend or a one-year anomaly.

Figure 9.7 summarized results for all crimes, irrespective of whether the *saiban-in* system applies to the crime. The next question is, is the overall pattern seen in Figure 9.7 also true of the specific crimes that are subject to lay judge trials? In order to probe this point, Figure 9.8 above shows the trends in longer-term sentences for two crimes that are subject to *saiban-in* trial: murder and burglary leading to death or injury.

Figure 9.8 shows that, as in Figure 9.7, a rapid surge in the percentage of longer-term sentences occurred between 2004 and 2008. Again, these were the first few years after the 2004 Criminal Code revision, when the longest non-life terms were extended to thirty years. For murder, the percentage of fifteen- to thirty-year terms rose rapidly after 2004 and continued to rise after the introduction of the *saiban-in* system. Defendants who were sentenced to fifteen- to thirty-year terms rose from 5.0% of all defendants found guilty of murder and sentenced to jail or prison terms in 2004, to 13.3% in 2008 to 15.8% in 2012 before falling somewhat during 2013 and 2014. For burglary leading to death or injury, the corresponding figures rose from 3.0% in 2004 to 8.8% in 2008, but then declined slightly after the launch of the new system in 2009. For both crimes, the percentage of longer sentences remain much higher compared to the pre-2004 period, despite moderating in the last few years.

Some observers have argued that the decline in death sentences and life sentences among murder and burglary leading to death cases has also impacted injury leading to death cases. They have argued that since the introduction of the *saiban*-in system, prosecutors have increasingly been charging cases as injury leading to death rather than as burglary leading to death or, especially, murder (e.g. Takeda 2014). The reason is that the burden of proof for intent is lighter for injury leading to death compared to murder. To what extent can we glean evidence for this claim from the existing data?

The sentencing trends for injury leading to death cases are shown in Figure 9.9. As noted earlier, the 1979–1998 figures draw on the *Annual Reports*, while the figures from 1999 onwards are from the *Hoso Jiho* (Saiko Saibansho Jimu Sokyoku Keijikyoku various years). Since the *Hoso Jiho* only presents the number of sentences per year for twenty- to thirty-year terms and ten- to twenty-year terms, the data shown in Figure 9.9 is for ten to thirty years rather than the fifteen- to thirty-year interval that was used in Figure 9.8. There is no death or life sentence for this category of crimes.

Figure 9.9 shows that between 1979 and 2003, the percentage of the heaviest sentences (between ten and thirty years) exceeded 1% of all jail or prison term sentences only in one year: 2001. But since 2004, the percentage of ten- to thirty-year sentences has never fallen below 1% and, since 2010, it has never dropped below 5%. From the post-2009 peak of 12.9% in 2011, the proportion of the heaviest ten- to

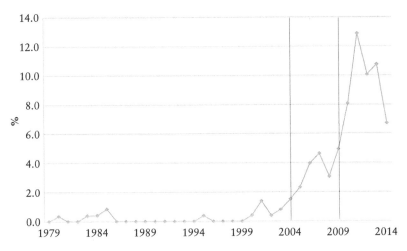

Figure 9.9 Percentage of those sentenced to more than ten years among those sentenced to jail or prison terms, injury leading to death, district court level, 1979–2014
Until 2004, the maximum sentence short of a life sentence was twenty years; since 2004, up to thirty years may be given. Also, until 2004, the minimum sentence was two years; since 2004, it has been three years.
Sources: Data between 1979 and 1989 are from Saiko Saibansho Jimu Sokyoku (various years [b]). Data between 1999 and 2014 are from Saiko Saibansho Jimu Sokyoku Keijikyoku (various years).

thirty-year sentences has fallen back to 6.7% in 2014, and it remains to be seen whether this decline will continue. Nevertheless, the 2014 figure remains much higher than the pre-2004, and even pre-2009, levels. Thus, while much more evidence is necessary, the data is consistent with the claim that many cases that could have been charged in the category of murder prior to the introduction of the *saiban-in* system are now increasingly being charged as injury leading to death. If so, this is indicative of a major impact of the new lay judge system on prosecutors' decisions.

Observers have also noted the increasing frequency of suspended sentences since the introduction of the *saiban-in* system. As Takamori (2015) points out, the surge in the longest-term sentences among injury leading to death cases has also coincided with a rapid rise in jail or prison terms with suspended sentences. Between 1979 and

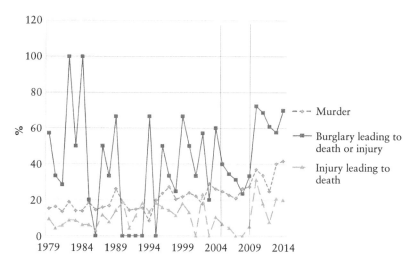

Figure 9.10 Percentage of suspended sentences with probation among
suspended sentences, murder, burglary leading to death or injury, and injury
leading to death cases, district court level, 1979–2014
Sources: Data for murder and burglary leading to death or injury are from
Saiko Saibansho Jimu Sokyoku (various years [b]). For injury leading to
death, data for 1979–98 are from Saiko Saibansho Jimu Sokyoku (various
years [b]); data for 1999–2014 are from Saiko Saibansho Jimu Sokyoku
Keijikyoku (various years).

2009, the percentage of suspended sentences among those sentenced
to jail or prison terms had surpassed 10% in only one year: 1993.
Since 2010, the percentage of suspended sentences has exceeded 10%
in four out of five years, peaking at 23% in 2010. Although more
data is necessary, the initial trends seem to suggest that the rise in
the longest term sentences does not represent a simple trend toward
harsher sentences but a rise in both the least severe and most severe
sentences.

Another issue has to do with probation. Figure 9.10 above shows the
trends in suspended sentences with probation for murder, burglary leading to death or injury, and injury leading to death, all of which are subject
to *saiban-in* trials. Under the Japanese probationary system, community
volunteers who have been trained by the state meet on a regular basis
with individuals who have been sentenced to suspended sentences with
probation and offer advice on finding employment, housing, and other

issues that would help to rehabilitate the individual. Figure 9.10 shows that for murder, the percentage of suspended sentences with probation has indeed increased markedly since the introduction of new system, and it has in fact reached the highest levels in the entire period. For burglary leading to death or injury, the rate of probationary suspended sentences has leapt up to levels not seen since the 1990s. For injury leading to death as well, in 2010, the percentage of probationary suspended sentences jumped to 31.3%, the highest level in the thirty-five year period. Aside from 2012, the post-2010 figures have generally hovered around 20%, which are the highest levels recorded during the period, with the possible exception of the early 1990s. Note that the figures for burglary leading to death or injury fluctuate more because the number of cases for which suspended sentences are given for this category of crimes is much smaller, generally fewer than ten cases a year.

Shiroshita (2011) has speculated that this increase in suspended sentences with probation may be attributed to the fact that *saiban-in* are more interested than professional judges in the rehabilitation of defendants. This idea fits with the general impression that lay judges tend to be more lenient than professional judges. It should be noted, however, that the *saiban-in* system is not the only factor driving the increase in probationary sentences. Reform of the Offenders Rehabilitation Law in the mid-2000s made it easier for judges to hand out probationary suspended sentences, and the proportion of such sentences began to rise in 2009, just as the *saiban-in* system was being introduced.[10]

One way to assess the effect of *saiban-in* trials on the rise in probationary suspended sentences is to compare the percentage of such sentences for crimes that are subject to *saiban-in* trials against those that are not. Figure 9.11 shows the results for non-*saiban-in* trials, i.e. trials that involve professional judges only.

Figure 9.11 shows a mixed picture regarding the sentencing tendencies of professional judges acting on their own. According to Figure 9.11, suspended sentences with probation appear to be on the rise among theft and extortion cases. There appears to be no change, or perhaps even a decline, in the frequency of probations for fraud and unintended injury. In sum, the data on these other categories of crime suggests that the increase in probations among murder and burglary leading to death cases cannot be attributed solely to the introduction of the *saiban-in* system.

---

[10] I thank Takayuki Shimaya for pointing this out.

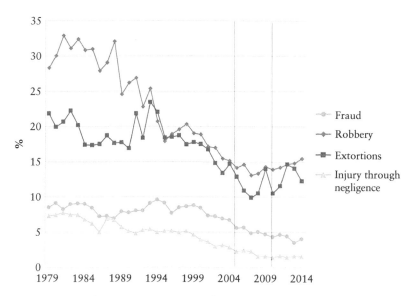

Figure 9.11 Probations as percentage of suspended sentences, crimes not subject to lay judge trials, district court level, 1979–2014
Source: Saiko Saibansho Jimu Sokyoku (various years [b]).

Changes in Procedure

How, and to what extent, has the introduction of the *saiban-in* system changed government practices in criminal procedures more broadly? The increased transparency of the criminal procedures as a result of the introduction of the *saiban-in* system may make the judiciary and prosecution more cautious in its practices. This section examines whether, and to what extent, the new system has impacted three aspects of criminal procedures: the bringing of charges, detaining of defendants, and releasing of defendants. Each will be examined in turn.

Johnson (2002) argued that Japanese prosecutors enjoy broader discretion than American prosecutors in choosing which cases to charge. How has the exercise of this discretion changed since the new system came into effect? This analysis is particularly important because it can also affect how we interpret the data on verdicts and sentencing that were presented previously. Have prosecutors filed a greater or smaller proportion of charges against individuals since the introduction of the *saiban-in* system? If so, then the new system may be having

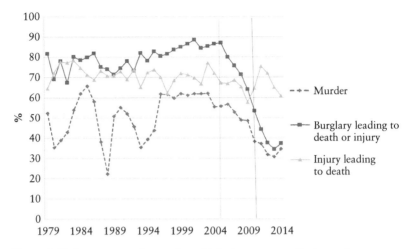

Figure 9.12 Percentage of cases for which charges were filed, murder, burglary leading to death or injury, and injury leading to death, 1979–2014
Source: Homusho (various years).

an even bigger impact than the verdict and sentencing data suggest. Figure 9.12 above shows the percentage of cases charged by prosecutors among those that were booked by the police between 1979–2014 for the three major crimes for which *saiban-in* trials are held: murder, burglary leading to death or injury, and injury leading to death. This data is available from the *Annual Report of Statistics on Prosecution* (Homusho various years). Figure 9.13 then shows the figures for the main categories of crimes that are not subject to *saiban-in* trial: theft, burglary, fraud, and injury through negligence. Unlike the *Annual Report of Judicial Statistics*, the burglary figures in the *Annual Report of Statistics on Prosecution* do not include those types of burglary cases that are subject to lay judge trial, so it is possible to use them in this analysis.

Figure 9.12 shows that since the introduction of the *saiban-in* system, the percentage of charges brought by prosecutors has declined markedly for murder and for burglary leading to death or injury. 48.9% of murder arrests by the police were charged by prosecutors in 2008, just before the introduction of the new system. By 2010, the figure had fallen to 38.3%, and in 2013, it was just 30.7%. Similarly, 71.4% of burglaries leading to death or injury arrests were charged by prosecutors in 2008, but only 53.5% in 2010 and 34.4% in 2013. Thus, there is evidence that crimes subject to *saiban-in* trials have been charged much less frequently since the introduction of the system. On the other hand, injury leading to death, shown in Figure 9.12, does not exhibit a significant decline in the percentage of cases being charged.

This data makes it seem at least plausible that prosecutors are holding back from filing charges due to their knowledge of the greater difficulty of winning a conviction in *saiban-in* trials. Here again, though, the decline in the percentage of cases being charged as a percentage of those that were booked by the police has probably not been driven solely by the introduction of the new lay judge system. The percentage of charges brought for these cases had been declining even before the introduction of the *saiban-in* system in 2009, though it is possible that the decline since 2004 reflected prosecutors' anticipation of the effects of the new system. Even though the trends were already downward, the introduction of the new system has reinforced and accelerated them.[11]

These figures on the frequency of charges also make the higher acquittal rates and more lenient sentencing among murder cases shown earlier all the more remarkable. Acquittal rates have increased and sentencing has generally become less harsh, despite the fact that a smaller percentage of cases booked by police are being charged as murder by prosecutors.

The contrast with crimes that are not subject to lay judge trial is also revealing. Figure 9.13 shows that for theft, the percentage of cases charged was 42.4% in 2008 and 42.8% in 2010. In 2013, the figure was still 41.3%. Similarly, for unintended injury, the corresponding figures were 9.8%, 9.5%, and 9.5%. Changes for fraud have also been flat since 2009, and charges for burglary are actually up. Thus, the drop in the percentages seems much steeper for crimes that are subject to *saiban-in* trials than for those that are not. This is consistent with

---

[11] At least part of the reason for the decline in the percentage of cases charged may be the fact that *saiban-in* trials have been, somewhat surprisingly, more time-consuming than non-*saiban-in* trials (Saiko Saibansho Jimu Sokyoku [2012(c)]). Between 2006 and 2008, before the introduction of the *saiban-in* trials, an average case required 6.6 months to resolve; between 2009 and May 2012, the corresponding figure was 8.5 months (ibid). Almost 70% of this time is spent on pre-trial conference procedures.

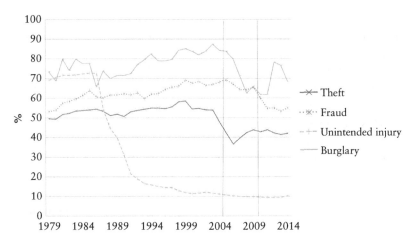

Figure 9.13 Percentage of cases for which charges were filed, 1979–2014, crimes not subject to lay judge trial
Source: Homusho (various years).

the impression that the new system has changed prosecutors' behavior in a pro-defendant direction.

Observers have also pointed to significant change in the practice of holding and releasing defendants since the *saiban-in* system was introduced (e.g. "Koryu Seikyu" 2015). After an individual has been arrested, Japanese prosecutors can request a warrant from the courts to detain the individual for up to ten days (renewable for another ten days).[12] Figure 9.14 shows the trends in the percentage of denied requests for detention warrants.

Figure 9.14 shows that the percentage of denied requests for warrants has risen markedly since the passage of the system in 2004. From a low of just 0.3% of denied requests in 2003, the figure rose to 1.1% in 2008, just before the introduction of the *saiban-in* system. The figures continued to rise thereafter and reached 2.7% in 2014, by far the highest levels seen in the past thirty-five years. Although the specific impact of the *saiban-in* system on this trend is hard to judge, the data is certainly consistent with the view that it has had an effect, including

---

[12] Some have criticized this system, which allows police and prosecutors to question arrested individuals intensively, as leading to false confessions and wrongful trials (e.g. Imamura 2008).

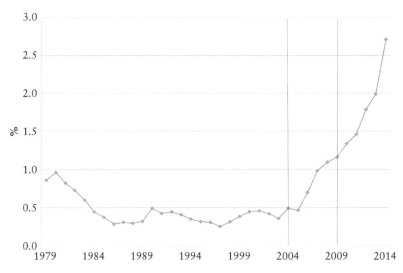

Figure 9.14 Request for warrants for detention denied, 1979–2014
Source: Saiko Saibansho Jimu Sokyoku (various years[b]).

by anticipation during the 2004–8 period. Note that the prosecution may be expected to learn from the rising rate of denied requests and become more careful. So over the longer run, this percentage may be expected to decline. But at least during the initial years after the system was launched, the courts appear to have become much more active in turning down requests.

Observers have also asserted that the introduction of the lay judge system could lead to a rise in the percentage of defendants who are released prior to the conclusion of the trial (e.g. *Asahi Shimbun* April 21, 2008). Under the new system, defendants are not permitted to present evidence that has not been agreed upon between the defense and the prosecution prior to the start of trial; thus, some experts argue that once the trial begins, defendants can be released without the risk that they would tamper with evidence (ibid). To what extent has the introduction of the *saiban-in* system affected trends in the release of defendants? Figure 9.15 is shown below.

As shown in Figure 9.15, between the late 1980s and early 2000s, the courts had become increasingly reluctant to release detained defendants before their final ruling. This began to change after the system

Figure 9.15 Percentage of detainees released before final judgment,
1979–2014
Source: Saiko Saibansho Jimu Sokyoku (various years[b]).

was passed in 2004; after hitting an all-time low of 11.5% in 2003,
the percentage of detained defendants released prior to their final ruling rose to 14.5% in 2008. It continued to rise steadily following the
introduction of the *saiban-in* system, to 23.9% in 2014, the highest
rate in a quarter-century. Again, the specific impact of the *saiban-in*
system on this trend is hard to judge, but the data is consistent with the
view that it has had an impact, in a pro-defendant direction.

Effects on Lay Judges
Thus far, this chapter has focused primarily on the *saiban-in* system's
impacts on court trial outcomes and criminal procedures. Another
important question to address is how the *saiban-in* system has affected
those who have served as lay judges. As seen in Chapter 2, an influential line of justification for jury trials is that they serve as a "school
for democracy" where citizens learn to deliberate with their fellow-
citizens and, in so doing, become more civic-minded. Indeed, this was
one of the reasons why Tocqueville gave high praise to the American
jury system (Tocqueville 1840/2000). To what extent has the *saiban-in*
system served this function in Japan?

Since the introduction of the system in 2009, the Supreme Court of Japan has conducted extensive surveys of individuals who served as *saiban-in*. According to the *Saiban-in* Report alluded to earlier in this chapter, over the first three years of the new system, 95.5% of former lay judges surveyed indicated that serving as a lay judge either was a "very good experience" or a "good experience" (Saiko Saibansho Jimu Sokyoku 2012[c]: 120). The figure has been largely consistent thereafter; for instance, the 2014 survey found that 95.9% responded that serving as a lay judge either was a "very good experience" or a "good experience" (Saiko Saibansho 2015). This is despite the fact that a majority of citizens had not initially looked forward to serving as a lay judge; over the first three years, 52.5% of those who served either "had very much not wanted to serve" or "had not wanted to serve" (Saiko Saibansho Jimu Sokyoku 2012[c]). These findings parallel those of studies of jurors in the United States, who also typically do not look forward to serving (Guinther 1998) but come out of the experience with a sense of satisfaction about what they learned (Diamond 1993).

The *Saiban-in* Report unfortunately did not include detailed survey questions on *why* the lay judges thought that their experiences were "good." It did, however, pose an open-ended question that asked respondents to elaborate on their reasons. Among the respondents who did respond to this open-ended question, 48.4% indicated that they had learned a great deal about the courts (calculated from Saiko Saibansho Jimu Sokyoku 2012[c]: 181). 10.5% indicated that serving as jurors had provided an opportunity for in-depth discussion with fellow citizens and to become exposed to views that they would not have otherwise encountered (ibid).

One former Japanese lay judge noted: "Normally I do not even watch the news or read the newspaper. But serving as a lay judge was a great experience because it has made me more interested in the real world . . . I would like my child to have an opportunity to serve, too" (ibid: 121). Another wrote, "[Serving as a juror] exposed me to a very different world to the one I had been accustomed to . . . The experience made me think a lot more about what I, as a member of society, could do to reduce crime" (ibid). Since these were responses to an open-ended question, which the overwhelming majority of respondents skipped (only 288 of 21,000 former *saiban-in* surveyed completed this open-ended section), it is not clear how representative they are.

One driver of the positive impressions of the lay judges about the new system seems to be the perception that the deliberations with professional judges were congenial. Despite the "mixed" jury design of the Japanese system in which lay judges deliberate alongside professional judges, which scholars suggest may cool lay judges' enthusiasm to participate, 76.7% of former *saiban-in* indicated that they did not feel uncomfortable speaking up (ibid: 122). 74.1% of respondents also replied that sufficient discussions had occurred before reaching a ruling (ibid: 126). Thus, far from a superficial change in institutions, the lay judge system in Japan indeed appears to be having real effects on those who participate in it, in line with Tocqueville's expectations.

Effects of the New Jury System in South Korea

As noted thus far in this book, the transfer of powers from professional judges to jurors/lay judges was most extensive in Spain, while it was more limited in Japan and most limited in South Korea. In Spain and Japan, cases that fall into a certain category of crime essentially must be tried by lay judge trial. Jurors in Spain deliberate and rule on verdict separately from professional judges, whereas they deliberate together in Japan. Professional judges in Korea, on the other hand, have the legal authority to rule on whether or not a trial should be judged by jury trial or bench trial. In addition, jurors' rulings do not constrain professional judges in Korea, while in Spain and Japan, the rulings of jurors/lay judges are binding. What has been the impact thus far of the more extensive transfer of powers in Japan and Spain compared to Korea in terms of verdict and sentencing?

There is some data on how sentencing patterns have changed in South Korea since the introduction of the new jury system in 2007. In South Korea, defendants must petition the courts for a jury trial, and so far, the professional judges have liberally exercised their right to reject defendants' petitions for a jury trial (recall that this discretion is severely limited for professional judges in Japan). Choi (2013a: 94) reports that during the first five years after the introduction of the new Korean system, only 38.2% of the defendants' petitions for their cases to be decided by a jury were accepted by the professional judges. According to Lee (2016: 123), a total of 1,464 cases were tried by jury trial in the first seven years of Korea's new system, or the equivalent of 209.1 cases per year. This is a much smaller number of cases compared to the roughly 1,000 to 1,500 cases that are tried by lay judges in Japan every year (Saiko Saibansho Jimu Sokyoku various years[a]), even taking into account South Korea's smaller population.

How, and to what extent, has the new jury system impacted verdict and sentencing patterns? Between January 2008 and October 2010, the conviction rate in jury trials in South Korea was 71.5%, as opposed to 77.7% in trials involving only professional judges (Kim et al. 2013; n = 323).[13] Although this difference suggests that jurors may be more lenient, the fact that the professional judges exercised a gatekeeping function means that it is hard to assess the extent of the jury's impact. There is stronger evidence for the idea of divergent tendencies of Korean professional judges and laypersons in the finding of Kim et al. (2013) that between January 2008 and October 2010, jurors and judges (who, recall, deliberate separately in the Korean system) reached the same verdict in 91.4% of cases. When the jurors and professional judges disagreed, the professional judges were typically more likely to declare the defendant guilty. More research is needed on the impact of the Korean reforms.

On sentencing, Lee (2016) reports that between 2008 and 2014, judges and jurors agreed in 89.3% of all cases. Judges' sentences were more than one year longer than juries' recommendations in 6.4% of all cases, whereas the jury's recommendations were harsher than the professional judges' sentence by more than one year in 4.4% of all cases.

The Korean case thus parallels the Japanese case in coinciding with more frequent acquittals and more lenient sentencing in the wake of the introduction of new jury/lay judge systems. Indeed, the Korean differences in verdicts and sentencing before and after the reform may superficially seem greater than the differences that were observed in the Japanese case. But it cannot necessarily be said that the effects of the Korean reform have been greater than the effects of the Japanese reforms. First, it should be stressed that because of the institutional differences in the categories of crimes that are subject to jury/lay judge trial in Japan and South Korea, it is difficult to directly compare changes in verdict and sentencing patterns in the two countries since the introduction of their respective systems. Another issue is that other

---

[13] This finding parallels that of Eisenberg et al. (2005), which also finds that judges have a lower conviction threshold than jurors. In contrast, Bliesener (2006) reports that in Germany, lay judges often favor harsher sentences than professional judges.

contemporaneous factors may have been responsible for the changes in Korea, as this chapter extensively examined for the case of Japan. Moreover, there is a potential problem of endogeneity in the South Korean case, in that professional judges may be more likely to agree to include jurors in the process when they believe the prosecution's case is weaker. Some of these questions could be answered with more systematic comparative assessment of crimes that were subject to jury trial versus those that were not, in the Korean case.

Effects of the New Jury System in Spain

Spain transferred extensive powers from professional judges to jurors when it instituted its *Ley del Jurado* in 1995. The law offers a long list of crimes for which a jury must be empaneled, and the judge must accept the jury's decision. Spain has in fact held a larger number of jury trials compared to Japan or South Korea, although the number has been steadily declining. As noted in Chapter 8, the number of jury trials in Spanish *juzgados de instrucción* (magistrates' courts), *juzgados de primera instancia e instrucción* (courts of first instance), and since 2005, the new *juzgados de violencia contra la mujer* (violence against women courts) has decreased steadily from a high of 785 in 1998, which was soon after the jury system began, to only 364 in 2014 (this and all further data from Consejo General del Poder Judicial 2015). The decrease in the number of jury trials is even more impressive if one considers the increase in Spain's population over that period. By that measure, 1998 was the high point with 1.97 jury trials per 100,000 inhabitants; by 2014 it was down to 0.78 jury trials per 100,000 inhabitants. Juries have also been empaneled for cases at *audiencias provinciales* ("provincial courts," which serve as courts of second instance), and the number of jury trials has also fallen at this level, albeit less rapidly. In 1998 there were 404 jury trials; the number of jury trials then peaked at 448 in 2002; it then hit a low of 308 in 2008; and by 2014 it had recovered to 346. Despite the decline in the number of jury trials, when all of these figures are combined there were just over 700 cases a year in 2014, which means that Spain still has more jury trials each year on a per-population basis than Japan.

In addition to the reasons offered by Jimeno-Bulnes (2011) that were discussed in Chapter 8, a report by the Spanish newspaper *El País* suggests that the decline in the number of jury trials has been engineered by Spanish professional prosecutors and judges who are exploiting a loophole in the jury law (Crespo 2015). The law does not specifically state what should happen in the event that a criminal suspect is accused of multiple crimes, some of which require jury trial and others of which do not. The professionals have decided that in this situation, they can do without the jury. Some prosecutors may even be choosing to add a lesser charge simply to avoid having to deal with a jury. This is an interesting example of how a strong reform on paper can be weakened in its implementation.

How, and to what extent, has the new Spanish jury system impacted verdict and sentencing patterns? The available data does not allow a clear answer to this question. Since 1998, the number of guilty verdicts by juries has hovered around 90%. The high was 91.6% in 2002; the low was 86.0% in 2008; in 2014, the number stood at 90.4%. Conviction rates for these categories of crimes prior to the launch of the jury law are not available. However, conviction rates since the jury law was enacted for other, lesser crimes that do not require a jury trial are available. The overall conviction rate for jury trials since 1996 has been 89.2%; meanwhile, for *procedimientos sumarios* (summary proceedings) it has been 84.7% and for *procedimientos abreviados* (abbreviated proceedings) it has been 80%. These are useful figures, but without data that allows for comparison to the prior period, it is difficult to assess whether the Spanish reform has had the same pro-defendant effects as in the cases of Japan and Korea.

Impressionistically it would appear that the reform has generally had a pro-defendant impact. Juries have acquitted defendants in several high profile cases, which has led conservative politicians to try to undo the reform. Moreover, the *El País* article cited above notes that Joaquim Bosch, the head of the left wing judges' group called *Jueces por la Democracia* (Judges for Democracy), remains strongly in favor of the new system and hopes that the abovementioned loophole will be closed to allow more cases to be tried by juries.

It is also notable that the Spanish law permits appeals to higher courts (*tribunales superiores de justicia*) of sentences delivered by magistrates in jury trials, but not of the jury's verdicts in those trials (Gómez 2009). (It is possible to appeal against magistrate's actions that may have affected the jury's verdict.) The number of appeals of sentences has fluctuated, from 120 in 1999 to 178 in 2003, back down to 121 in 2009, and again up to 171 in 2012, until settling back down to 166 in 2014. The percentage of successful appeals, however, has risen over the years, from a low of 22.5% in 2004 to a high of 33.6% in 2014.

Unfortunately, it is not clear how many of these decisions on appeal resulted in longer or shorter sentences than those that were initially imposed; in Spain, both prosecutors and defendants can appeal to a higher court. There have also been appeals of jury trial outcomes to the Supreme Court, typically about seventy to a hundred each year since 2000. For the years 2012–14, the Supreme Court either partially or fully revoked 23.4% of lower court decisions, although in most cases this did not mean changing the lower court's sentence.

More research is needed on the impact of the Spanish reforms.

Conclusions

This chapter has shown that the introduction of the new *saiban-in* system has had considerable effects on the procedure and substance of criminal justice in Japan. Regarding verdicts, there has been a rise in the percentage of acquittals. On sentencing, contrary to what some have argued, the launch of the new system has not produced generally stiffer sentences. In fact, there has been a general decline in the rate of death sentences and life sentences, although it should be reiterated that this chapter did not examine rape-related cases, which scholars have often pointed to as seeing harsher sentencing. There has also been a rise in the percentage of suspended sentences with probation, although the evidence as to whether this trend has been driven by the introduction of the new system is mixed. Note that many of these changes were already underway by the time that the new system was introduced, but the system appears to have reinforced and accelerated them to some extent; and in part the prior trends may have been the result of judges and prosecutors anticipating the effects of the new system. The new system's effects were also clearly in line with the wishes of some of the new left-oriented politicians and lawyers who pushed most strongly for the system to be introduced, although perhaps the effects have not been as extensive as they had hoped.

On criminal procedures, the effects have been more dramatic. The *saiban-in* system has seemingly led to a large drop in the percentage of cases charged among cases booked by the police, a rise in the percentage of denied requests for detentions, and a rise in the percentage of detainees released before final ruling. Thus, the system appears to have caused Japanese prosecutors to select more carefully which cases to charge. One might say that the rights of defendants appear to have been strengthened. Here again, changes were already underway prior to the launch of the new system, but the new system has certainly not reversed those changes and appears to have reinforced them.

On several occasions, this chapter has noted that many of the changes that occurred after the introduction of the *saiban-in* system were already underway prior to the introduction of the system. It has pointed to a number of factors that conceivably may have led to changes in Japanese court behavior before the lay judge system was launched. For instance, changes in the maximum non-life prison or jail terms, as well as reforms of the Offenders' Rehabilitation Law, are likely to have impacted court behavior. Nevertheless, another potentially important factor driving changes in court behavior in the years before the launch of the new system may have been the anticipation of the new system itself. As noted at the outset of this chapter, the Japanese courts held more than 630 mock *saiban-in* trials across the country in cooperation with the Ministry of Justice and the Japan Federation of Bar Associations between 2004, when the *saiban-in* system was passed, and 2009, when the system came into effect (Moriya 2015: 14). Thus, the courts had a reasonably good sense of how the lay judges were likely to rule, even before the system formally came into effect. Indeed, in conjunction with several leading legal scholars, the Japanese Supreme Court conducted a detailed study on the findings yielded from the mock trials (Saiko Saibansho Jimu Sokyoku Keijikyoku 2009). It is possible that professional judges were able to adjust their behavior in anticipation of the formal launch of the system in 2009. A more systematic assessment of the relative impact of these factors is beyond the scope of this book but presents an important avenue for future inquiry.

Finally, the Japanese data show that lay judges have found the experience to be a positive one that enriched their understanding of the justice system. This civic engagement effect was another goal of many new left-oriented politicians and lawyers who pushed most forcefully for the system to be introduced.

In Korea as well, there is initial evidence to suggest that the new jury system, when professional judges allow it to operate, has led to more lenient verdicts. But more research is necessary on the actual extent of the effects in Korea, and even more so Spain, as well as the relative effects of the Japanese, Korean, and Spanish reforms.

10 | Conclusions

Most established democracies have jury or lay judge systems with histories that go back for centuries, and in such countries, the institution is often taken for granted. Upon closer inspection, however, it is a truly extraordinary institution within the democratic polity. Serving as a juror or lay judge presents the average citizen with a rare opportunity to directly engage in state decision-making. This aspect of the jury/lay judge system sets it apart from most other avenues for participation, such as voting or signing petitions. Jury/lay judge systems also represent one of the few formal institutions for collective citizen deliberation that theorists of deliberative democracy such as Jürgen Habermas, Jane Mansbridge, and James Fishkin have so celebrated. This deliberative function sets the jury/lay judge system apart from other channels for direct decision-making, such as the referendum or ballot initiative. Yet despite their significance, jury/lay judge systems have not received systematic comparative treatment within the field of political science, let alone an examination of why different countries design their jury/lay judge systems in markedly different ways. This book has thus begun to fill a major gap in the scholarly literature.

This topic of jury/lay judge systems is all the more important because since the early 1990s, several developed democracies, notably Japan, South Korea, and Spain, have launched new jury/lay judge systems. In addition, Taiwan has been engaged in serious discussions toward the introduction of a new system. Not only did these countries create new jury/lay judge systems, but they also designed them to empower citizens and undermine the power of professional judges to markedly different degrees. For instance, the rulings of jurors/lay judges are binding on professional judges in Japan and Spain, but they are not binding in South Korea or the proposed system in Taiwan.

What factors account for the differences in the extent to which the four countries have empowered juries/lay judges? Why did these different states choose to cede powers from professionals to the citizenry to varying extents? This book has drawn on both mixed-method analysis of the Japanese case and comparative case studies of Taiwan, Spain, and South Korea to probe these issues. The book has reported the results of quantitative content analyses of over fifty years of legislative debates over the jury/lay judge system in the Japanese parliament, and qualitative process-tracing of the precise mechanisms that shaped the design of the new Japanese lay judge system. The book has also presented the results of in-depth original field research on the case of Taiwan, which as of late 2016 has not yet introduced a new jury/lay judge system despite considerable support for the idea across the political spectrum. Finally, the book has also presented shorter case studies of Spain and South Korea. Note also that although this book has focused on the variations in new jury/lay judge systems among developed democracies that have recently adopted such systems, future studies should examine the variations in institutional design among states that have recently adopted such systems in the developing world as well.

The basic theoretical contention of this book has been that the degree to which power is transferred from professional judges to lay judges/ jurors depends on the strength of new left-oriented political parties at the time that the judicial reform issue emerges onto the political agenda. This book has put forth a two-step framework that accounts for the configuration of new jury/lay judge systems in developed democracies. First, regarding the *preferences* for a weaker or stronger reform, parties that adopt new left issues to a greater extent are more likely to favor jury/lay judge systems that transfer more powers from professional judges to jury/lay judges. As Herbert Kitschelt has noted, these new left-oriented parties have come to emphasize not only the achievement of substantive policy outcomes, but also the "quality of the process" through which those outcomes come about. The jury/lay judge system is just the kind of procedural innovation that new left-oriented parties tend to embrace. Second, the extent to which new left-oriented parties' preferences may materialize in the form of real legislation depends crucially on the relative power of those parties within the overall political system.

Japan presented a particularly crucial case for this study because it had the longest history of democracy among the four countries at the time that the reform emerged onto the policy agenda, and thus also had the most entrenched professional judicial bureaucracy, yet it introduced a lay judge system that transferred considerable powers to the lay judges. The case study of Japan showed that new left-oriented parties in Japan were more likely than other parties to push for a greater transfer of power from professional judges to jurors/lay judges. The case study of Japan also found that the impact of new left-oriented parties over the actual design of new jury/lay judge systems was contingent upon these parties' broader political power positions vis-à-vis other parties around the time that the issue was under debate.

For the Taiwanese case, the book showed that in the early 2010s the ruling conservative Kuomintang (KMT) proposed a system in which the rulings of lay judges would merely be advisory, in effect allowing the professional judges to preserve much of their powers. By contrast, the more new left-oriented Democratic Progressive Party (DPP) favored a much more extensive transfer of power away from the professional judges. The DPP's political influence was limited by its lack of control of either the executive or legislative branch at the time when the issue emerged onto the political agenda, however. In the end, the KMT administration of President Ma was unable to push through even its modest reform due to the divergent interests of KMT legislators.

For the case of Spain, the book showed that the ruling Socialist Party, which was new left-oriented, successfully pushed through a system in 1995 that transferred extensive powers away from professional judges to jurors. The Socialists were supported in this initiative by other new left-oriented parties and also regionalist parties. The conservative Partido Popular, however, did not favor such a robust reform.

In South Korea, the new left-oriented President Roh was in office during the mid-2000s, but his party was less consistently new left-oriented than its counterparts in Japan, Spain, or Taiwan. Moreover, the conservative opposition held a majority in the legislature for much of his term. This constellation of factors led to a jury system in which the rulings of jurors were nonbinding, only transferring very limited powers from professional judges to the jurors.

The book's findings shed new light on the issue of judicial independence, which has become more salient in political science and policy debates in recent decades. Scholars have pointed to various reforms that have made judges more independent from *politicians* in a wide variety of countries. But new jury/lay judge systems undermine the independence of judges vis-à-vis the *public*. Future studies should assess the *combined* effect of both of these global changes – i.e. the strengthening of judicial independence from politics and the weakening of judicial independence from public opinion – on judges' professional autonomy in different countries.

One point that can already be made about these two faces of judicial independence is that they do not appear to be highly correlated. Neither existing theories of judicial independence nor the fact of judicial independence itself can account for the extent to which states transfer powers from professional judges to jurors/lay judges. For instance, proponents of "political insurance theory" have claimed that ruling parties facing electoral defeat will seek to reinforce judicial independence from politicians. Conceivably, a similar motivation could have led them to be wary of undermining judicial independence vis-à-vis the public. But in Spain, a very vulnerable Socialist Party chose to enact a strong jury system that even had jurisdiction over cases of official corruption. In addition, existing studies generally rank judicial independence from politics to be higher in Japan and lower in the other cases, but there is little correlation between countries' scores on this measure and the extent to which states transferred powers away from professional judges.

The present book has focused on the political factors that have shaped the design of *new* jury/lay judge systems, specifically on how the strength of new left-oriented parties impacts the extent to which powers are transferred from professional judges to jurors/lay judges. But a similar framework may also be useful for explaining reforms of existing jury/lay judge systems. For instance, the Spanish case showed that even after a new jury system had been introduced, the conservative PP was tempted on several occasions to roll back the jury system, while new left-oriented and regionalist parties tried to defend the 1995 reforms.

Reforms of existing jury/lay judge systems have occurred even in several developed democracies with well-established traditions of lay participation over the last few decades, including England and France. Whether, and to what extent, the framework advanced in the present book may also account for reforms of longstanding existing jury systems is an important question for further research. Are new left-oriented parties more likely to favor reforms of existing jury/lay judge systems that transfer more powers away from professional judges to jurors/lay judges? Conversely, are parties that are less new left-oriented more likely to promote reforms that enhance the autonomy of professional judges? These and many more questions about the reform of judicial procedures in established jury/lay judge systems should be closely investigated in future studies.

The theory presented in this book may also help to illuminate why some developed democracies that still lack jury/lay judge systems continue to see little partisan momentum for introducing such systems. As shown in the empirical chapters of the book, new left-oriented parties are more likely to push for jury/lay judge systems that undermine the powers of professional judges to a greater extent. This is in part due to their new left ideology of "government of participation," but also in part due to their identity as insurgents against the professional establishment. The insurgent, anti-professional character of new left-oriented parties is particularly intense in post-developmental states. But it might be that if a leftist party had succeeded in staying in power for a relatively long stretch of time in earlier decades, it could have developed a close relationship with the judiciary, in turn defusing its enthusiasm for pushing for measures that would undermine the power of professional judges, even as it adopted new left positions on other issues, such as the environment. A case in point may be the Netherlands, which conspicuously lacks a jury/lay judge system, and whose center-left party was in power for long stretches in the postwar era, although further study is necessary.

Broader Implications

The findings from this book yield at least three broader implications for the study of comparative politics. Each will be addressed in turn below.

The Political Impact of the New Left Cleavage

First, the book follows earlier work on democratization by O'Donnell and Schmitter (1986) and Luebbert (1991), among others, which suggests that decisions to invite the broader public to participate in public affairs materialize as a result of bargaining among political elites. While the general public may at times help to propel the issue of expanding participation onto the policymaking agenda, its power to determine the specific extent and form of public participation is limited. As shown in Chapter 1, countries that exhibited higher levels of public distrust vis-à-vis professional judges did not necessarily introduce lay judge systems that undermined the powers of professional judges to a greater degree.

More consequential for the design of new jury/lay judge systems is the level of distrust that particular *political parties* may exhibit toward professional judges, and the relative power of those parties within the overall party system. This finding accords with studies of democratization, which have often found that the traditional left historically favored the expansion of the suffrage, while the right opposed it (Rueschemeyer et al. 1992; Tilly 1997; Przeworski 2009). Meanwhile, the right in many Anglo-Saxon countries often favored mass conscription during World War I, while the traditional left typically sought to resist it (Adams and Poirier 1987; Levi 1996). More broadly, the book's argument echoes the point advanced recently by scholars of democratization that partisan dynamics crucially shaped the trajectory of democratization in nineteenth-century Europe (Capoccia and Ziblatt 2010; Ertman 2010).

But the classic left-right split over economic issues is no longer the only partisan cleavage that is relevant for shaping policy outcomes. Rather, the book has demonstrated the real political impact of the new left policy dimension. In his groundbreaking work, Herbert Kitschelt (1994) showed that many formerly "old" left political parties in developed democracies have increasingly transformed themselves into champions of new left and postmaterialist issues in recent decades. Scholars have subsequently confirmed that this "transformation" of leftist parties has had real policy impact. For instance, many studies show that industrialized countries with stronger new left-oriented parties in fact tend to adopt more extensive environmental policies (e.g. Neumayer 2003; Agnone 2007; Knill et al. 2010).

Expansion of the suffrage and opposition to the draft were among the core political agendas for the nascent new left, both in the United States and other developed democracies during the Vietnam War era (Foley 2003; Symons and Cahill 2005). As noted in the opening chapter, introducing a new jury/lay judge system has similarities *both* to the expansion of the suffrage and the introduction of mass conscription. While jury/lay judge systems give citizens a greater voice in the judicial decision-making process, participation in this process is an obligation, not a right. While the new left had opposed conscription during its earlier years, it has eagerly embraced the introduction of a strong jury/lay judge systems as another form of civic obligation.

A large proportion of the studies that examine the policy impact of new left-oriented parties have focused on substantive issue-areas such as environmental policy, but the new left is interested not only in the substance of policy but also in the quality of the decision-making process. Few studies have systematically assessed the impact of the new left on the state decision-making process itself.[1] This book has shown that the relative strength of the new left accounts for the cross-national variations in the configuration of new jury/lay judge systems.

This book thus represents some first steps toward systematically testing how new left-oriented parties impact not only the substance of state policy, but also the institutions of state decision-making. The study indeed confirms that cross-national differences in the relative power of new left-oriented parties within the overall party system account for variations in the extent to which ordinary people gained power over the shaping of criminal trial outcomes.

In addition, the case studies in this book also suggest that the new left versus right *cleavage* may often be more important in shaping parties' preferences vis-à-vis jury/lay judge systems than differences in the degree of new left-orientation among new left-oriented parties. To take an example, the Democratic Party of Japan (DPJ) in Japan was rated by both expert surveys and the Comparative Manifesto Project as being less new left-oriented than the JSP, but the DPJ and SPD adopted very similar judicial policy positions in comparison with the positions of the conservative Liberal Democratic Party (LDP). By contrast, Taiwan's KMT enjoyed a monopoly of power and therefore did not have to compromise with new left-oriented parties as the LDP did, even though the KMT's own legislators ended up failing to enact President Ma's modest reform. This is a point that deserves further inquiry.

---

[1] Some works that also hint at this include Dalton et al. (2003), Andersen and Bjørkland (1990), and Müller (1990). There also exists a sizable body of work that has examined how the new left-orientation of parties affects their positions on European integration, which typically find the more extreme new left-oriented parties to be more likely to oppose integration, and vice versa (e.g. Hooghe et al. 2002; Marks et al. 2006). European integration is an important issue for parties that are concerned with the quality of policy-making process, since it removes policy-making authority from the national level, in effect disenfranchising national publics. But these studies have focused on parties' preferences toward policy, rather than on their capacity to bring about policy change *per se*.

Experts and Policymaking

Second, the findings from this book suggest that despite the highly technical nature of the judicial field, major policy changes in this issue area are still largely driven by partisan dynamics rather than legal professionals. For instance, many of the legislators of the Committee on Judicial Affairs in the Japanese parliament also had legal backgrounds, but they rarely took positions that were out of step with their parties' ideological positions. Thus, political affiliation was more important than professional background in shaping their positions on supposedly technical issues. Moreover, although the technical details of the reform may be hammered out by "non-partisan" experts, politicians play a key role in shaping the broader direction of reform. For instance, Chapter 5 showed that politicians in Japan played a key gatekeeping function in deciding *which* experts would be invited into the policymaking process.

The assessment of the role of experts in the policymaking process presented in this book thus stands in contrast to the implication left by some of the "epistemic community" literature. According to Haas (1992: 3), an "epistemic community" is a highly cohesive group of experts that is characterized by "shared principled and normative beliefs," "shared causal beliefs," "shared notions of validity," and "a common policy enterprise." But in all four countries examined in this book, legal experts in the judicial policymaking process hardly comprised such a cohesive "community." In all four countries, judges typically were the most reluctant to introduce a system of public participation in criminal trials and sought to preserve their own powers as much as possible. Many private attorneys, by contrast, were eager to undermine the powers of professional judges, although to varying degrees in different countries. Other legal experts were all over the map. Moreover, as noted above, although the politicians who were involved in the judicial policymaking process often had legal training, they split largely along party lines. Politicians with legal expertise who belonged to new left-oriented parties tended to favor a greater transfer of power from professional judges to jurors/lay judges, while those who belonged to conservative or old left-oriented parties typically favored a more modest transfer of power.

The cases presented in this volume also highlight the fact that some experts may even be eager to open decision-making channels to nonexperts. The typical view of experts is that they jealously guard their policymaking jurisdictions and that they are reluctant to cede powers to the ignorant public (Fischer 2000). This was certainly true of most professional judges in the four countries, who consistently sought a system that would enable them to retain more of their powers. But in all four countries, many politicians with legal expertise as well as many private attorneys and even some judges eagerly pushed for the nonexpert general public to play a greater role in criminal rulings. The cases support Okayama (2012)'s point that the dichotomy that is often drawn between experts and nonexperts may at times be exaggerated. Different philosophies, standpoints, and even rivalries within the expert community can push some experts to promote a transfer of decision-making powers to nonexperts, while others prefer to leave those powers to legal experts alone.

This insight into the greater relative importance of partisan dynamics and ideology over professional expertise also highlights the possibility that politicians may at times enact particular institutional designs on the basis of wrong assumptions about their likely effects. For instance, the LDP advocated a system with fewer numbers of lay judges due to the belief that this would help to preserve the power of professional judges, despite the fact that the scholarly literature typically finds the contrary to be true. The opposition parties wanted more lay judges, based on the same mistaken assumption.

The realm of judicial politics may be more similar to the sphere of economic policy-making than is typically recognized. As in the area of economic policy, there are deep rifts among experts on the desirable course of action in the field of judicial policy, rifts that typically reflect more fundamental ideological differences. Moreover, the impact of these different camps of judicial experts is highly contingent on political and institutional factors, much as Hall (1989) found in his classic study of the power of economic ideas.

Implications for the Study of Japan and Other Post-Developmental States

Third, this book also yields broader implications for the subfield of Japanese politics as well as the politics of other post-developmental states more broadly. In the past, to study policymaking in Japan meant studying the LDP, its internal decision-making apparatus, and its relationship with the bureaucracy. Today, the LDP is still a major part of the policymaking process, but it is only a part. Scholars of Japanese politics have pointed to the growing impact of opposition parties and coalition dynamics in the policymaking process since the late 1990s (e.g. Kamikawa 2010; Tsuji 2012). Divided legislatures and coalition politics have become a frequent feature of Japanese policymaking in the last two decades. Scholars of Japanese politics have argued that this situation has allowed coalition partners, such as the Komeito and opposition parties, such as the DPJ, to exert considerable influence over policymaking in Japan, even when the LDP runs the Cabinet. Therefore, new left-oriented ideas have gained access to the policy-making process (Tsuji 2012). The present study reinforces these findings.

Scholars of Japanese politics have often bemoaned the weakness of "new politics" in Japan (e.g. Schreurs 2002). This book, however, shows that there is a new left partisan cleavage in Japan and that this cleavage is meaningful for parties' issue positions, even if it may not have top-tier salience for many voters. Indeed, as recent studies have stressed, the intensity of partisan divides is analytically distinct from their electoral salience (Helbling and Tresch 2011; Hoeglinger 2016). Expert surveys by Kato (2014) show that while policy distance between the LDP and the opposition parties in Japan on new left issues is often greater than for economic issues, new left issues are usually less salient for votes than economic issues. The present book shows, however, that partisan cleavages that are less salient electorally may nevertheless impact the substance of policy in important ways.

The findings from the book also highlight the point that countries such as Japan that adopt more restrictive policies toward civil society groups do not necessarily also limit the transfer of powers to jurors/lay judges. Pekkanen (2006) in particular has shown how Japan's restrictive policies toward civil society have impeded the growth of large advocacy groups. A recent study on the restrictiveness of regulations toward NGOs in different countries also finds Japan to have relatively restrictive policies, while Spain has relatively permissive policies, and South Korea's policies fall somewhere in between (Bloodgood et al. 2014). But among the cases under study in this book, there is little correlation between the restrictiveness of a country's policies vis-à-vis civil society and the extent to which that country empowered jurors/lay judges. Spain, with relatively permissive policies toward civil society, did also empower jurors to a substantial degree. But Japan empowered its lay judges more than South Korea. The book thus suggests that the factors that push the state to empower civil society groups to a greater extent may be different than those that lead it to transfer more powers to individual citizens.

All of the countries taken up in this book were historically known as "developmental states": states that prioritized the channeling of national resources toward the task of rapid industrialization, over citizen input and transparency. The book can be read as a partial answer to the question of what happens to developmental states once they have achieved development. The findings from this book show that states may dismantle their developmental state apparatus to varying degrees in different countries. Some countries may begin to allow considerable public input into decision-making processes, while others may preserve the power of state actors to a much greater extent. Partisan dynamics may play a crucial role in shaping the extent to which states dismantle their developmental state apparatuses. They certainly have played a crucial role in determining who judges.

References

Abramson, Jeffrey (1994), *We, the Jury: The Jury System and the Ideal of Democracy*. New York: Basic Books.

Adams, James, Michael Clark, Lawrence Ezrow, and Garrett Glasgow (2006), "Are Niche Parties Fundamentally Different than Mainstream Parties? The Causes and the Electoral Consequences of West European Parties' Policy Shifts, 1976–1998," *American Journal of Political Science*, vol. 50, no. 3: 513–29.

Adams, Ralph James Q., and Philip P. Poirier (1987), *Conscription Controversy in Great Britain, 1900–18*. Columbus, OH: Ohio State University Press.

Agnone, Jon (2007), "Amplifying Public Opinion: The Policy Impact of the US Environmental Movement," *Social Forces*, vol. 85, no. 4: 1593–620.

Amsden, Alice (1989), *Asia's Next Giant: South Korea and Late Industrialization*. New York: Oxford University Press.

Andersen, Jørgen Goul, and Tor Bjørklund (1990), "Structural Changes and New Cleavages: The Progress Parties in Denmark and Norway," *Acta Sociologica*, vol. 33, no. 3: 195–217.

Arrington, Celeste L. (2014), "Leprosy, Legal Mobilization, and the Public Sphere in Japan and South Korea," *Law & Society Review*, vol. 48, no. 3: 563–93.

Asaba, Yuki (2009), "Kankokuni okeru Seito Shisutemuno Henyo [The Transformation of the Korean Party System]," *Yamaguchi Kenritsu Daigaku Gakujutsu Joho*, vol. 2: 16–29.

(2013), "Presidentialism in Korea: A Strong President and a Weak Government," in Yuko Kasuya, ed., *Presidents, Assemblies, and Policy-Making in Asia*. New York: Palgrave Macmillan.

Asaba, Yuki, Yutaka Onishi, and Ikumi Haruki (2010), "Kankokuni okeru Senkyo Saikuru Fuicchino Seitou Seijieno Eikyo [President Lee Myung-bak's Government Formation in Korea: A Missing Link of Electoral Cycle in Party Politics]," *Leviathan*, vol. 47: 65–88.

Ashibe, Nobuyoshi (1997), *Kenpo (Shinpan) [Constitutional Law (New Edition)]*. Tokyo: Iwanami Shoten.

Bakker, Ryan, and Sara B. Hobolt (2013), "Measuring Party Positions," in Geoffrey Evans and Nan Dirk de Graaf, eds., *Political Choice Matters: Explaining the Strength of Class and Religious Cleavages in Cross-National Perspective*. Oxford: Oxford University Press.

Bakker, Ryan, Catherine De Vries, Erica Edwards et al. (2015), "Measuring Party Positions in Europe: The Chapel Hill Expert Survey Trend File, 1999–2010". *Party Politics*, vol. 21, no. 1: 143–52.

Bauhr, Monika, and Marcia Grimes, "Indignation or Resignation: The Implications of Transparency for Societal Accountability," *Governance*, vol. 27, no. 2: 291–320.

Bennett, Mark W. (2010), "Unraveling the Gordian Knot of Implicit Bias in Jury Selection: The Problems of Judge-Dominated Voir Dire, the Failed Promise of Batson, and Proposed Solutions," *Harvard Law & Policy Review*, vol. 4, no. 1: 149–71.

Benoit, Kenneth, and Michael Laver (2006), *Party Policy in Modern Democracies*. New York and London: Routledge.

(2007), "Estimating Party Policy Positions: Comparing Expert Surveys and Hand-Coded Content Analysis," *Electoral Studies*, vol. 26, no. 1: 90–107.

Beramendi, Pablo, and David Rueda (2007), "Social Democracy Constrained: Indirect Taxation in Industrialized Democracies," *British Journal of Political Science*, vol. 37, no. 4: 619–41.

Bergalli, Roberto (1995), "The Spanish Attempt to Build a Democratic Criminal Justice System," in Vincenzo Ruggiero, Mick Ryan, and Joe Sim, eds., *Western European Penal Systems: A Critical Anatomy*. London: Sage.

Bergara, Mario, Barak Richman, and Pablo T. Spiller (2003), "Modeling Supreme Court Strategic Decision Making: The Congressional Constraint," *Legislative Studies Quarterly*, vol. 28, no. 2: 247–80.

Berger, Joseph, B. Cohen Bernard, and Morris Zelditch, Jr. (1972), "Status Characteristics and Social Interactions," *American Sociological Review*, vol. 37, no. 3: 241–55.

Bergoglio, Maria Inés (2003), "Argentina: The Effects of Democratic Institutionalization," in Lawrence M. Friedman and Rogelio Perez-Perdomo, eds., *Legal Culture in the Age of Globalization: Latin America and Latin Europe*. Stanford, CA: Stanford University Press.

Black, Ryan C., and Ryan J. Owens (2009), "Agenda Setting in the Supreme Court: The Collision of Policy and Jurisprudence," *Journal of Politics*, vol. 71, no. 3: 1062–75.

Bliesener, Thomas (2006), "Lay Judges in the German Criminal Court: Social-Psychological Aspects of the German Criminal Justice System," in Martin F. Kaplan and Ana M. Martin, eds., *Understanding World*

Jury Systems through Social Psychological Research. New York: Psychology Press, pp. 179–97.

Bloeser, Andrew J., Carl McCurley, and Jeffery J. Mondak (2012), "Jury Service as Civic Engagement Determinants of Jury Summons Compliance," *American Politics Research*, vol. 40, no. 2: 179–204.

Bloodgood, Elizabeth A., Joannie Tremblay-Boire, and Aseem Prakash (2014), "National Styles of NGO Regulation," *Nonprofit and Voluntary Sector Quarterly*, vol. 43, no. 4: 716–36.

Bobek, Michal (2015), "Judicial Selection, Lay Participation, and Judicial Culture in the Czech Republic: A Study in a Central European (non) Transformation," in Sophie Turenne, ed., *Fair Reflection of Society in Judicial Systems: A Comparative Study*. Cham, Switzerland: Springer International Publishing.

Bohman, James, and William Rehg (1997), "Introduction," in James Bohman and William Rehg, eds., *Deliberative Democracy: Essays on Reason and Politics*. Cambridge, MA: MIT Press.

Bolleyer, Nicole (2012), "New Party Organization in Western Europe: Of Party Hierarchies, Stratarchies, and Federations," *Party Politics*, vol. 18, no. 3: 315–36.

Bouissou, Jean-Marie (2001), "Party Factions and the Politics of Coalition: Japanese Politics under the 'System of 1955'," *Electoral Studies*, vol. 20, no. 4: 581–602.

Bowler, Shaun, Kevin Esterling, and Dallas Holmes (2014), "GOTJ: Get Out the Juror," *Political Behavior*, vol. 36, no. 3: 515–33.

Bräuninger, Thomas, and Thomas König (1999), "The Checks and Balances of Party Federalism: German Federal Government in a Divided Legislature". *European Journal of Political Research*, vol. 36, no. 2: 207–34.

Brown, Rupert (2000), *Group Processes: Dynamics within and between Groups*. Oxford: Blackwell Publishers.

Budge, Ian (2000), "Expert Judgements of Party Policy Positions: Uses and Limitations in Political Research," *European Journal of Political Research*, vol. 37, no. 1: 103–13.

Budge, Ian, Hans-Dieter Klingemann, Andrea Volkens, Judith Bara, and Eric Tanenbaum (2001), *Mapping Policy Preferences: Estimates for Parties, Electors, and Governments, 1945–1998*. Oxford: Oxford University Press.

Burke, Edmund (2008), *The Evils of Revolution*. London: Penguin Books.

Calder, Kent E. (1988), *Crisis and Compensation: Public Policy and Political Stability in Japan, 1949–1986*. Princeton, NJ: Princeton University Press.

(1993), *Strategic Capitalism: Private Business and Public Purpose in Japanese Industrial Finance*. Princeton, NJ: Princeton University Press.

Callander, Stephen, and Patrick Hummel (2014), "Preemptive Policy Experimentation," *Econometrica*, vol. 82, no. 4: 1509–28.

Capoccia, Giovanni, and Daniel Ziblatt (2010), "The Historical Turn in Democratization Studies: A New Research Agenda for Europe and Beyond," *Comparative Political Studies*, vol. 43, no. 8–9: 931–68.

Casper, Gerhard, and Hans Zeisel (1972), "Lay Judges in the German Criminal Courts," *The Journal of Legal Studies*, vol. 1, no. 1: 135–91.

Center for Jury Studies (n.d.), "The State-of-the-States Survey of Jury Improvements Efforts: Executive Summary," available at www.ncsc-jurystudies.org/~/media/Microsites/Files/CJS/SOS/sos_exec_sum.ashx, accessed February 7, 2015.

Chambers, Simone (2003), "Deliberative Democratic Theory," *Annual Review of Political Science*, vol. 6: 307–26.

Chang, Hsun Chia (2009), "Taiwan ni okeru Shiho Kaikaku ni tsuite [Judicial Reform in Taiwan]," *Kanagawa Law Journal*, vol. 2: 39–41.

Chen, Yun-Tsai (2012), "Taiwan ni okeru Jinmin Kanshin Shiko Jorei Soan nitsuite [On the Lay Observer Trial System Bill]," *Ronkyu Jurisuto*, vol. 2: 90–5.

Chen, Weitseng, and Jimmy Chiashin Hsu (2014), "Horizontal Accountability in a Polarized New Democracy: The Case of Post-Democratization Taiwan," *Australian Journal of Asian Law*, vol. 15, no. 2: 1–19.

Chiou, Lian-gong (1998), "Taiwan ni okeru Shiho Kaikakuno Ugoki [Developments in Taiwanese Judicial Reform]," *Ho no Shihai*, vol. 108: 99–111.

Chiu, Hsuan-ju, and Chao-fen Peng (2001), "Taiwan ni okuru Hono Juyoto Tenkai [The Acceptance and Development of Law in Taiwan]," *Jurisconsultus*, vol. 10: 151–66.

Cho, Kuk (2002), "The Unfinished Criminal Procedure Revolution of Post-Democratization South Korea," *Denver Journal of International Law & Policy*, vol. 30, no. 3: 377–94.

(2008), "The Newly Introduced Criminal Jury Trial in Korea: A Historic Step Towards 'Criminal Justice by the People'," *Australian Journal of Asian Law*, vol. 10, no. 2: 268–89.

Choi, Jong-Sik (2008), "Kankokuni okeru Kokuminno Keiji Saiban Sanyo Seido [The Korean Criminal Jury]," *Keiji Bengo*, vol. 53: 163–69.

(2013a), "Korean Citizen Participation in Criminal Trials: The Present Situation and Problems," *International Journal of Law, Crime, and Justice*, vol. 42, no. 2: 83–102.

(2013b), "Kankokuni okeru Kokumin Sanyo Keiji Saiban Seidono Saishu Keitai [The Final Form of the Korean Jury System]," *Horitsu Jiho*, vol. 85, no. 10: 88–94.

Chud, Adam M., and Michael L. Berman (2000), "Six-Member Juries: Does Size Really Matter?" *Tennessee Law Review*, vol. 67, no. 3: 743–63.

Chung, Li-hua and Jake Chung (2016), "Tsai Says Second Judicial Reform to be All-Inclusive," *Taipei Times*, November 26, available at www .taipeitimes.com/News/taiwan/archives/2016/11/26/2003660022, accessed December 26, 2016.

Clark, Tom S. (2009), "The Separation of Powers, Court Curbing, and Judicial Legitimacy," *American Journal of Political Science*, vol. 53, no. 4: 971–89.

Coleman, John J. (1999), "Unified Government, Divided Government, and Party Responsiveness," *American Political Science Review*, vol. 93, no. 4: 821–35.

Consejo General del Poder Judicial (2015), "Ley del Jurado (III)," *Datos de Justicia Boletín de information Estadistica*, No. 40, Junio, available at www.poderjudicial.es/cgpj/es/Temas/Estadistica-Judicial/Estudios-e-Informes/Datos-de-Justicia/, accessed January 2, 2017.

Corey, Zachary, and Valerie P. Hans (2010), "Japan's New Lay Judge System: Deliberative Democracy in Action," *Asia-Pacific Law & Policy Journal*, vol. 12, no. 1: 72–94.

Courts of Denmark (n.d.), "A Closer Look at the Courts of Denmark: Lay Judges and Jurors," available at www.domstol.dk/om/publikationer/ HtmlPublikationer/Profil/Profilbrochure%20-%20UK/kap08.html, accessed March 18, 2016.

Crespo, Virginia Martínez (2015), "Los Casos Tramitados con la Ley del Jurado Caen a la Mitad en 20 Años," *El País*, July 14, available at http://politica.elpais.com/politica/2015/07/14/actualidad/ 1436875597_983440.html, accessed January 2, 2017.

Dainow, Russell (1967), "The Civil Law and Common Law: Some Points of Comparison," *American Journal of Comparative Law*, vol. 15, no. 3: 419–35.

Dalton, Russell J. (2008), "The Quantity and the Quality of Party Systems," *Comparative Political Studies*, vol. 41, no. 7: 899–920.

(2009), "Economics, Environmentalism, and Party Alignments: A Note on Partisan Change in Advanced Industrial Democracies," *European Journal of Political Research*, vol. 48, no. 2: 161–75.

Dalton, Russell J., Susan E. Scarrow, and Bruce E. Cain (2003), "New Forms of Democracy? Reform and Transformation of Democratic Institutions," in Bruce E. Cain, Russell J. Dalton, and Susan E. Scarrow, eds., *Democracy Transformed? Expanding Political Opportunities in Advanced Industrial Democracies*. Oxford: Oxford University Press.

Dalton, Russell J., and Aiji Tanaka (2007), "The Patterns of Party Polarization in East Asia," *Journal of East Asian Studies*, vol. 7, no. 2: 203–23.

Dammer, Harry, and Jay Albanese (2013), *Comparative Criminal Justice Systems*. Belmont, CA: Cengage Learning.

Davison, Phil (1993), "Gonzalez Brings Independents into Spain's Cabinet: The Left Wing is Shut Out of New Government," *Independent*, July 14, 1993, available at www.independent.co.uk/news/world/europe/gonzalez-brings-independents-into-spains-cabinet-the-left-wing-is-shut-out-of-new-government-1484781.html, accessed April 8, 2016.

Dawson, John P. (1960), *A History of Lay Judges*. Cambridge: Harvard University Press.

Deguchi, Yuichi (2000), "GHQno Shiho Kaikaku Koso kara Mita Senryouki Ho Keiju [Legal Transplantation During the Occupation Era as Seen from the GHQ's Vision for Judicial Reforms]," *Hogaku Seijigaku Kenkyu*, no. 44: 351–84.

   (2001), "GHQ no Shiho Kaikaku Kosoto Kokuminnno Shiho Sanka [The GHQ's Vision for Judicial Reforms and Popular Participation in the Judicial System]," *Hogaku Seijigaku Ronkyu*, no. 49: 149–81.

Delli Carpini, Michael X., Fay Lomax Cook, and Lawrence R. Jacobs (2004), "Public Deliberation, Discursive Participation, and Citizen Engagement: A Review of the Empirical Literature," *Annual Review of Political Science*, vol. 7: 315–44.

Democratic Progressive Party (n.d.), "Basic Policies," available at www.dpp.org.tw/upload/history/20100604120114_link.pdf, accessed April 18, 2015.

Devine, Dennis J., D. Clayton Laura, Benjamin B. Dunford, Rasmy Seying, and Jennifer Pryce (2001), "Jury Decision Making: 45 years of Empirical Research on Deliberating Groups," *Psychology, Public Policy, and Law*, vol. 7, no. 3: 622–727.

De Winter, Lieven (1998), "Conclusion: Toward a Comparative Analysis," in Lieven De Winter and Huri Türsan, eds., *Regionalist Parties in Western Europe*. London and New York: Routledge.

Diamond, Sheri Seidman (1993), "What Jurors Think," in Robert E. Litan, ed., *Verdict: Assessing the Civil Jury System*. Washington, DC: The Brookings Institution.

Diesen, Christian (2001), "Lay Judges in Sweden: A Short Introduction," *Revue Internationale de Droite Pénal*, vol. 72, no. 1–2: 313–15.

Dobrovolskaia, Anna (2016), *The Development of Jury Service in Japan: A Square Block in a Round Hole?* Abingdon: Routledge.

Doheny, Shane, and Claire O'Neill (2010), "Becoming Deliberative Citizens: The Moral Learning Process of the Citizen Juror," *Political Studies*, vol. 58, no. 4: 630–48.

Donovan, James M. (2010), *Juries and the Transformation of Criminal Justice in France in the Nineteenth and Twentieth Centuries*. Chapel Hill, NC: University of North Carolina Press.

Dryzek, John S. (2000), *Deliberative Democracy and Beyond: Liberals, Critics, Contestations*. Oxford: Oxford University Press.

Duch, Raymond M., and Michaell A. Taylor (1993), "Postmaterialism and the Economic Condition," *American Journal of Political Science*, vol. 37, no. 3: 747–79.

Eda, Satsuki (2000), "Shiminga Shuyakuno Shihoe [Towards a Justice System in which the Citizens are the Protagonists]," available at www .eda-jp.com/dpj/shihou.html, accessed February 19, 2015.

(2002), "Shiminga Shuyakuno Shiho [A Justice System in which the Citizens are the Protagonists]," available at www.eda-jp.com/satsuki/ 2002/shihou.html, accessed November 3, 2016.

Eisenberg, Theodore, Paula. L. Hannaford-Agor, Valerie P. Hans et al. (2005), "Judge-Jury Agreement in Criminal Cases: A Partial Replication of Kalven and Zeisel's *The American Jury*". *Journal of Empirical Legal Studies*, vol. 2, no. 1: 171–207.

Eisenberg, Theodore, Paula L. Hannaford-Agor, Michael Heise et al. (2006), "Juries, Judges, and Punitive Damages: Empirical Analyses Using the Civil Justice Survey of State Courts 1992, 1996, and 2001 Data," *Journal of Empirical Legal Studies*, vol. 3, no. 2: 263–95.

Eisenberg, Theodore, Neil LaFountain, Brian Ostrom, and David Rottman (2002), "Juries, Judges, and Punitive Damages: An Empirical Study," *Cornell Law Review*, vol. 87, no. 3: 743–82.

Eisenberg, Thomas, Michael Heise, Nicole L. Waters, and Martin T. Wells (2010), "The Decision to Award Punitive Damages: An Empirical Study," *Journal of Legal Analysis*, vol. 2, no. 2: 577–620.

Encarnación, Omar G. (2008), *Spanish Politics*. Cambridge: Polity Press.

Epstein, David, and Sharyn O'Halloran (1999), *Delegating Powers: A Transaction Cost Politics Approach to Policymaking under Separate Powers*. Cambridge: Cambridge University Press.

Ertman, Thomas (2010), "The Great Reform Act of 1832 and British Democratization," *Comparative Political Studies*, vol. 43, no. 8–9: 1000–22.

Feld, Lars P., and Stefan Voigt (2003), "Economic Growth and Judicial Independence: Cross-Country Evidence Using a New Set of Indicators," *European Journal of Political Economy*, vol. 19, no. 3: 497–527.

Fell, Dafydd (2005), *Party Politics in Taiwan: Party Change and the Democratic Evolution of Taiwan, 1991–2004*. Abingdon: Routledge.

(2007), "Partisan Issue Competition in Contemporary Taiwan: Is Taiwan's Democracy Dead?" *Chinese History and Society*, vol. 32: 23–39.

(2011), "The Polarization of Taiwan's Party Competition in the DPP Era," in Robert Ash and Penny Prime, eds., *Taiwan's Democracy and Future: Economic and Political Challenges*. London: Routledge.

(2013), "Impact of Candidate Selection Systems on Election Results: Evidence from Taiwan before and after the Change in Electoral Systems," *The China Quarterly*, vol. 213: 152–71.

Finkel, Jodi (2005), "Judicial Reform as Insurance Policy: Mexico in the 1990s," *Latin American Politics & Society*, vol. 47, no. 1: 87–113.

(2008), *Judicial Reform as Insurance: Argentina, Peru, and Mexico in the 1990s* Notre Dame, IN: University of Notre Dame Press.

Fischer, Frank (2000), *Citizens, Experts, and the Environment: The Politics of Local Knowledge*. Durham and London: Duke University Press.

Fishkin, James S. (2009), *When the People Speak: Deliberative Democracy and Public Consultation*. Oxford: Oxford University Press.

Flynn, George Q. (2002), *Conscription and Democracy: The Draft in France, Great Britain, and the United States*. Westport, CT: Greenwood Press.

Foley, Michael S. (2003), *Confronting the War Machine: Draft Resistance during the Vietnam War*. Chapel Hill and London: University of North Carolina Press.

Foote, Daniel H. (2014), "Citizen Participation: Appraising the Saiban' in System," *Michigan State International Law Review*, vol. 22, no. 3: 755–75.

Franzmann, Simon, and André Kaiser (2006), "Locating Political Parties in Policy Space: A Re-Analysis of Party Manifesto Data," *Party Politics*, vol. 12, no. 2: 163–88.

Fujimura, Naofumi (2013), "A New Day, A New Way: The Post Allocation of the Democratic Party of Japan under the Mixed-Member Majoritarian System," *Japan Forum*, vol. 25, no. 2: 259–92.

Fukumoto, Kentaro (2000), *Nihonno Kokkai Seiji: Zen Seifu Rippono Bunseki [Legislative Politics in Japan: An Analysis of All Legislation]*. Tokyo: Tokyo Daigaku Shuppankai.

(2004), "Shijo Ronso Shohyo Masuyama Mikitaka cho Gikai Seidoto Nihon Seiji Giji Un'ei no Keiryo Seijigaku wo Megutte [Debating Mikitaka Masuyama's *Agenda Power in the Japanese Diet*]," *Leviathan*, vol. 35: 152–9.

Fukurai, Hiroshi (2011), "Japan's Quasi-Jury and Grand Jury Systems as Deliberative Agents of Social Change: De-Colonial Strategies and Deliberative Participatory Democracy," *Chicago-Kent Law Review*, vol. 86, no. 2: 789–830.

Fukurai, Hiroshi, Kay-Wah Chan, and Setsuo Miyazawa (2010), "The Resurgence of Lay Adjudicatory Systems in East Asia," *Asia-Pacific Law and Policy Journal*, vol. 12: i–xi.

Fukurai, Hiroshi, Clark Robert Knudtson, and Susan Irene Lopez (2009), "Is Mexico Ready for a Jury Trial?: Comparative Analysis of Lay

Justice Systems in Mexico, the United States, Japan, New Zealand, South Korea, and Ireland," *Mexican Law Review*, vol. 2, no. 1: 3–44.

Fukurai, Hiroshi, and Valerie P. Hans (2012), "Special Feature: The Future of Lay Adjudication in Korea and Japan," *Yonsei Law Journal*, vol. 3, no. 1: 25–35.

Fukushima, Mizuho (2001), "Shiho Seido Kaikaku Shingikai Chukan Hokokuni tsuite [On the Interim Report of the Justice System Reform Council]," *Shakai Minshu*, vol. 550: 111–13.

Fukuyama, Tatsuo (2002), "Taiwan: Shiho Zenryoikini wataru 'Kaizo' [Taiwan: Remaking the Entire Judicial System]," *Ajiken World Trend*, vol. 77: 12–15.

Furukawa, Teijiro (2004), "Shiho Seido Kaikakuni tsuite [On Judicial Reforms]," *Shiho Kaikaku Chosa Shitsuho*, vol. 3: 2–24.

Gadbin-George, Geraldine (2012), "Towards a Mutation of the Language of Criminal Trial in French and British Courts? The Influence of the Part Played by Juries on Judges' Discourse," *Comparative Law Review*, vol. 3, no. 2: 1–22.

Gallup Korea (n.d.), "The President's Job Approval Rating Since 1988," available at www.gallup.co.kr/english/social.asp, accessed December 14, 2016.

Gastil, John, Laura W. Black, E. Pierre Deess, and Jay Leighter (2008), "From Group Member to Democratic Citizen: How Deliberating with Fellow Jurors Reshapes Civic Attitudes," *Human Communication Research*, vol. 34, no. 1: 137–69.

Gastil, John, E. Pierre Deess, and Phil Weiser (2002), "Civic Awakening in the Jury Room: A Test of the Connection between Jury deliberation and Political Participation," *Journal of Politics*, vol. 64, no. 2: 585–95.

Gastil, John, E. Pierre Deess, Philip J. Weiser, and Cindy Simmons (2010), *The Jury and Democracy: How Jury Deliberation Promotes Civic Engagement and Political Participation*. Oxford: Oxford University Press.

Gastil, John, and Philip J. Weiser (2006), "Jury Service as an Invitation to Citizenship: Assessing the Civil Value of Institutionalized Deliberation," *Policy Studies Journal*, vol. 34, no. 4: 605–27.

Gee, Graham (2015), *The Politics of Judicial Independence in the UK's Changing Constitution*. Cambridge: Cambridge University Press.

Giles, Micheal W., and Thomas D. Lancaster (1989), "Political Transition, Social Development, and Legal Mobilization in Spain," *American Political Science Review*, vol. 83, no. 3: 817–33.

Ginsburg, Tom (2001), "Dismantling the Developmental State? Administrative Procedure Reform in Japan and Korea," *American Journal of Comparative Law*, vol. 49, no. 4: 585–625.

(2003), *Judicial Review in New Democracies: Constitutional Courts in Asian Cases*. Cambridge: Cambridge University Press.

(2010), "The Constitutional Court and the Judicialization of Korean Politics," in Andrew Harding and Penelope Nicholson, eds., *New Courts in Asia*. Abingdon: Routledge.

(2012), "Competitive Modernization: The Politics of Legal and State Reform in Northeast Asia," Presented at the Conference on State and Asia, Leiden, Netherlands, December 2012, available at http://media.leidenuniv.nl/legacy/tom-ginsburg.pdf, accessed March 5, 2015.

Glaeser, Edward L., and Andrei Shleifer (2002), "Legal Origins," *The Quarterly Journal of Economics*, vol. 117, no. 4: 1193–229.

Gómez, Arturo Todoli (2009), "El Recurso de Apelación contra la Sentencia en el Proceso ante el Tribunal del Jurado," *Noticias Jurídicas*, July 1, available at http://noticias.juridicas.com/conocimiento/articulos-doctrinales/4467-el-recurso-de-apelacion-contra-la-sentencia-en-el-proceso-ante-el-tribunal-del-jurado/, accessed January 2, 2017.

Guinther, John (1998), *The Jury in America*. New York: Facts on File.

Gunther, Richard, and José Ramón Montero (2009), *The Politics of Spain*. Cambridge: Cambridge University Press.

Gutmann, Amy, and Dennis Thompson (1996), *Democracy and Disagreement: Why Moral Conflict Cannot be Avoided in Politics, and What Should be Done about It*. Cambridge, MA: Harvard University Press.

(2004), *Why Deliberative Democracy?* Princeton, NJ: Princeton University Press.

Ha, Tae-Hoon (2010), "Shimin Dantai kara mita Kokumin Sanyo Saiban [The Korean Jury from the Perspective of Civil Society]," *Hogaku Seminar*, vol. 55, no. 6: 42–5.

Haas, Peter M. (1992), "Introduction: Epistemic Communities and International Policy Coordination," *International Organization*, vol. 46, no. 1: 1–35.

Hall, Peter A., ed. (1989), *The Political Power of Economic Ideas: Keynesianism Across Nations*. Princeton, NJ: Princeton University Press.

Hamai, Koichi, and Tom Ellis (2008), "Genbatsuka: Growing Penal Populism and the Changing Role of Public Prosecutors in Japan?" *Hanzai Shakaigaku Kenkyu*, vol. 33: 67–92.

Han, In-Sup (2015), "Kankokuno Kokumin Sanyo Saiban (Baishin-in Saiban) [The Jury Trial in South Korea]," *Hogaku Seminar*, vol. 60, no. 8: 62–8.

Han, Sang Hoon, and Kwangbai Park (2012), "Citizen Participation in Criminal Trials of Korea: A Statistical Portrait of the First Four Years," *Yonse Law Journal*, vol. 3: 55–66.

Hanashi, Yasuhiro (2004), "Kokkai deno Shitsumon Iken Hyomei 16kai (Jimito Giinchu Saita [Posed Sixteen Questions and Comments in the Parliament: The Most Among LDP Dietmembers]," available at www .hanashiyasuhiro.com/3679, accessed July 22, 2015.

Hans, Valerie P. (2008), "Jury Systems Around the World," *Annual Review of Law and Social Science*, vol. 4: 275–97.

Hans, Valerie P., and Claire M. Germain (2011), "The French Jury at a Crossroads," *Chicago-Kent Law Review*, vol. 86: 737–68.

Harada, Kunio (2013), "Saiban-in Saibanni okeru Ryokei Keiko [Trends in Sentencing Patterns Under the Saiban-in Trials]," *Keio Hogaku*, vol. 27: 161–87.

Harvey, Anna, and Barry Friedman (2006), "Pulling Punches: Congressional Constraints on the Supreme Court's Constitutional Rulings, 1987–2000," *Legislative Studies Quarterly*, vol. 31, no. 4: 533–62.

Helbling, Marc, and Anke Tresch (2011), "Measuring Party Positions and Issue Salience from Media Coverage: Discussing and Cross-Validating New Indicators," *Electoral Studies*, vol. 30, no. 1: 174–83.

Hellmann, Olli (2014), "Party System Institutionalization Without Parties: Evidence from Korea," *Journal of East Asian Studies*, vol. 14, no. 1: 53–84.

Helmke, Gretchen (2002), "The Logic of Strategic Defection: Court-Executive Relations in Argentina under Dictatorship and Democracy," *American Political Science Review*, vol. 96, no. 2: 291–303.

(2005), *Courts under Constraints: Judges, Generals, and Presidents in Argentina*. Cambridge: Cambridge University Press.

Helmke, Gretchen, and Frances Rosenbluth (2009), "Regimes and the Rule of Law: Judicial Independence in Comparative Perspective," *Annual Review of Political Science*, vol. 12: 345–66.

Hendler, Catedra (2005), "Jury Trials in Argentina," Paper Presented at the Annual Meeting of the Law and Society Association, Las Vegas, NV, available at www.catedrahendler.org/doctrina_in.php?id=31, accessed February 15, 2015.

Hendler, Edmundo (2008/9), "Lay Participation in Argentina: Old History, Recent Experience," *Southwestern Journal of International Law*, vol. 15, no. 1: 1–30.

Heo, Uk, and Hans Stockton (2005), "The Impact of Democratic Transition on Elections and Parties in South Korea," *Party Politics*, vol. 11, no. 6: 674–88.

Herron, Erik S., and Kirk A. Randazzo (2003), "The Relationship between Independence and Judicial Review in Post-Communist Courts," *Journal of Politics*, vol. 65, no. 2: 422–38.

Hersch, Joni, and W. Kip Viscusi (2004), "Punitive Damages: How Judges and Juries Perform," *The Journal of Legal Studies*, vol. 33, no. 1: 1–36.

Heuer, Larry, and Steven Penrod (1994), "Trial Complexity: A Field Investigation of Its Meaning and its Effects," *Law and Human Behavior*, vol. 18, no. 1: 29–51.

Higuchi, Naoto, Midori Ito, Shunsuke Tanabe, and Mitsuru Matsutani (2009), "Explaining Japan's Lack of Green Parties: A Socio-Milieu Approach," Paper Presented at the XXI World Congress of the International Political Science Association, Santiago, Chile.

Hirschl, Ran (2002), *Towards Juristocracy: The Origins and Consequences of the New Constitutionalism*. Cambridge: Harvard University Press.

Hix, Simon, and Hae-Won Jun (2009), "Party Behavior in the Parliamentary Arena: The Case of the Korean National Assembly," *Party Politics*, vol. 15, no. 6: 667–94.

Ho, Ming-Sho (2005), "Weakened State and Movement: The Paradox of Taiwanese Environmental Politics after the Power Transfer," *Journal of Contemporary China*, vol. 14, no. 43: 339–52.

Hoeglinger, Dominic (2016), "The Politicisation of European Integration in Domestic Election Campaigns," *West European Politics*, vol. 39, no. 1: 44–63.

Hofferbert, Richard I., and Hans-Dieter Klingemann (1990), "The Policy Impact of Party Programmes and Government Declarations in the Federal Republic of Germany," *European Journal of Political Research*, vol. 18, no. 3: 277–304.

Holsti, Ole (1998/9), "A Widening Gap between the U.S. Military and Civilian Society? Some Evidence, 1976–99," *International Security*, vol. 23, no. 3: 5–42.

Homusho (various years), *Kensatsu Tokei Nenpo [Annual Report of Statistics on Prosecution]*. Tokyo: Homu Daijin Kanbo Shiho Hoseichosabu Chosa Tokeika.

Honjo, Takeshi (2003), "Saiban-in no Ryokei Sanka [Participation of Saiban-in in the Sentencing Process]," *Hitotsubashi Ronso*, vol. 129, no. 1: 22–40.

Hooghe, Liesbet, Gary Marks, and Carole J. Wilson (2002), "Does Left/ Right Structure Party Positions on European Integration?" *Comparative Political Studies*, vol. 35, no. 8: 965–89.

Hoover, Dennis R., and Kevin R. den Dulk (2004), "Christian Conservatives Go to Court: Religion and Legal Mobilization in the United States and Canada," *International Political Science Review*, vol. 25, no. 1: 9–34.

Hopkin, Jonathan (1999), *Party Formation and Democratic Transition in Spain: The Creation and Collapse of the Union of the Democratic Centre*. New York: St. Martin's Press.

Horan, Jacqueline (2005), "Perceptions of the Civil Jury System," *Monash University Law Review*, vol. 31, no. 1: 134–51.

House of Councillors (n.d.), "Sangiinno Aramashi [Makeup of the House of Councillors]," available at www.sangiin.go.jp/japanese/aramashi/ keyword/kaiha.html, accessed February 18, 2015.

Howell, William, E. Scott Adler, Charles Cameron, and Charles Riemann (2000), "Divided Government and the Legislative Productivity of Congress, 1945–94," *Legislative Studies Quarterly*, vol. 25, no. 2: 285–312.

Huang, Kuo-Chang, Kong-Pin Chen, and Chang-Chin Lin (2010), "Does the Type of Criminal Defense Counsel Affect Case Outcomes? A Natural Experiment in Taiwan," *International Review of Law and Economics*, vol. 30, no. 2: 113–27.

Huang, Kuo-Chang, and Chang-Ching Lin (2013), "Rescuing Confidence in the Judicial System: Introducing Lay Participation in Taiwan," *Journal of Empirical Legal Studies*, vol. 10, no. 3: 542–69.

Huber, John, and Ronald Inglehart (1995), "Expert Interpretations of Party Space and Party Locations in 42 Societies," *Party Politics*, vol. 1, no. 1: 73–111.

Huber, John D., and Charles R. Shipan (2002), *Deliberate Discretion? The Institutional Foundations of Bureaucratic Autonomy*. Cambridge: Cambridge University Press.

Huckfeldt, Robert, Paul E. Johnson, and John Sprague (2004), *Political Disagreement: The Survival of Diverse Opinions within Communication Networks*. Cambridge: Cambridge University Press.

Husa, Jaakko (2004), "Classification of Legal Families Today: Is it Time for a Memorial Hymn?" *Revue International de Droit Comparé*, vol. 56, no. 1: 11–38.

Iaryczower, Matías, Pablo T. Spiller, and Mariano Tommasi (2002), "Judicial Independence in Unstable Environments, Argentina 1935–1998," *American Journal of Political Science*, vol. 46, no. 4: 699–716.

Iaryczower, Matias, Pablo T. Spiller, and Mariano Tommasi (2006), "Judicial Lobbying: the Politics of Labor Law Constitutional Interpretation," *American Political Science Review*, vol. 100, no. 1: 85–97.

Ibusuki, Makoto (2010), "Quo Vadis?: First Year Inspection to Japanese Mixed Jury Trial," *Asian-Pacific Law & Policy Journal*, vol. 12, no. 1: 24–58.

Iimuro, Katsuhiko (2000), "Saraba Omakase Shiho [Taking Control of the Judicial Process]," *Shiho Kaikaku*, vol. 2, no. 2: 53–6.

Imamura, Kaku (2008), *Enzai Bengoshi [Defense Lawyers for Wrongful Convictions]*. Tokyo: Shumposha.

Imaseki, Motonari (2013), "Kenryokuka shita Kensatsu Shinsakai [The Prosecutorial Review Commission Gains Powers]," *Yomiuri Online*, available at www.yomiuri.co.jp/adv/wol/opinion/society_130318.html, accessed March 28, 2016.

Inglehart, Ronald (1988), "The Renaissance of Political Culture," *American Political Science Review*, vol. 82, no. 4: 1203–30.

Inoguchi, Takashi (1987), "Japan 1960–1980: Party Programmes in Elections," in Ian Budge, ed., *Ideology, Strategy, and Party Change: Spatial Analyses of Post-War Election Programmes in 19 Democracies*. New York: Cambridge University Press.

Inoguchi, Takashi, and Tomoaki Iwai (1987), *"Zoku Giin" no Kenkyu [A Study of "Zoku" Dietmembers]*. Tokyo: Nihon Keizai Shimbunsha.

Ito, Kazuko (2011), "'Nejire Kokkai' ni okeru Kokkai Shingino Shoso [The Various Aspects of Deliberations in the Divided Diet]," *Hokudai Hogaku Ronshu*, vol. 61, no. 5: 1730–56.

Jackson, John D., and Nikolay P. Kovalev (2006/7), "Lay Adjudication and Human Rights in Europe," *Columbia Journal of European Law*, vol. 13: 83–123.

Janowitz, Morris (1983), *The Reconstruction of Patriotism: Education for Civic Consciousness*. Chicago: University of Chicago Press.

Jennings, M. Kent (1987), "Residues of a Movement: The Aging of the American Protest Generation," *American Political Science Review*, vol. 81, no. 2: 367–82.

(2002), "Generation Units and the Student Protest Movement in the United States: An Intra- and Intergenerational Analysis," *Political Psychology*, vol. 23, no. 2: 303–24.

"Jihaku Nerau Koryu, Mitomenu Hoko [A Decline in Rejection of Detentions for the Sake of Inducing Confessions]," *Asahi Shimbun*, April 21, 2008.

Jeon, Jin Young, and Satoshi Machidori (2015), "Seitono Ittaiseiha Ikanishite Kakuho Sarerunoka [How is Party Discipline Achieved]?" in Won-Taek Kang, Yuki Asaba, and Seon Gyu Go, eds., *Nikkan Seiji Seido Hikaku [Comparing Japanese and Korean Political Institutions]*. Tokyo: Keio Daigaku Shuppankai.

Jimeno-Bulnes, Mar (2004), "Lay Participation in Spain: The Jury System," *International Criminal Justice Review*, vol. 14: 164–85.

(2007), "A Different Story Line for 12 Angry Men: Verdicts Reached by Majority Rule-The Spanish Perspective," *Chicago-Kent Law Review*, vol. 82, no. 2: 759–75.

(2011), "Jury Selection and Jury Trial in Spain: Between Theory and Practice," *Chicago-Kent Law Review*, vol. 86, no. 2: 585–612.

Jiyu, Minshuto (1998), "Shiho Seido Tokubetsu Chosakai Houkoku 21-seiki no Shihono Tashikana Shishin [A Solid Framework for the Justice System for the 21st Century: A Report by the Special Research Commission on the Justice System]," *Jiyuto Seigi*, vol. 49, no. 8: 194–7.

(2000), "21-seiki no Shiho no Tashikana Ippo [A Firm Step Forward for the Judicial System in the 21st Century]," *Jiyu to Seigi*, vol. 51, no. 7: 136–48.

Johnson, Chalmers (1982), *MITI and the Japanese Miracle: The Growth of Industrial Policy: 1925–1975*. Stanford, CA: Stanford University Press.

Johnson, David (2002), *The Japanese Way of Justice*. Oxford: Oxford University Press.

(2008), "Japanese Punishment in Comparative Perspective," *Japanese Journal of Sociological Criminology*, vol. 33: 46–66.

Jou, Willy (2011), "How do Citizens in East Asian Democracies Understand Left and Right?" *Japanese Journal of Political Science*, vol. 12, no. 1: 33–55.

Judicial Yuan (n.d.), "Results from Survey on Advisory Jury System," conducted November 1–5, 2012, available at www.judicial.gov.tw/GuanShen/study03.asp, accessed July 14, 2015.

(2012), "Ssu fa yuan jen min kuan shen chih tu yen i tzu liao hui pien (Documents on the Judicial Yuan's Discussions over the Lay Observer System [Part 1 of 2])," available at www.judicial.gov.tw/LayParticipation/download/%E5%8F%B8%E6%B3%95%E9%99%A2%E4%BA%BA%E6%B0%91%E8%A7%80%E5%AF%A9%E5%88%B6%E5%BA%A6%E7%A0%94%E8%AD%B0%E8%B3%87%E6%96%99%E5%BD%99%E7%B7%A8(%E4%B8%8A).pdf, accessed July 7, 2015.

(2014), *Statute on the Pilot Implementation of the Advisory Jury System in Trial (Draft)*. Taipei: Judicial Yuan.

Ka, Sangjoon, and Junya Nishino (2015), "Shissei Chusubuni Kansuru Nikkan Hikaku [Comparing Japan and Korea's Core Executive]," in Won-Taek Kang, Yuki Asaba, and Seon Gyu Go, eds., *Nikkan Seiji Seido Hikaku [Comparing Japanese and Korean Political Institutions]*. Tokyo: Keio Daigaku Shuppankai.

Kaarbo, Juliet (1996), "Power and Influence in Foreign Policy Decision Making: The Role of Junior Coalition Partners in German and Israeli Foreign Policy," *International Studies Quarterly*, vol. 40, no. 4: 501–30.

(2008), "Coalition Cabinet Decision Making: Institutional and Psychological Factors," *International Studies Review*, vol. 10, no. 1: 57–86.

Kage, Rieko (2015), "Nihonnni okueru Saiban-in Seidono Sosetsu [The Founding of the Saiban-in System in Japan]," in Yuriko Takahashi, ed., *Akauntabiriti Kaikakuno Seijigaku*. Tokyo: Yuhikaku.

Kalven, Harry Jr., and Hans Zeisel (1966), *The American Jury*. Boston, MA: Little, Brown.

Kamikawa, Ryunoshin (2010), *Koizumi Kaikakuno Seijigaku [Analyzing Koizumi's Reforms]*. Tokyo: Toyo Keizai Shimposha.

Kanda, Hiroki (2014), "Sengo Shuyo Seitono Hensento Kokkainai Seiryokuno Suii [The Postwar Evolution of Major Parties in Japan and Their Pariamentary Seat Shares]," *Refarensu*, vol. 64, no. 6: 41–64.

Kang, Won-Taek, and Yuki Asaba (2015), "Bunkatsu Seifuno Nikkan Hikaku [Comparing Divided Government in Japan and South Korea]," in Won-Taek Kang, Yuki Asaba, and Seon Gyu Go, eds., *Nikkan Seiji Seido Hikaku [Comparing Japanese and Korean Political Institutions]*. Tokyo: Keio Gijuku Daigaku Shuppankai.

Kaplan, Martin F., and Ana M. Martin (1999), "Effects of Differential Status of Group Members on Process and Outcome of Deliberation," *Group Processes and Intergroup Relations*, vol. 2, no. 4: 347–64.

Kaplan, Martin F., and Ana M. Martín, eds. (2006), *Understanding World Jury Systems Through Social Psychological Research*. New York and Hove: Psychology Press.

Kaplan, Martin F., Ana M. Martín, and Janine Hertel (2014), "Issues and Prospects in European Juries: An Overview," in Martin F. Kaplan and Ana M. Martín, eds., *Understanding World Jury Systems Through Social Psychological Research*. New York and Hove: Psychology Press.

Kasuya, Yuko (2013a), "Introduction," in Yuko Kasuya, ed., *Presidents, Assemblies, and Policy-Making in Asia*. New York: Palgrave Macmillan.

(2013b), "A Framework for Analysing Presidential-Legislative Relations in Asia," in Yuko Kasuya, ed., *Presidents, Assemblies, and Policy-Making in Asia*. New York: Palgrave Macmillan.

Kato, Junko (2003), *Regressive Taxation and the Welfare State: Path Dependence and Policy Diffusion*. Cambridge: Cambridge University Press.

(2014), "Expert Survey Results in Japan 1996–2012," available at www .katoj.j.u-tokyo.ac.jp/, accessed March 3, 2015.

Katzenstein, Peter J. (1985). *Small States in World Markets: Industrial Policy in Europe*. Ithaca, NY: Cornell University Press.

Keizai Doyukai (1994), *Gendai Nihonno Byorito Shoho [The Pathologies of Contemporary Japan: Prescriptions]*. Tokyo: Keizai Doyukai.

(1997), *Gurobarukani Taiosuru Kigyo Hoseino Seibiwo Mezashite [Towards a Corporate Law System that Responds to Globalization]*. Tokyo: Keizai Doyukai.

Kelly, Terrence (2004), "Unlocking the Iron Cage: Public Administration in the Deliberative Democratic Theory of Jürgen Habermas," *Administration & Society*, vol. 36, no. 1: 38–61.

Kier, Elizabeth (1999), *Imagining War: French and British Military Doctrine Between the Wars*. Princeton: Princeton University Press.

Kim, Sangjoon, Jaihyun Park, Kwangbai Park, and Jin-Sup Eom (2013), "Judge-Jury Agreement in Criminal Cases: The First Three Years of the Korean Jury System," *Journal of Empirical Legal Studies*, vol. 10, no. 1: 35–53.

Kim, Wonik (2010), "Does Class Matter? Social Cleavages in South Korea's Electoral Politics in the Era of Neoliberalism," *Review of Political Economy*, vol. 22, no. 4: 589–616.

Kimura, Masato (2015), "Muchini Motozku Chobatsu Ishiki? [Misinformed Citizen and Death Penalty]," *Takachiho Ronso*, vol. 50, no. 2: 23–46.

Kitschelt, Herbert (1994), *The Transformation of European Social Democracy*. Cambridge: Cambridge University Press.

(2013), *Democratic Accountability and Linkages Project*. Durham, NC: Duke University.

Klingemann, Hans-Dieter (1995), "Party Positions and Voter Orientations," in Hans-Dieter Klingemann and Dieter Fuchs, eds., *Citizens and the State*. Oxford and New York: Oxford University Press, pp. 183–205.

Klingemann, Hans-Dieter, Andrea Volkens, Judith Bara, Ian Budge, and Michael McDonald (2006), *Mapping Policy Preferences II: Estimates for Parties, Electors, and Governments in Eastern Europe, European Union, and OECD 1990–2003*. Oxford: Oxford University Press.

Knill, Christoph, Marc Debus, and Stephan Heichel (2010), "Do Parties Matter in Internationalised Policy Areas? The Impact of Political Parties on Environmental Policy Outputs in 18 OECD Countries, 1970–2000," *European Journal of Political Research*, vol. 49, no. 3: 301–36.

Knutsen, Oddbjørn (1998), "Expert Judgments on the Left-Right Location of Political Parties: A Longitudinal Study," *West European Politics*, vol. 21, no. 2: 63–94.

Koga, Tsuyoshi, Yasue Kirimura, and Makito Okumura (2010), "Teikoku Gikai oyobi Kokkaino Rippo Tokei [Statistics on Legislation in the Imperial Diet and the Postwar Diet]," *Refarensu*, vol. 60, no. 11: 117–55.

Koike, Shintaro (2016), "Ryokei Handanno Arikata [Sentencing]," *Keiho Zasshi*, vol. 55, no. 2: 346–60.

Kojima, Toru (2015), "Saiban-in Saibanni yoru Ryokeino Henka [Changes in Sentencing since the Introduction of the Saiban-in System]," *Chukyo Hogaku*, vol. 49, no. 3–4, 169–97.

König, Thomas, Moritz Marbach, and Moritz Osnabrügge (2013), "Estimating Party Positions across Countries and Time—A Dynamic Latent Variable Model for Manifesto Data," *Political Analysis*, vol. 21, no. 4: 468–91.

"Koryu Seikyu Kyakka Kyuzo [A Steep Increase in Rejected Requests for Detention Warrants]" (2015), *Mainichi Shimbun*, December 24.

Kovalev, Nikolai (2010), *Criminal Justice Reform in Russia, Ukraine, and the Former Republics of the Soviet Union: Trial by Jury and Mixed Courts*. Lewiston, NY: Edwin Mellen Press.

Kovalev, Nikolai, and Gulnar Suleymenova (2010), "New Kazakhstani Quasi-Jury System: Challenges, Trends and Reforms," *International Journal of Law, Crime and Justice*, vol. 38, no. 4: 261–78.

Krebs, Ron R. (2006), *Fighting for Rights: Military Service and the Politics of Citizenship*. Ithaca, NY: Cornell University Press.

Kudo, Mika (2004a), "Kankoku Shiho Kaikaku Iinkaito Nichibenren Chosano Gaiyo [The Korean Reform Committee and Overview of the JFBA Study Team]," *Shiho Kaikaku Chosa Shitsuho*, vol. 4: 2–13.

(2004b), "Kankokuno Shiho Kaikaku kara Manabu [Learning from Korea's Judicial Reforms]," *Hogaku Seminar*, vol. 49, no. 11: 59–63.

Kutnjak Ivković, Sanja (1999), *Lay Participation in Criminal Trials: The Case of Croatia*. Lanham, MD: Austin and Winfield Publishers.

Langbein, John H. (1981), "Mixed Court and Jury Court: Could the Continental Alternative Fill the American Need?" *Law & Social Inquiry*, vol. 6, no. 1: 195–219.

Langer, Máximo (2004), "From Legal Transplants to Legal Translations: The Globalization of Plea-Bargaining and the Americanization Thesis in Criminal Procedure," *Harvard International Law Journal*, vol. 45, no. 1: 1–64.

Laver, Michael J., and Kenneth Benoit (2005), "Estimating Party Positions: Japan in Comparative Context," *Japanese Journal of Political Science*, vol. 6, no. 2: 187–209.

Laver, Michael J., and Ian Budge (1992), "Measuring Policy Distances and Modelling Coalition Formation," in Michael J. Laver and Ian Budge, eds., *Party Policy and Government Coalitions*. New York: St. Martin's Press.

Laver, Michael, and W. Ben Hunt (1992), *Policy and Party Competition*. New York: Routledge.

Leal, David L. (1999), "It's Not Just a Job: Military Service and Latino Political Participation," *Political Behavior*, vol. 21, no. 2: 153–74.

Lee, Dong-hee (2011a), "Kankoku Kokumin Sanyo Saibanno Genjo to Kadai (Jou) [The Korean Jury System: Current State and Issues for the Future (Part 1)]," *Kikan Keiji Bengo*, vol. 67: 182–93.

(2011b), "Kankoku Kokumin Sanyo Saibanno Genjo to Kadai (Ge) [The Korean Jury System: Current State and Issues for the Future (Part 2)]," *Kikan Keiji Bengo*, vol. 68: 197–204.

Lee, Eun-Mo (2008), "Kankokuno Kokumin Sanyo Saiban Seidono Naiyoto Mondaiten [An Introduction of the New Civil Participatory Criminal Trials System in Korea]," *Nomos*, vol. 23: 65–76.

Lee, Jae-Hyup (2009), "Getting Citizens Involved: Civic Participation in Judicial Decision-Making in Korea," *University of Pennsylvania East Asia Law Review*, vol. 4, no. 2: 177–207.

Lee, John Sanghyun (2016), "Transplanting Jury Trials in South Korean Legal Soils: Comparative Analysis with Jury Trials in the United States," *Asian Journal of Criminology*, vol. 11, no. 2: 111–33.

Legislative Yuan (n.d.), "Minutes of the Legislative Yuan," available at http://lci.ly.gov.tw/LyLCEW/lcivAgendarec.action#pageName_searchResult =1, accessed March 21, 2016.

Leib, Ethan J. (2007), "A Comparison of Criminal Jury Decision Rules in Democratic Countries," *Ohio State Journal of Criminal Law*, vol. 5, no. 2: 629–44.

Lehmann, Pola, Theres Matthie, Nicolas Merz, Sven Regel, and Annika Werner (2015), *Manifesto Corpus. Version: 2015–5*. Berlin: WZB Berlin Social Science Center.

Levi, Margaret (1996), "The Institution of Conscription," *Social Science History*, vol. 20, no. 1: 133–67.

(1997), *Consent, Dissent, and Patriotism*. Cambridge: Cambridge University Press.

Levine, Dennis J., Laura D. Clayton, Benjamin B. Dunford, Rasmy Seying, and Jennifer Pryce (2001), "Jury Decision Making: 45 Years of Empirical Research on Deliberating Groups," *Psychology, Public Policy, and Law*, vol. 7, no. 3: 622–727.

Linzer, Drew A., and Jeffrey K. Staton (2015), "A Global Measure of Judicial Independence, 1948–2012," *Journal of Law and Courts*, vol. 3, no. 2: 223–56.

Lloyd-Bostock, Sally, and Cheryl Thomas (1999), "The Decline of the 'Little Parliament': Juries and Jury Reform in England and Wales," *Law and Contemporary Problems*, vol. 62, no. 2: 7–40.

Luebbert, Gregory M. (1991), *Liberalism, Fascism, or Social Democracy: Social Classes and the Political Origins of Regimes in Interwar Europe*. New York and Oxford: Oxford University Press.

Lupu, Noam (2014), "Party Polarization and Mass Partisanship: A Comparative Perspective," *Political Behavior*, vol. 37, no. 2: 331–56.

McElwain, Kenneth Mori, and Christian G. Winkler (2015), "What's Unique about the Japanese Constitution?: A Comparative and Historical Analysis," *The Journal of Japanese Studies*, vol. 41, no. 2: 249–80.

Machura, Stefan (2001), "Interaction between Lay Assessors and Professional Judges in German Mixed Courts," *Revue Internationale de Droit Pénal*, vol. 72, no. 1–2: 451–79.

Mackerras, Malcolm, and Ian McAllister (1999), "Compulsory Voting, Party Stability and Electoral Advantage in Australia," *Electoral Studies*, vol. 18, no. 2: 217–33.

Maeda, Naoki (2014), "Liu Wen-ching Chen Yu-erh Jikento Amnesty International Nihonnon Setsuritsu [Contract Point between Taiwan Independent Movement in Japan and the Foundation of AI]," *Hiroshima Hogaku*, vol. 38, no. 2: 74–81.

Malsch, Marijke (2009), *Democracy in the Courts: Lay Participation in European Criminal Justice Systems*. Farnham: Ashgate.

Manow, Philip, and Simone Burkhart (2007), "Legislative Self-Restraint under Divided Government in Germany, 1976–2002," *Legislative Studies Quarterly*, vol. 32, no. 2: 167–91.

Marks, Gary, Liesbet Hooghe, Moira Nelson, and Erica Edwards (2006), "Party Competition and European Integration in the East and West: Different Structure, Same Causality," *Comparative Political Studies*, vol. 39, no. 2: 155–75.

Martín, Ana M., and Martin F. Kaplan (2006), "Psychological Perspectives on Spanish and Russian Juries," in Martin F. Kaplan and Ana M. Martín, eds., *Understanding World Jury Systems Through Social Psychological Research*. New York and Hove: Psychology Press.

Masuyama, Mikitaka (2000), "Is the Japanese Diet Consensual?" *Journal of Legislative Studies*, vol. 6, no. 4: 9–28.

  (2003), *Gikai Seidoto Nihon Seiji [Agenda Power in the Japanese Diet]*. Tokyo: Bokutakusha.

  (2004), "Ripponi Okeru Jikanto Eikyoryoku [Time and Influence over Legislation]," *Leviathan*, vol. 35: 160–3.

  (2006), "Ripponi Okeru Henkan vs. Taido Hyomei – Kokkai Shingito Futai Ketsugi [Legislative Gains versus Position Taking: How the Diet Makes Supplementary Resolutions]," *Leviathan*, vol. 38: 131–53.

Matsumoto, Mitsutoyo (2013), "Presidential Strength and Party Leadership in Taiwan," in Yuko Kasuya, ed., *Presidents, Assemblies, and Policy-Making in Asia*. New York: Palgrave Macmillan.

  (2014a), "Kunosuru Yoto: Taiwan no Handaitoryosei to Chugoku Kokuminto [Ruling Party in Distress: Semi-Presidentialism in Taiwan and the KMT]," *Chugoku Bunka Kenkyu*, vol. 27: 1–18.

  (2014b), "Taiwannno Han-Daitoryosei ni okeru Seisaku Kettei [Policymaking under Taiwan's Semi-Presidential System]," *Toyo Bunka*, vol. 94: 29–60.

Matsumoto, Shunta, and Akitaka Matsuo (2010), "Kokkai Giinwa Naze Iinkaide Hatsugen Surunoka? [Why Japan's Lower House Members Speak in Committes?]," *Senkyo Kenkyu*, no. 26-2: 84–103.

McCubbins, Mathew D., and Thomas Schwartz (1984), "Congressional Oversight Overlooked: Police Patrols versus Fire Alarms," *American Journal of Political Science*, vol. 28, no. 1: 165–79.

McGuire, Kevin T., and Gregory A. Caldeira (1993), "Lawyers, Organized Interests, and the Law of Obscenity: Agenda Setting in the Supreme Court," *American Political Science Review*, vol. 87, no. 3: 717–26.

Meguid, Bonnie (2005), "Competition Between Unequals: The Role of Mainstream Party Strategy in Niche Party Success," *American Political Science Review*, vol. 99, no. 3: 347–59.

Mendelberg, Tali (2002), "The Deliberative Citizen: Theory and Evidence," in MX Delli Carpini, Leonie Huddy, and Robert Shapiro, eds., *Research in Micropolitics: Political Decisionmaking, Deliberation and Participation*, vol. 6, no. 1: 151–93. Greenwich, CT: JAI Press.

Michels, Robert (1911[1999]), *Political Parties: A Sociological Study of the Oligarchical Tendencies of Modern Democracy*. New Brunswick, NJ: Transaction Publishers.

Min, Young-Sung (2011), "Kokumin Sanyo Saiban Seidono Gaiyoto Seiritsuno Keii [Outline of the Korean Jury System and How it Passed]," in Akira Goto, ed., *Higashi Ajia ni okeru Shiminno Keiji Shiho Sanka [Participation in the Criminal Process in East Asia]*. Tokyo: Kokusai Shoin.

(2012), "Kankokuno Kokumin Sanyo Saibanno Genjo to Kadai [The State of Korea Jury Trials and Issues Ahead]," *Horitsu Jiho*, vol. 84, no. 12: 58–62.

Minshuto (2003), "Saiban-in Seido Sekkeini Kansuru Kangaekata [Basic Approach for Designing the Saiban-in System]," available at http://archive.dpj.or.jp/news/?num=10611, accessed February 19, 2015.

Mitani, Taichiro (2013), *Zoho Seiji Seidoto shiteno Baishinsei [The Jury as a Political Institution, Enlarged and Revised Edition]*. Tokyo: Tokyo Daigaku Shuppankai.

Miyamoto, Yasuaki (2005), "Shiho Seido Kaikakuno Shiteki Kento Josetsu [A Prelude to the Examination of Judicial Reforms in Historical Perspective," *Gendai Hogaku*, vol. 10: 59–88.

Miyazawa, Setsuo (2008), "The Politics of Increasing Punitiveness and the Rising Populism in Japanese Criminal Justice Policy," *Punishment & Society*, vol. 10, no. 1: 47–77.

(2013), "Senshinkoku ni Okeru Hanzai Hasseiritsuno Jokyoto Nihonno Jokyoheno Kokusaiteki Kanshin [Crime Rates in Industrialized Democracies and the Interest in the Japanese Situation]," *Hanzai Shakaigaku Kenkyu*, vol. 38: 7–35.

Mizuno, Kunio (1999), "Shiho Seido Kaikaku Shingikaiwa Donoyouni Setsuritsu Saretaka [How the Justice System Reform Council was Established]," *Gekkan Shiho Kaikaku*, vol. 1, no. 1: 53–61.

Moriya, Katsuhiko (2015), "Hoshikkomaeni Jisshi sareta Hoso Sansha Shusaino Mogi Saiban [Mock Trials Sponsored by the Courts,

Prosecutors, and the Bar Association Before the Law Came Into Effect]," in Satoshi Mishima, ed., *Saiban-in Saibanno Hyogi Dezain [The Design of the Deliberation Scheme in Saiban-in Trials]*. Tokyo: Nihon Hyoronsha.

Moscovici, Serge (1985), "Social Influence and Conformity," in Gardner Lindzey and Elliot Aronson, eds., *Handbook of Social Psychology* (3rd Edition), Vol. 2. New York: Random House.

Muramatsu, Michio (1981), *Sengo Nihonno Kanryosei [The Postwar Japanese Bureaucracy]*. Tokyo: Toyo Keizai Shimposha.

Mutz, Diana C. (2002), "The Consequences of Cross-Cutting Networks for Political Participation," *American Journal of Political Science*, vol. 46, no. 4: 838–55.

National Diet Library (n.d.), "Kokkai Gijiroku Kensaku System [Search Engine for Japanese Parliamentary Minutes]," available at http://kokkai .ndl.go.jp/, accessed June 27, 2017.

Neumayer, Eric (2003), "Are Left-Wing Party Strength and Corporatism Good for the Environment? Evidence from Panel Analysis of Air Pollution in OECD Countries," *Ecological Economics*, vol. 45, no. 2: 203–20.

Nishino, Kiichi (2009), "Nihonkoku Kenpo to Baishinsei Sairon [The Japanese Constitution and the Jury System: A Reprise]," *Hosei Riron*, vol. 41, no. 2: 1–13.

O'Donnell, Guillermo, and Philippe C. Schmitter (1986), *Transitions from Authoritarian Rule: Tentative Conclusions about Uncertain Democracies*. Baltimore, MD: Johns Hopkins University Press.

Ogura, Yoshihisa (2013), "Saiban-in Seidono Tanjo (2) [The Birth of the Saiban-in System, Part 2]," *Kansai Daigaku Hogaku Ronshu*, vol. 62, no. 6: 2472–505.

Okayama, Hiroshi (2012), "Senmonsei Kenkyuno Saikosei [Reconsidering Studies of Political Expertise]," in Yu Uchiyama, Takeshi Ito, and Hiroshi Okayama, eds., *Senmonseino Seijigaku [The Politics of Expertise]*. Kyoto: Minerva Shobo.

Okimoto, Daniel I. (1989), *Between MITI and the Market: Japanese Industrial Policy for High Technology*. Stanford, CA: Stanford University Press.

Okumura, Makito (2009), "Daikan Minkokuno Gikai Seido [Legislative Institutions in the Republic of Korea]," *Refarensu*, vol. 59, no. 8: 97–125.

Onishi, Yutaka (2004), "Kankokuni okeru Ideology Seijino Fukkatsu [The Revival of Ideological Politics in Korea]," *Kokusai Mondai*, vol. 535: 17–30.

———— (2014), *Senshinkoku Kankokuno Yuutsu [Challenges Facing South Korea as a Developed Country]*. Tokyo: Chuo Koron Shinsha.

Oppermann, Kai, and Klaus Brummer (2014), "Patterns of Junior Partner Influence on the Foreign Policy of Coalition Governments," *The British Journal of Politics and International Relations*, vol. 16, no. 4: 555–71.

Oppler, Alfred C. (1976), *Legal Reform in Occupied Japan: A Participant Looks Back*. Princeton, NJ: Princeton University Press.

Ota, Shozo (2015), "Bengoshi kara Mita Keiji Shihoto Saibanin Seido (1): Gaikan [Criminal Justice and the Saiban-in System from the Perspective of Defense Lawyers, Part 1: Overview]," in Yoshiyuki Matsumura, Manako Kinoshita, and Shozo Ota, eds., *Nihonjin kara Mita Saiban-in Seido [The Lay Judge System as Seen by the Japanese People]*. Tokyo: Keiso Shobo.

Park, Hyunjun (2014), *Kankokugata Law School no Tanjo [The Birth of Korean-Style Law Schools]*. Okayama: Daigaku Kyoiku Shuppan.

Park, Ryan Y. (2010), "The Globalizing Jury Trial: Lessons and Insights from Korea," *American Journal of Comparative Law*, vol. 58, no. 3: 525–82.

Pekkanen, Robert (2006), *Japan's Dual Civil Society: Members without Advocates*. Stanford, CA: Stanford University Press.

Perry, H.W. (1991), *Deciding to Decide: Agenda-Setting in the United States Supreme Court*. Cambridge: Cambridge University Press.

Pierson, Paul (2004), *Politics in Time: History, Institutions, and Social Analysis*. Princeton, NJ: Princeton University Press.

Poguntke, Thomas (2002), "Green Parties in National Governments: From Protest to Acquiescence?" *Environmental Politics*, vol. 11, no. 1: 133–45.

Popova, Maria (2010), "Political Competition as an Obstacle to Judicial Independence: Evidence from Russia and Ukraine," *Comparative Political Studies*, vol. 43, no. 10: 1202–229.

(2012), *Politicized Justice in Emerging Democracies: A Study of Courts in Russia and Ukraine*. Cambridge: Cambridge University Press.

Pratt, John (2007), *Penal Populism*. Abingdon: Routledge.

Price, Vincent (2009), "Citizens Deliberating Online: Theory and Some Evidence," in Todd Davies and Seeta Pena Gangadharan, eds., *Online Deliberation: Design, Research, and Practice*. Stanford, CA: CSLI Publications.

Przeworski, Adam (2009), "Conquered or Granted? A History of Suffrage Extensions," *British Journal of Political Science*, vol. 39, no. 2: 291–321.

Ramnath, Kalyani (2013), "The Colonial Difference between Law and Fact: Notes on the Criminal Jury in India," *The Indian Economic and Social History Review*, vol. 50, no. 3: 341–63.

Ramseyer, J. Mark (2001), "Why Are Japanese Judges So Conservative in Politically Charged Cases?" *American Political Science Review*, vol. 95, no. 2: 331–44.

Ramseyer, J. Mark, and Frances M. Rosenbluth (1993), *Japan's Political Marketplace*. Cambridge, MA: Harvard University Press.

Rich, Timothy S. (2014), "Party Voting Cohesion in Mixed Member Legislative Systems: Evidence from Korea and Taiwan," *Legislative Studies Quarterly*, vol. 39, no. 1: 113–35.

Rigger, Shelley (2011), "The Politics of Constitutional Reform in Taiwan," in Robert Ash, John W. Garver, and Peneleope B. Prime, eds., *Taiwan's Democracy: Economic and Political Challenges*. Abingdon: Routledge.

Robbennolt, Jennifer K. (2005), "Evaluating Juries by Comparison to Judges: A Benchmark for Judging?" *Florida State University Law Review*, vol. 32, no. 2: 469–509.

Rogers, James R. (2001), "Information and Judicial Review: A Signaling Game of Legislative–Judicial Interaction," *American Journal of Political Science*, vol. 45, no. 1: 84–99.

Rueschemeyer, Dietrich, Evelyne Huber Stephens, and John D. Stephens (1992), *Capitalist Development and Democracy*. Chicago, IL: Chicago University Press.

Saiko Saibansho (n.d.), "Kensatsu Shinsakaino Juri Kensu, Giketsu Kensuto [Number of Cases Accepted and Processed by the Prosecutorial Review Commission]," available at www.courts.go.jp/vcms_lf/kensin toukeiH27.pdf, accessed March 28, 2016.

    (2015), "Saiban'into Keikenshani Taisuru Anketo Chosa Kekka Hokokusho (Heisei 26-nendo) [Results of Surveys of Former *Saiban-in*, FY2014]," available www.saibanin.courts.go.jp/vcms_lf/26-a-1.pdf, accessed July 6, 2017.

    (2016), "Saiban-in Seidoni tsuite (Saiban-in Shiko~Heisei 28nen 10-gatsumatsu Sokuho [On the *Saiban-in* System (From Introduction of the System to October 31, 2016)]," available at www.saibanin.courts.go.jp/vcms_lf/h28_10_saibaninsokuhou.pdf, accessed December 23, 2016.

Saiko Saibansho Jimu Sokyoku (2012[c]), "Saiban-in Saiban Jisshi Jokyono Kensho Hokokusho [Report on the Implementation of Saiban-in Trials]," available at www.saibanin.courts.go.jp/vcms_lf/hyousi_honbun .pdf, accessed February 2, 2016.

    (various years[a]), "Saiban-in Saibanno Jisshi Jokyotoni Kansuru Shiryo [Source on the Implementation of the *Saiban-in* Trials]," available at www.saibanin.courts.go.jp/topics/09_12_05-10jissi_jyoukyou.html, accessed February 2, 2016.

    (various years[b]), *Shiho Tokei Nenpo 2, Keijihen [Annual Report of Judicial Statistics. 2, Criminal Cases]*. Tokyo: Saiko Saibansho Jimu Sokyoku.

Saiko Saibansho Jimu Sokyoku Keijikyoku (2009), "Mogi Saibannno Seikato Kadai," *Hanrei Times*, vol. 60, no. 7: 8–52.

(various years), "Keiji Jikennno Gaikyo [General Situation of Criminal Cases]," *Hoso Jiho*.

Saito, Hiroshi (1999), "Shiho Seido Kaikaku [Judicial System Reform]," *Gekkan Shiho Kaikaku*, vol. 1, no. 1: 47–52.

Salamon, Lester M., Wojciech Sokolowski, and Associates (2004), *Global Civil Society: Dimensions of the Nonprofit Sector, Volume Two*. Bloomfield, CT: Kumarian Press.

Samuels, Richard J. (1987), *The Business of the Japanese State: Energy Markets in Comparative and Historical Perspective*. Ithaca, NY: Cornell University Press.

Samuels, David J., and Matthew S. Shugart (2010), *Presidents, Parties, and Prime Ministers: How the Separation of Powers Affects Party Organization and Behavior*. Cambridge: Cambridge University Press.

Sannabe, Atsushi (2014), "Are Hereditary Dietmembers Competent? An Analysis of the Data of the Activities in the House of Representatives," Waseda Institute for Advanced Study Working Paper No. 2014-003, available at http://dspace.wul.waseda.ac.jp/dspace/bitstream/2065/44486/1/DiscussionPaper_2014_003_Sannabe.pdf, accessed February 12, 2015.

Sato, Koji (1981), *Kenpo [Constitutional Law]*. Tokyo: Seirin Shoin Shinsha.

Sato, Koji, and Yoshimitsu Aoyama (2001), "Tokubetsu Taidan Shiho Seido Kaikaku Shingikaiwo Furikaeru [Special Discussion: Looking Back on the Debates in the Justice System Reform Council]," *Juristo*, vol. 1208: 10–24.

Scarrow, Susan E. (2003), "Making Elections More Direct? Reducing the Role of Parties in Elections," in Bruce E. Cain, Russell J. Dalton, and Susan E. Scarrow, eds., *Democracy Transformed? Expanding Political Opportunities in Advanced Industrial Democracies*. Oxford: Oxford University Press.

Schmitter, Philippe C. (1974), "Still the Century of Corporatism?" *The Review of Politics*, vol. 36, no. 1: 85–131.

Schreurs, Miranda A. (2002), *Environmental Politics in Japan, Germany, and the United States*. Cambridge: Cambridge University Press.

Schumacher, Gijs, Catherine E. de Vries, and Barbara Vis (2013), "Why Do Parties Change Positions? Party Organization and Environmental Incentives," *The Journal of Politics*, vol. 75, no. 2: 464–77.

Schofer, Evan, and Ann Hironaka (2005), "The Effects of World Society on Environmental Protection Outcomes," *Social Forces*, vol. 84, no. 1: 25–47.

Schofer, Evan, and John W. Meyer (2005), "The Worldwide Expansion of Higher Education in the Twentieth Century," *American Sociological Review*, vol. 70, no. 6: 898–920.

Segal, Jeffrey A., and Harold J. Spaeth (1993), *The Supreme Court and the Attitudinal Model*. Cambridge: Cambridge University Press.

(2002), *The Supreme Court and the Attitudinal Model Revisited*. Cambridge: Cambridge University Press.

Sheng, Shing-Yuan (2009), "The Dynamic Triangles among Constituencies, Parties, and Legislators: A Comparison Before and After the Reform of Electoral System," Paper Presented to the Annual Meeting of the American Political Science Association, Seattle, WA.

Sheyn, Elizabeth R. (2010), "A Foothold for Real Democracy in Eastern Europe: How Instituting Jury Trials in Ukraine Can Bring about Meaningful Governmental and Juridical Reforms and Can Help Spread These Reforms Across Eastern Europe," *Vanderbilt Journal of Transnational Law*, vol. 43, no. 3, 649–700.

Shin, Dong Woon (2012), "Kankokuni okeru Kokumin Sanyo Saibanno Aratana Tenkai [New Developments in the Korean Jury System]," *Keijiho Journal*, no. 32: 102–11.

(2014), "Kankoku [South Korea]," *Kanagawa Daigaku Hogaku Kenkyusho Kenkyushoho*, vol. 32: 89–108.

Shiomi, Toshitaka (1975), "Nihonno Shiho Kaikaku [Judicial Reform in Japan]," in Tokyo Daigaku Shakai Kagaku Kenkyusho, ed., *Sengo Kaikaku 4: Shiho Kaikaku [Postwar Reforms, vol. 4: Judicial Reforms]*. Tokyo: Tokyo Daigaku Shuppankai.

Shiroshita, Yuji (2011), "Saiban-in Saibanni okeru Ryokeino Dokoto Kadai [Trends in Saiban-in Trial Sentencing Patterns and Issues for the Future]," *Hanzaito Hiko*, vol. 170: 60–85.

(2013), "Saiban-in Saiban ni okeru Ryokei Handan [Sentencing under the Saiban-in System]," in Yuji Shiratori, ed., *Keiji Sibanni okeru Shinrigaku Shinrikanteino Kanosei [Progress in Psychology and Psychological Expertise in Criminal Court]*. Tokyo: Nihon Hyoronsha, pp. 215–48.

Shishido, Kuniaki, and Noriko Iwai (2010), "JGSS Ruiseki Detani Miru Nihonjinno Ishikito Kodono Henka [Trends of Japanese Values and Behavioral Patterns Based on JGSS Cumulative Data 2000–2008]," *JGSS Research Series Monograph*, available at http://jgss.daishodai .ac.jp/research/monographs/jgssm10/jgssm10_01.pdf, accessed February 10, 2014.

Shogan, Colleen J. (2007), "Anti-Intellectualism in the Modern Presidency: A Republican Populism," *Perspectives on Politics*, vol. 5, no. 2: 295–303.

Shugart, Matthew Soberg (2005), "Semi-Presidential Systems: Dual Executive and Mixed Authority Patterns," *French Politics*, vol. 3, no. 3: 323–51.

Shugart, Matthew Soberg, and John M. Carey (1992), *Presidents and Assemblies: Constitutional Design and Electoral Dynamics*. Cambridge: Cambridge University Press.

Simmons, Beth A., Frank Dobbin, and Geoffrey Garrett (2006), "Introduction: The International Diffusion of Liberalism," *International Organization*, vol. 60, no. 4: 781–810.

Songer, Donald R., Jeffrey A. Segal, and Charles M. Cameron (1994), "The Hierarchy of Justice: Testing a Principal-Agent Model of Supreme Court-Circuit Court Interactions," *American Journal of Political Science*, vol. 38, no. 3: 673–96.

Spoon, Jae-Jae, Sara B. Hobolt, and Catherine E. de Vries (2014), "Going Green: Explaining Issue Competition on the Environment," *European Journal of Political Research*, vol. 53, no. 2: 363–80.

Steinberg, David I., and Myung Shin (2006), "Tensions in South Korean Political Parties in Transitions: From Entourage to Ideology?" *Asian Survey*, vol. 46, no. 4: 517–37.

Stephenson, Matthew C. (2003), "'When the Devil Turns. . .': The Political Foundations of Independent Judicial Review," *The Journal of Legal Studies*, vol. 32, no. 1: 59–89.

Strodbeck, Fred L., Rita M. James, and Charles Hawkins (1957), "Social Status in Jury Deliberations," *American Sociological Review*, vol. 22, no. 6: 713–19.

Sui, Cindy (2010), "Taiwan Judges on Corruption Charges," *BBC News*, November 8, available at www.bbc.com/news/world-asia-pacific-11711199, accessed June 7, 2015.

Suzuki, Ken (2004), "Taiwan no Shiho Seido Kaikaku: Nihon eno Shisa [Judicial Reforms in Taiwan: Implications for Japan]," *Hogaku Seminar*, vol. 599: 64–7.

Symons, Beverly, and Rowan Cahill (2005), *A Turbulent Decade: Social Protest Movements and the Labour Movement, 1965–1975*. Sydney: Sydney Branch, Australian Society for the Study of Labour History.

Taiwan Jury Association (2014), *Pei shen tuan mei guo xian ti yan [A Fresh Experience of the US Jury System]*. Taipei: Mi Le Culture Press.

Taiwan Indicators Survey Research (n.d.), available at www.tisr.com .tw/?p=5452#more-5452, accessed July 7, 2015.

Takamori, Nobuhiro (2015), "Saiban-in Saibanno Jisshi Jokyo ni Tsuite [On the Implementation of the Saiban-in Trials]," *Hanzaito Hiko*, no. 179: 139–60.

Takeda, Masahiro (2014), "Kensatsuwa Taisho Jikenwo Shinchoni Kiso [Prosecution Carefully Selecting Which Cases to Indict]," *Journalism*, vol. 292: 136–43.

Tani, Katsuhiro (2002), "Shiho Seido Kaikaku Shingikaino Seiji Katei [Political Process in the Judicial Reform Council]," *Hoshakaigaku*, vol. 57: 153–69.

(2004), "Saiban-in Seidono Rippo Kateino Kensho [Investigating the Legislative Process of the Saiban-in System]," *Meijo Hogaku*, vol. 54, no. 1–2: 355–414.

Taniguchi, Naoko, and Christian Winkler (2015), "Sekaino Nakano Nihonno Seito: Seito Koyaku Coding ni yoru Kokusai Hikaku [Japanese Political Parties in the World: An International Comparison Based on Party Manifesto Codings," Paper Presented at the Japan Electoral Studies Association, Kumamoto, Japan.

Tanioka, Ichiro (2007), "Hanko Hikono Shitsuto Ryowo Sokuteisuru Kijun Zukurini Mukete [Guideline for Measuring Quality and Quantity of Crime & Delinquency]," *Hanzai Shakaigaku Kenkyu*, vol. 32: 76–86.

Thaman, Stephen C. (1995), "The Resurrection of Trial by Jury in Russia," *Stanford Journal of International Law*, vol. 31, no. 1: 61–274.

(1997), "Spain Returns to Trial by Jury," *Hastings International and Comparative Law Review*, vol. 21: 241–537.

(1999), "Europe's New Jury Systems: The Cases of Spain and Russia," *Law and Contemporary Problems*, vol. 62, no. 2: 233–59.

(2002), "Latin America's First Modern System of Lay Participation: The Reform of Inquisitorial Justice in Venezuela," in Andreas Donatsch, Marc Foster, and Cristian Schwarzenegger, eds., *Strafrecht, Strafprozessrecht Und Menschenrechte. Festschrift Für Stefan Trechsel*. Zurich: Schulthess.

(2007), "The Nullification of the Russian Jury: Lessons for Jury-Inspired Reform in Eurasia and beyond," *Cornell International Law Journal*, vol. 40, no. 2: 355–428.

Thies, Michael F., and Yuki Yanai (2014), "Bicameralism vs. Parliamentarism: Lessons from Japan's Twisted Diet," *Senkyo Kenkyu*, vol. 30, no. 2: 60–74.

Thompson, Dennis F. (2008), "Deliberative Democratic Theory and Empirical Political Science". *Annual Review of Political Science*, vol. 11: 497–520.

Tilly, Charles C. (1997), "The Top-Down and Bottom-Up Construction of Democracy," in Eva Etzioni-Halevy, ed., *Classes and Elites in Democracy and Democratization*. New York: Garland Publishing.

Tocqueville, Alexis de (1840/2000), *Democracy in America*. Translated by Harvey C. Mansfield and Delba Winthrop. Chicago and London: The University of Chicago Press.

Tokyo Bar Association, ed. (1992), *Baishin Saiban [Jury Trials]*. Tokyo: Gyosei.

Toshitani, Nobuyoshi (1975), "Sengo Kaikakuto Kokuminno Shiho Sanka [Postwar Reforms and Popular Participation in the Judicial System]," in Tokyo Daigaku Shakai Kagaku Kenkyusho, ed., *Sengo Kaikaku 4:*

Shiho Kaikaku [Postwar Reforms, vol. 4: Judicial Reforms]. Tokyo: Tokyo Daigaku Shuppankai.

(1984), "Nihonno Baishinho [The Prewar Japanese Jury Law]," *Jiyuto Seigi*, vol. 35, no. 13: 4–12.

Traest, Philip (2001), "The Jury in Belgium," *Revue Internationale de Droit Pénal*, vol. 72, no. 1: 27–50.

Tsai, Yun-Chu (2012), "Legislatives in Taiwan: New Electoral Rules, New Representative Roles, and Experienced Politicians," Paper Presented at the Annual Meeting of the American Political Science Association, New Orleans, LA.

Tsai, Ing-wen (2015), "VOTE 2016: Tsai Ing-wen's Judicial Reform Platform," available at http://thinking-taiwan.com/vote-2016-tsai-ing-wens-judicial-reform-platform/, accessed March 20, 2016.

Tsuchiya, Yoshiaki (2005), *Shiminno Shihowa Jitsugen Shitaka [Did A Citizen-Centric Judicial System Come About?]*. Tokyo: Kadensha.

Tsuji, Yuki (2012), *Kazoku Shugiteki Fukushi Regimeno Saihento Gender Seiji [Realignment of the Familialist Welfare Regime and Gender Politics]*. Kyoto: Minerva Shobo.

Tsuji, Hironori (2015), *Saiban-in-ho/Keiji Soshoho [Act on Criminal Trials with Participation of Saiban-in/Code of Criminal Procedure]*. Tokyo: Shoji Homu.

Turner, Ralph V. (1968), "The Origins of the Medieval English Jury: Frankish, English, or Scandinavian?" *The Journal of British Studies*, vol. 7, no. 2: 1–10.

Ueno, Nobuko (1998), "Kyutenpo de Susumu Jiminto Shiho Seido Tokubetsu Chosakaino 'Shiho Kaikaku' Teigen [LDP Special Research Commission on the Justice System's Proposals for 'Judicial Reform': Hastily Put Together]," *Ho to Minshushugi*, vol. 326: 55–7.

Umakoshi, Toru (2010), *Kankoku Daigaku Kaikakuno Dainamizumu [The Dynamics of Korean University System Reform]*. Tokyo: Yushindo.

United States Courts (n.d.), "New Public Law Affects Jury Selection and Service," available at www.uscourts.gov/News/TheThirdBranch/08-12-01/New_Public_Law_Affects_Jury_Selection_and_Service.aspx, accessed January 28, 2015.

Upham, Frank K. (1987), *Law and Social Change in Postwar Japan*. Cambridge: Harvard University Press.

Vanberg, Georg (2005), *The Politics of Constitutional Review in Germany*. Cambridge: Cambridge University Press.

Vanoverbeke, Dmitri (2015), *Juries in the Japanese Legal System: The Continuing Struggle for Citizen Participation and Democracy*. London: Routledge.

Vidmar, Neil (2000), "The Jury Elsewhere in the World," in Neil Vidmar, ed., *World Jury Systems*. Oxford: Oxford University Press.

Vidmar, Neil, and Matthew W. Wolfe (2009), "Punitive Damages," *Annual Review of Law and Social Science*, vol. 5: 179–99.

Volkens, Andrea (2007), "Strengths and Weaknesses of Approaches to Measuring Policy Positions of Parties," *Electoral Studies*, vol. 26, no. 1: 108–20.

Wade, Robert (1990), *Governing the Market: Economic Theory and the Role of Government in East Asian Industrialization*. Princeton, NJ: Princeton University Press.

Wang, Jaw-Perng (2006), "Taiwan Keiji Shiho Kaikakuno Seiko [The Success of Criminal Justice Reform in Taiwan]," *Meijo Hogaku*, vol. 55, no. 4: 1–34.

(2011), "The Evolution and Revolution of Taiwan's Criminal Justice," *Taiwan in Comparative Perspective*, vol. 3: 8–29.

Wang, Zhuoyu, and Hiroshi Fukurai (2010), "Popular Legal Participation in China and Japan," *International Journal of Law, Crime and Justice*, vol. 38, no. 4: 236–60.

Watson, Alan (1974), *Legal Transplants: An Approach to Comparative Law*. Athens and London: University of Georgia Press.

Weber, Ingram (2009), "The New Japanese Jury System: Empowering the Public, Preservation Continental Justice," *East Asia Law Review*, vol. 4, no. 1: 125–76.

Wilson, Matthew J., Fukurai Hiroshi, and Maruta Takashi (2015), *Japan and Civil Jury Trials: The Convergence of Forces*. Northampton, MA: Edward Elgar.

Woo-Cumings, Meredith, ed. (1999), *The Developmental State*. Ithaca, NY: Cornell University Press.

Wuthnow, Robert (1994), *Sharing the Journey: Support Groups and America's New Quest for Community*. New York: Free Press.

Yamamoto, Satoshi (2015), "Saiban-in Saibanno Jisshi Jokyo Bunseki karamiru Shiminno Seigikan [Japanese Citizens' Sense of Justice as Seen in the Analysis of the Implementation of the Saiban-in Trials]," *NCCD Japan*, vol. 50: 61–87.

Yamazaki, Ushio (2001), "Shiho Seido Kaikakuwo Furikaette [Looking Back on the Judicial Reforms]," *Shiho Hoseibu Kiho*, vol. 108: 1–3.

Yanase, Noboru (2007), "Saiban-in Hono Rippo Katei (1) [Legislating the Saiban-in Law (Part 1)]," *Shinshu Daigaku Hogaku Ronshu*, vol. 8: 99–140.

(2008), "Saiban-in Hono Rippo Katei (3) [Legislating the Saiban-in Law (Part 3)]," *Shinshu Daigaku Hogaku Ronshu*, vol. 10: 119–64.

Yasuoka, Okiharu (2009), *Seiji Shudono Jidai [The Era of Political Leadership]*. Tokyo: Chuo Koron Shinsha.

Yonekura, Tsutomu (2012), "Jijitsu Ninteito Ryokeino Ryomenkara Mieru Jubatsuka Genbastuka Gensho [The Increasing Severity of Punishments from the Perspective of both Factual Determination and Sentencing]," *Ho to Minshu Shugi*, vol. 474: 63–5.

Yoon, Yong-Taek (2001), "Kankokuni okeru Shiho Seidono Hensento Shiho Kaikakuno Genjo [Changes in the Korean Judicial System and the Current State of Judicial Reforms]," *Shakai Taiseito Ho*, vol. 2: 2–20.

Index

.